the Jacobite Song

POLITICAL MYTH AND NATIONAL IDENTITY

AUP titles of related interest

POPULAR LITERATURE IN VICTORIAN SCOTLAND
language, fiction and the press
William Donaldson

THE PROTEAN SCOT
the crisis of identity in eighteenth century
Scottish literature
Kenneth Simpson

ABERDEEN AND THE ENLIGHTENMENT
edited with an introduction by
Jennifer J Carter and Joan H Pittock

MUSTER ROLL OF PRINCE CHARLES EDWARD STUART'S ARMY
1745-46
editors Alastair Livingstone of Bachuil, Christian W H Aikman and Betty Stuart Hall

THE HISTORY OF SCOTTISH LITERATURE
in four volumes
general editor: Cairns Craig
Volume 1   Origins to 1660, *editor R D S Jack*
Volume 2   1660 to 1800, *editor Andrew Hook*
Volume 3   Nineteenth century, *editor Douglas Gifford*
Volume 4   Twentieth century, *editor Cairns Craig*

THE GREIG DUNCAN FOLK SONG COLLECTION
editors Patrick Shuldhan-Shaw and Emily B Lyle
Volume 1   Nautical, military and historical songs
Volume 2   Narrative songs
Volume 3   Songs of the countryside, home and social life
Volume 4   Songs of courtship, night visiting songs and songs about particular people

the Jacobite Song

POLITICAL MYTH AND NATIONAL IDENTITY

WILLIAM DONALDSON

ABERDEEN UNIVERSITY PRESS

First published 1988
Aberdeen University Press
A member of the Pergamon Group

© William Donaldson 1988

British Library Cataloguing in Publication Data

Donaldson, William, *1944-*
    The Jacobite Song: political myth and national identity
    1. Songs in English. Special Subject. Scotland. Nationalism,
    1707-1815
    2. Scotland. Political events 1707–1850. Cultural aspects
    I. Title
    784.7′19411
    941.107
    ISBN 0 08 036576 0
        0 08 036405 5 Pbk

PRINTED IN GREAT BRITAIN
THE UNIVERSITY PRESS
ABERDEEN

CONTENTS

v

LIST OF ILLUSTRATIONS

PREFACE

During the later eighteenth and early nineteenth centuries the identity of Scotland underwent rapid and profound change. After centuries of conflict between the Highlands and Lowlands a unified national image was achieved; Scots of every kind, regardless of ethnic, linguistic or regional background, began to consider themselves as part of an essentially Celtic nation. This book examines how this came about.

Scottish politics in the first half of the eighteenth century were dominated by the struggle between Whigs and Jacobites following the fall of the Stuarts in 1688-9. The issues were not narrowly dynastic. The main aim of the Whigs in supporting the House of Hanover was to preserve the Union of 1707 upon which their power in Scotland was based. Likewise the major political goal of the Jacobites was to dissolve the Union and maintain the independence of the Scottish nation within a distinctively Scottish state. The Whigs won; and one of the fruits of success was the privilege of writing the official histories and authoritatively interpreting the past. Generations of Whig historians consequently laboured to present the fall of the Stuarts and the Union of 1707 as inevitable and good. This remains the prevailing orthodoxy. Most writers on Scottish culture appear to consider the Scottish identity as having been fatally compromised in 1707 and as having undergone progressive disintegration thereafter. They picture long centuries of decline punctuated by brief, inexplicable, 'revivals' as in Ramsay, Fergusson, Burns, Scott, Hogg, Stevenson, MacDiarmid, Grassic Gibbon, and so on.

This study deals with the Jacobite tradition, particularly its contribution to the history of ideas. It traces the growth of a heroic legendary history, and its role in maintaining and defining a distinctively Scottish world-picture in the century after the Union. It focuses attention on popular song, the dominant cultural form of the period, and the implications of the evolution of a new genre, the Jacobite song, within it. It argues that instead of merely reflecting popular attitudes and beliefs, popular song was capable of generating important cultural change, and that by its agency, the elements that were to transform Scotland into the 'land of the mountain and the flood' were in place a decade before the birth of Scott.

Finally it suggests that Scottish popular culture possessed great strength and coherence, and that the central theme of Jacobite song, summed up in the notion of 'Awa Whigs awa' continued to inform the Scottish world-picture in the period following the Union—(up to and including, arguably, Hugh MacDiarmid and his followers in the 'Scottish Renaissance'. during the present century).

This study deals with the Lowland world-picture during the eighteenth and early nineteenth centuries. It has relatively little to say, therefore, about Jacobite songs in Gaelic. For an account of these, the reader should consult John Lorne Campbell's authoritative *Highland Songs of the Forty-Five* (Edinburgh 1984, first published 1933). Likewise, it does not discuss Sir Walter Scott in detail; Scott's novels were the principal means by which Scottish Jacobitism was represented outside Scotland, but he was not significant as a creator of Jacobite songs.

The texts themselves are cited, wherever possible, from original sources. Authorial comments are placed within square brackets, and elisions indicated in the normal manner. A sample of the more important tunes is given in an appendix.

This study could not have been written without the advice and support of many individuals and institutions, although its conclusions are my own. I wish particularly to thank the staff of Aberdeen University Library, the National Library of Scotland and the Scottish Record Office. My special thanks are due to the Rt Hon The Earl of Dalhousie, and Mr David Dundas, for their generous permission to reproduce material from their family papers; and also the Keeper of the Scottish Record Office and the Trustees of the National Library of Scotland for material in their possession. I wish to thank also the editors of the *Scottish Literary Journal* and *Cencrastus* for permission to use material in chapters 6 and 10 which first appeared in an earlier form in the pages of their journals. Finally I wish to express a profound debt of gratitude, accumulated during the course of many years, to Mr Thomas Crawford and Mr Donald J Withrington.

Chapter One
INTRODUCTION

In November 1688 James VII and II abandoned his throne and fled to France, and one of the most serious and protracted succession crises in European history began. Three civil wars were fought and almost every aspect of life from the nature of kingship and the state, to church government and doctrine, the structure of society, even the definition of culture, was caught up in it.

The Jacobite era is one of the most familiar in Scottish history, and the military side of the story—Claverhouse and Killiecrankie, the '15 and Sheriffmuir, the '45, Culloden and Bonnie Prince Charlie—has been retold many times. But the more important cultural side of Jacobitism, its effect upon the shaping of ideas, its role in transforming the image and identity of Scotland, is still little known.[1]

For more than half a century after the '45, Jacobitism was a forbidden subject (a sufficient indication of the shattering impact of the rising upon the British establishment). It was not until 1814 and the publication of *Waverley* that it became fashionable and the great wave of Jacobite *Kitsch* was launched upon the world. An enormous publishing boom followed, with distinct peaks during the 1890s and within the last decade when the subject has again begun to attract serious attention. Jacobitism has been discussed by all the major historical schools. It has been variously interpreted as a dynastic squabble, a victory for constitutional government over absolutism, the final struggle between the various racial elements in the national make-up—(the decisive encounter between Celt and Saxon)—as the triumph of a modern over a traditional type of society, or as a stepping stone in the long battle between civilisation and barbarism.[2]

Only one proposition seems to have commanded general assent: that the Jacobite movement in Scotland gave birth to a matchless body of popular poetry and song. Robert Burns declared that 'the Scotish Muses were all Jacobites'[3] and few have subsequently disagreed.

Joseph Ritson the English ballad-collector stated in the introduction to his edition of *Scotish Songs* (London 1794) that

> The gallant attempt made by a delicate young prince to recover the throne of his ancestors, in 1745, seems to have been hailed by the Scotish muse with her most brilliant strains. On no occasion did ever such a multitude of songs appear, of which several are among the finest specimens of lyrical composition.[4]

General David Stewart of Garth who along with Scott stage-managed the famous visit of George IV to Edinburgh in 1822 was equally enthusiastic: 'we find', he wrote in his *Sketches of the Character, Manners, and Present State of the Highlanders of Scotland* (Edinburgh 1821),

> that the whole power of national song, during that period, inclined towards the ancient dynasty; and the whole force of the ludicrous, the popular, and the pathetic, volunteered in the Jacobite service.[5]

It was Stewart, indeed, who was responsible for the Highland Society of London's commission to James Hogg, the Ettrick Shepherd, for *The Jacobite Relics of Scotland* (Edinburgh 1819-21). This became the standard work on Jacobite song, an inexhaustible quarry for later collectors, and a demonstration, to all appearances conclusive, that Jacobite minstrelsy was one of the major branches of Scottish song. 'It has always been admitted', said Hogg,

> that our Jacobite songs and tunes are the best that the country ever produced. The apophthegm is so well established in popular opinion, that it is never controverted, and has become in a manner proverbial.[6]

This took place at a particularly interesting time in the history of European culture. Democratic and nationalist theories were transforming the way people looked at society. The Romantic movement was at its height, and along with it, important new ideas about the links between creativity and social class. Much of this came from Germany, where patriotic scholars were viewing with dismay the traditional dominance of France and the relative paucity of major works of German literature during the previous centuries. They began to advance the notion that the traditional provider of 'literature', the bourgeois intelligentsia, was incapable of contributing to a truly national culture because it had become rootless and *déraciné*; the really distinctive voice was to be found amongst the common people, the folk. They were the custodians of the national *Geist* and from them all creative virtue flowed. The foundation, then, upon which the whole superstructure of German cultural supremacy was to be built, was popular song and tale, and scholars like the brothers Grimm, diligently applied themselves to laying it.[7]

These ideas were scarcely new to the Scots who had already arrived, although by a different route, at roughly the same spot on the cultural map. Like the Germans, the Scots had for centuries been overshadowed by a more powerful neighbour and had suffered a similar loss of high art. At the same time, they had early grasped the notion that their culture was a popular one, and that the inspiration for even the most sophisticated poet should be the language and traditions of the common people. During the eighteenth and nineteenth centuries they produced a brilliant succession of poets, collectors, and editors of popular material, working in vernacular Scots. The popular art-song became the dominant literary form, so much so that it is difficult to think of a poet of any consequence at this time who was not also a song writer— sometimes, like Robert Burns and James Hogg, of outstanding excellence. This new enthusiasm for popular song was eagerly exploited by the Scots. They adapted German ideas and developed the concept of 'National Song', launching Scottish culture into the nineteenth century upon a tidal wave of buoyancy and optimism. Thus, for example, John Struthers, in *The Harp of Caledonia* (Glasgow 1819):

> that [poets] have...a very considerable influence upon the destinies of individuals and communities, is undeniable. The question 'What will a child learn sooner than a song?' has always been, and probably must for ever be negatively answered: and so long as songs continue to be the first things committed to memory, so long will they continue to form and to influence modes of thinking, that the hand of death alone can obliterate. Of consequence, if a national character is once formed, song is the most happy expedient for rendering it permanent...How much this particular feature of Scottish song strengthens the Amor Patriae, for which Scotsmen are so remarkably distinguished, and of which every country knows something that has ever heard her warpipes play, or seen her tartans wave...would not be easy, perhaps it is altogether impossible, to calculate.[8]

By the middle of the nineteenth century, Jacobite song stood second only to love-song in the popular canon. Acceptance of its excellence was a touchstone of national awareness and pride and an enormous weight of popular sentiment lay behind remarks like the following from the distinguished patriot and classicist Professor John Stuart Blackie. They appear in his book *Scottish Song Its Wealth, Wisdom, and Social Significance* (Edinburgh 1889):

> The Jacobite Songs...are the finest combination of poetry, patriotism, and war that the history of literature knows...we have in the Jacobite ballads, I hesitate not to say, the finest and most complete collection that the popular literature of any country can boast. These ballads have the double advantage of being at once real contemporary history, and real popular poetry of the most classical type...this grand procession of native Scottish song is a continuous record of notable facts, as well as a consistent unity of lyrical art.[9]

Here, then, we have the unanimous opinion of some of the most respected poets and scholars in the eighteenth and nineteenth century: Burns, Ritson, Stewart, Hogg, and Blackie. Their views still represent the general consensus on the subject.

There is only one snag.

Not one of them is telling the truth.

With the exception of Struthers, who may very possibly be right, none of the views quoted above bears examnation,

Let us consider, firstly, what has been passed down to us as apparently authentic songs dealing with contemporary events. Here are half a dozen titles which might be volunteered by any ordinary person asked to produce examples of 'Jacobite song': *The Skye Boat Song* ('Speed bonny boat like a bird on the wing/"Onward" the sailors cry;/Carry the lad that's born to be king/Over the sea to Skye'); *Ye Jacobites by name*, ('Ye Jacobites by name, give an ear, give an ear;/Ye Jacobites by name, give an ear;/Ye Jacobites by name/Your fautes I will proclaim,/Your doctrines I maun blame,/You shall hear.—'); *Come o'er the stream Charlie*, ('Come o'er the stream, Charlie,/Dear Charlie, brave Charlie;/Come o'er the stream, Charlie,/And dine with M'Lean;'); *Cam' ye by Athol?* ('Cam ye by Athol, lad wi' the philabeg,/Down by the Tummel, or banks o' the Garry,/Saw ye our lads, wi' their bonnets and white cockades,/Leaving their mountains to follow

Prince Charlie?'); *The Hundred Pipers*, ('Wi' a hundred pipers an' a', an' a',/Wi'
a hundred pipers an' a', an' a';/We'll up an'gie them a blaw, a blaw,/Wi' a hundred
pipers an' a', an' a".); *Wha'll be king but Charlie?* ('The news frae Moidart cam'
yestreen,/Will soon gar mony ferlie;/For ships o' war hae just come in,/And landit
Royal Charlie'.); *Will ye no come back again?*('Bonnie Charlie's noo awa'/Safely
o'er the friendly main/Mony a heart will break in twa/Should he no' come back
again;'); *Wae's me for Prince Charlie*, ('A wee bird cam' to our ha' door,/He
warbled sweet and clearly,/An' aye the o'ercome o' his sang/Was 'Wae's me for
Prince Charlie!' ').

None of these songs was in existence before 1780. They were written by
Robert Burns, James Hogg, Lady Nairne and other named songwriters during the
nineteenth century. One, 'The Skye Boat Song' is the work of an Englishman,
Harold Boulton, and was published during the 1880s.[10]

Most of them purport to be contemporary with the events they describe, and
some were explicitly presented as such by their writers, and the same is true of
the overwhelming majority of what the songbooks of Scotland contain under the
heading 'Jacobite Songs'. Is there anything, then, to prevent the conclusion that
they are fakes, brilliant fakes perhaps, but fakes notwithstanding?

And who knew about this? Robert Burns, certainly. After all, he single-handedly
invented the later Jacobite song as an independent type, (although he acknowledged
few of the pieces during his lifetime). Hogg likewise, who cheerfully passed off his
own compositions as genuine specimens of antiquity with the ink still wet on them.
A handful of collectors and editors, like Robert Chambers and Gavin Greig, and
that is about all. What passed current amongst the rest, was an illusion. Perhaps
they did not want to know. After all, the Jacobite songs represented the very
summit of the popular lyric in Scotland, supposedly the direct expression of an
inspired peasantry under the pressure of great events. Upon this Scottish claims
to cultural and ethnic superiority absolutely depended. If they were bogus the
whole edifice came crashing to the ground. This could not be allowed to happen.[11]
And so the real contemporary song-poetry of the period was largely consigned to
oblivion, along with the damaging insights it contained. Of course the Scottish
muses were not all Jacobites. If they had been there would have been more than
the handful of contemporary songs like 'Up and Warn a' Willie' and (possibly)
'Johnnie Cope' which managed to struggle into the run-of-the-mill nineteenth
century collections. But most Jacobite songs died with the events that gave them
birth. Nor before the '45 were Jacobite songs in any way exceptional. Some, it is
true, had wit and energy, but most were quite ephemeral, crudely made, and
wholly lacking in artistic merit as ordinarily conceived. Whig songwriters wrote
quite as many good (and bad) songs as their Jacobite counterparts.

Burns, then, was creating a myth, and must have been aware that he was doing
so. Why?

The answer is as complex as the man himself. It takes us back to the beginning
of the eighteenth century, and beyond into the realm of legendary history. We will
see how a basically mythologising tendency survived intact into the modern period
and how the ancient theme of 'Guid Auld Lang Syne' was combined with the
'Matter of Prince Charlie' to create a complex body of political myth which
profoundly affected the national identity in the century after the Union.

Chapter Two

'GUID AULD LANG SYNE'

The principles of modern historiography have, whether we are aware of it or not, deeply conditioned the way that most of us look at the world. These are intended, broadly speaking, to be 'scientific' and derive, as far as the different nature of the pursuits allow, from the methodology, of the physical and biological sciences during the nineteenth century. It is felt that history should be exact, empirical, and objective, and the underlying assumption is that the past possesses objective reality, accessible to the techniques of disciplined enquiry; it is something tangible and fixed and operating in accordance with definite, although as yet undiscovered, laws.

It would be convenient if this were true. But the real past is quite inaccessible. It is gone and nobody can recover it, any more than they can re-live earlier stages of their own lives. Of course we can manufacture simulacra: as the autobiographer and the historian do. But we must not be deluded by this. What they produce is something which resembles the past, not the past itself. We live in a continuous present and shape what we call the past to suit our immediate needs—as the historians did when they assumed the mantle of the empirical sciences.[1]

The prestige of 'empirical' history has obscured the fact that there are other, perhaps equally plausible, ways of looking at the past. One of them was current amongst the early eighteenth century Scots.

They had an alternative history, quite different from our one, and it expressed who they thought they were, where they thought they had been, and where they thought they were going to. It was made up of a tissue of myth and legend stretching back into the remotest antiquity, and provided a heroic backdrop against which they viewed themselves, a frame for their thinking, and the driving force behind their politics. They called it 'Guid Auld Lang Syne'.

Few of the historians of Scotland during the last hundred years or so have so much as alluded to the rich and antique pedigree that the Scots once claimed for themselves, and which for centuries corroborated their title to the land of Scotland and their right to political autonomy within it. Yet until well into the modern period the mythic past coloured the world view of all Scotsmen and inspired many of them to passionate political commitment.[2]

At the heart of the matter lay a vital principle underpinning not only the state but the whole social order, and summarised by the portentous doctrine of the Divine Right of Kings. It was a diffuse and complex theory, but in its simplest form it held that Kings enjoyed the patriarchal rights granted to Adam as the first

5

man. As the earliest and best government was paternal, so hereditary right was
the most natural expression of legitimacy in the state and in society. Kings were
the vicegerents of God who alone had power over them as creator and King of
Men and they derived their authority from Him and not from the People under
any form of original contract.[3]

As the rights of kings were of old extent, however, the debate about their powers
took highly distinctive forms depending on the experience of the states involved.
This was especially true in Scotland, where the fountainhead of authority was held
to be King Fergus I, who had founded the kingdom in 330 BC. The difficulty about
Fergus was that he had never existed: he was a myth.

From about the end of the Dark Ages onwards we begin to have record of the
charter-myths of the various European nations. These are late forms in the main,
deeply affected by literacy and chiefly classical or pseudo-classical in inspiration.
Their function at its simplest, was to establish original title to lands, and to
invest the contemporary state with an aura of imperial grandeur, and they chiefly
concerned the exploits of eponymous foundation heroes like Francio of France,
Danus of Denmark, and Brutus the Trojan in England.[4]

In the most popular version of the legend given by Geoffrey of Monmouth,
Brutus, fleeing from the sack of Troy, settled in Britain, drove out the giants who
possessed it, and endowed it with arts, arms and government. At his death, he
divided the island between his three sons, the northern part falling to the portion
of Albannact the youngest. If this was to be taken seriously, then the Kings of
England, as Brutus's heirs, had clear title to the crown of Scotland.

But the Scots had their own foundation myth which not only established their
right to independent existence but gave them an equal and opposite claim to
supremacy over the whole of Britain.

If the English claimed descent from the Trojans, they traced theirs from the
victorious Greeks, and from the Egyptians, who were the most ancient race of
all—unless one counted the Scythians, whom the Scots also included carefully in
their family tree.[5]

The Scottish charter myth took several different forms, but most versions began
with the progenitor of Clan-na-Gaedhal, Gathelus Glas, Prince of Athens, a kind
of Hellenic Rob Roy who, after a career of energetic brigandage in Macedonia and
Achaia, took service with the Pharaoh in Egypt. He rose to high command and
with his friend Moses he routed the Indians and Moors then threatening the
kingdom on the Nile.

He was rewarded with the hand of Scota, daughter of the Pharaoh, and at the
time of the Exodus, when the land was visited with plague and destruction,
Gathelus and Scota gathered their followers and took to the sea, bearing with them
a mighty stone of destiny upon which was written the prophecy:

Ni fallat fatum Scoti quocunque locatum lapidem invenient regnare tenentur ibidem:

> The Scottis sall bruke that realme as native ground,
> Gif weirdis faill nocht, quhair evir this chair is found.

They established their first kingdom in Spain, and thereafter sent various
expeditions to Ireland, settling permanently there about the year 1300 BC. The

Scots in Ireland then began to colonise Scotland and the isles, and a separate monarchy in the Milesian line was founded by Fergus I in the year 330 BC. After him reigned forty-five kings until Fergus II, son of Erch, in about AD 403.[6]

By the early eighteenth century the charter legend was beginning to be questioned in academic circles, although it continued to enjoy a wide popular appeal. It could still be found in the pages of antiquaries and genealogists of a more old-fashioned turn who laboriously traced the descent of the Stuart kings through Fergus to Milesius, and thence through Noah to Adam and the beginning of the world.[7]

This was not so eccentric as it may seem. It represented a well established intellectual practice based on the Universal History of Jerome and Orosius, and although serious historians seldom now began their work with an account of the Creation (as Fordun and Wyntoun had done), the old world-view continued to permeate theology and politics, and to colour constitutional speculation.

The basic principle was that history, instead of being meaninglessly cyclical as the ancients had believed, was linear: it had a beginning a middle and an end, and stretched from the six days of Creation to the Last Day and the Apocalypse. It represented man's confidence in the symmetry of the created order, and embodied his conclusions about the continuous manifestation of Providence through time.[8] It also provided a powerful stimulus to the manufacture of legendary history as generations of European intellectuals struggled to accommodate their national histories to the inherited cosmic scheme, and gave the supporters of monarchy the widest possible field of operation in pursuing the ideal of Legitimacy. Accordingly, in 1705, we find the Jacobite antiquary Mathew Kennedy extending the Stuart genealogy by sixty-one progenitors to Milesius, and by twenty-one degrees inclusively beyond him to Noah.[9]

The main difficulty in using such material was that it could be made to prove anything: indeed it had been generated by political controversy in the first place.

It was in response to English claims of supremacy in the thirteenth and fourteenth centuries, for example, that the earlier parts of the legendary history of Scotland were developed and systematised. Edward 1 rested his claim to the overlordship of Scotland squarely upon the Brutus myth, and when the dispute was referred to the Pope, the Scottish Procurators were furnished with whole tracts of pseudo-history from home in order to circumvent him. They appealed to their own myth, and advanced a counter-claim to supremacy over Britain based upon the title of Mordred of Lothian to the throne of Uther Pendragon.[10]

The effective answer to Edward's arguments was given at Bannockburn, but the paper war continued for centuries, flaring into life whenever relations between the two kingdoms became strained. English legendary history was still being used against the Scots at the time of the Union. Indeed the last parliament of Scotland ordered one particularly offensive tract to be publicly burnt.[11]

Whatever their political convictions, all Scots concurred in one central tenet of national pride: their country, by virtue of the succession, was the most ancient political fabric in Europe, perhaps in the world. Here, for example, is the historian Patrick Abercromby in the first volume of his *Martial Atchievements of the Scots Nation*, published in Edinburgh in 1711 by Robert Freebairn, who later became printer to the Old Pretender during the '15:

Scotland boasts of an uninterrupted Series of 112 Sovereigns, that, till this time, have sway'd its Scepter, since *Fergus i.* who began to Reign 330 Years before the Christian Aera commenc'd: Than which, there's nothing so glorious, nothing equal or secondary in its kind. By this Account, *Scotland* has remain'd a Monarchy, and Monarchs of the same unspotted Blood and Royal Line have Govern'd it, upwards of 2000 Years: Whereas, according to their own Historians *France* has lasted hitherto but 1309; *Spain* 1306; *England* 918; *Poland* 719; *Denmark* 920; *Swedland* 900; The Empire of the *Romans* in *Germany* 831; and that of the *Turks* but 420. The Empire or Kingdom of *China*, 'tis own'd, is of an Older Date than *Scotland*; but then, six several times, upon their own Records, the Race of their Kings has been chang'd by Civil Wars, and they have been four times Conquer'd by Foreign and Barbarous Forces; Nay, at this very Day, a *Tartar* Race sits on the Throne instead of a Chinese...Thus 'tis evident, that all *Scots-men*, however opposite as to their other Principles, agree nevertheless in this one concerning their Kings, and that after a Tract of Two Thousand revolving Years, They are not yet weary'd with the *Fergusian* Sway, a Blessing granted by Heaven to no one Prince or Family upon Earth, besides King *Fergus* and his Sacred Line.[12]

This powerful idea was one of the main grounds of opposition to the Union during the last session of the Scottish parliament, both within and without doors. The Seafield Papers speak of the violent hostility of the common people, noting that 'the very name and antiquity of the Kingdom was of great weight with them'[13]; and the opposition invoked it with passionate eloquence. Here, for example, is Lord Belhaven, speaking on the first Article of the Treaty, on 2 November 1706:

this affair...is of the last consequence unto this nation; I shall mind this honourable House, that we are the successors of our noble predecessors, who founded our Monarchy, framed our laws, ammended, altered, and corrected them, from time to time, as the affairs and circumstances of the nation did require, without the assistance or advice of any foreign power or potentate; and who, during the time of two thousand years, have handed them down to us, a free and independent nation, with the hazard of their lives and fortunes: shall we not then argue for that which our progenitors have purchased for us at so dear a rate, and with so much immortal honour and glory? GOD forbid...if our posterity, after we are dead and gone, shall find themselves under an ill-made bargain, and shall have recourse unto our records, and see who have been the managers of that treaty, by which they have suffered so much when they read their names, they will certainly conclude and say, Ah! our nation has been reduced to the last extremity at the time of this treaty; all our great *chieftains*, all our great Peers and considerable men, who used formerly to defend the rights and liberties of the nation, have been all killed and dead in the bed of honour, before ever the nation was reduced to condescend to such mean and contemptible terms. Where are the names of the chief men of the noble families of *Stewarts, Hamiltons, Grahams, Campbells, Gordons, Johnstons, Humes, Murrays, Kerrs, &c?* Where are the great officers of the crown, the *Hereditary Lords, High Constable,* and *Marshal of Scotland?* They have certainly all been extinguished, and now we are slaves for ever.[14]

Belhaven pleaded for a federal union, if there had to be one at all, because under the proposed terms the Scots had to give up their very independence while the English conceded practically nothing.

'Good GOD!' he exclaimed, 'What is this? An entire surrender'. He was overcome, and sat down, and wept, and several other members spoke before he was able to continue.[15]

The speech reached a wide audience. It was versified, and widely circulated in cheap prints under the title 'Belhaven's Vision'. It is extremely long, and covers most of the notable happenings during the last thousand years or so, but the gist of it is given below:

> While all the World to this Day,
> Since *Nimrod* did a Sceptre sway,
> Ensigns for sov'reign Power display,
>   Shall it be told,
> We, for a little shining Clay,
>   A Kingdom sold?
>
> I see an Independent STATE,
> Repenting when it is too late,
> They did ignobly abdicate
>   An ancient CROWN,
> Which their Ancestors Blood and Sweat
>   Had handed down...
>
> The Sun two thousand times did fly
> Round the twelve Chambers of the Sky,
> Since *Fergus* form'd our MONARCHY;
>   And to this Hour,
> Our Laws have been controuled by
>   No foreign Pow'r.
>
> And now, shall sham Equivalent
> Incorporate us out of Sense,
> To throw away our PARLIAMENT
>   Which did secure
> Our Laws, and put our own Defence
>   In our own Pow'r?...
>
> Our *Stewarts*, unto peaceful JAMES,
> *Gordons, Kers, Campbels, Murrays, Grahams,*
> Hero's from *Tyber* known to *Thames,*
>   For Freedom stood;
> And dy'd the Fields, in purple Streams
>   Of hostile Blood.
>
> Our Valiant BRUCE, and *Wallace* wight,
> Did neatly some Mens Doublets dight;
> Our CLANS, in Lith and Limb, were tight;
>   Their *Claymores*
> The lofty EAGLE thrice did fright,
>   From ALBION'S Shores.
>
> Are now the Spirits of the SCOTS
> Shrunk into *English* Cabbage-stocks,
> When *Hannibal* at our Gates knocks,
>   And waiteth on,
> His Grace out of this House to box,
>   And break his Throne?...

> Brave BELHAVEN having spoke,
> It might have pierc'd a Heart of Rock,
> O CALEDON! with rueful Look
>   And Voice he cry'd;
> Then bath'd in Tears, went Home, and broke
>   His Heart, and dy'd.[16]

A heroic popular history had developed which pictured Scotland as a nation under arms, the embodiment of patriotic virtue, replete with heroes in every age, and resolutely preserving her independence through centuries of conflict. This was not the exclusive preserve of any party, but reflected a patriotic pride widely current in the later seventeenth and early eighteenth centuries.

Its value as a stimulus to public virtue was widely acknowledged. The Jacobite writer Dr George Mackenzie expressed it thus in his *Lives and Characters Of the most Eminent Writers of the Scots Nation* (Edinburgh 1708-1722):

> *The Moral and Intellectual Conduct of Men's Lives is, in a great Part, Owing to the Observations which they make, either upon the Vertues or Failures of Others; and accordingly as they Imitate them, so they prove either Vicious or Vertuous. Hence it is, that all the Wise Nations in the World, have, with great Care and Diligence, transmitted to their Posterity, the Lives and Actions of their Illustrious Predecessors, that they, seeing the Rewards and Honours that were conferr'd upon them for their Vertues, might be thereby excited to Imitate them in their Actions.*[17]

Most educated Scots at this time were responsive to the heroic military ideals enshrined in their national history. They regarded themselves as representatives of the same tradition, and it provided them with a pattern of conduct to which they turned repeatedly for inspiration and guidance.

It is difficult to recapture that ethos now, especially as space permits only the barest summary, but the story varied little from historian to historian, and a similar spirit marked all their works. They told of how after settling in the mainland, the Fergusian Scots vanquished the warlike Picts and united the whole of the North under their control; how they halted the Roman Eagles on the shoulders of the Grampians, and bade defiance in turn to Britons, Saxons, Danes, and Normans, 'retreating into Woods, Mountains and such like Recesses...arm'd and guarded, with Hunger, Cold, and an obstinate Love of Liberty'.[18]

The annals spoke of the Scots' prodigious feats of arms in Arthurian times and how during their league with Charlemagne, they had conquered the Moors and founded the University of Paris. The tale became if anything more epic as it went on, reaching its apogee with Bruce and Wallace and the Wars of Independence— 'as great Heroes as any Countrey or age ever produced', wrote David Symson in his *Genealogical and Historical Account of the Illustrious Name of Stuart* (1712).[19]

For many centuries, their careers formed an inspiring backcloth to public affairs in Scotland especially at periods of crisis or danger. Whenever later generations sought to disparage their own times or to pay the highest tribute to great contemporaries, it was to this heroic vision that they turned as the epitome of the Scottish experience.

We can see this in the early eighteenth century Jacobite song 'Caledon, O Caledon how wretched is thy fate'. This is wholly contemporary in its political purpose and its condemnation of the Scots for abandoning their allegiance to the Stuarts; but a burning pride in heroic past achievement is by far the most powerful emotion:

> IN Days of Yore you was renown'd,
> Conspicuous was your FAME,
> All Nations did your Valour Praise,
> And Loyalty Proclaim;
>   You did your Ancient Rights maintain,
> And Liberties defend,
> And scorn'd to have it thought that you
> On *England* did depend.
>   UNTO your Kings you did adhere,
> Stood by the Royal Race;
> With them you Honour great did gain,
> And Paths of Glory trace;
>   With Royal STEWART at your Head
> All Enemies oppose,
> And like our brave Couragious *Clans*,
> In Pieces cut your foes...[20]

The author of the anonymous 'Elegy on the Death of that most illustrious PRINCE JAMES DUKE OF HAMILTON', dating from about 1711, places his subject within a similar framework, comparing him

> With the brave HEROS of the Scotish Race
> 'Mongst Royal STUARTS, and couragious GRAHAMES
> BRUCE, WALLACE, GORDONS, all immortal NAMES
> Of noble Birth, and nobler by renown
> For famous actions over the World known...[21]

It was all the more poignant as an ideal because the conditions which had made it possible were under severe threat.

In 1603 King James VI left his ancient kingdom and the Union of the Crowns began amid 'a great deal of Sorrow and Lamentation...And indeed it was no wonder; for tho' the Accession to the Crowns of *England* and *Ireland* made King *James* a much greater King, yet it made *Scotland* a much lesser nation'.[22]

The removal of the court and much of the apparatus of central government was followed by a century of decline, ending in the Treaty of Union in 1707, which seemed to many contemporaries to mark the final disappearance of Scotland from the map of Europe.

It was during these years that the theme of 'Guid Auld Lang Syne' began to make its appearance in political poetry, recalling golden ages of political independence, social autonomy, and pure uncomplicated heroism tragically compromised and lost. Its compressed power of association appears in the following simple tribute to royalist virtue, whose effect depends wholly upon its use:

> The great MONTROSE the brave DUNDEE
> Were Heroes in their time
> And never spard their Blood to spill
> For auld lang Syne.[23]

The theme permeated political poetry, but it was used most effectively by Tory and Jacobite writers who were able to add to its characteristic sense of *ubi sunt* the cutting edge of contemporary application:

> Oh fy for *Bruce* and *Wallace* now
> For *Randolph, Montrose, Airly;*
> This wicked generation's curst
> And hes done nothing fairly;
>
> Come, let us have our king again
> And set us as we were, jo,
> Then every man will have his ain
> And ill we need not fear, jo.[24]

Scotland's identity and independence had already suffered as a result of the Union of the Crowns; now the parliament and the royal house were to go under the Hanover succession and the Treaty of Union. As the century went on and it dawned on the Scottish right that after generations of see-sawing revolution and counter-revolution, maybe this time they could not stop the Whigs and Presbyterians, the appeal of the heroic past became even more attractive. The resulting fusion of contemporary politics with largely mythical perspectives can be seen clearly in '*The true* Scots *Mens Lament for the Loss of the Rights of their Ancient Kingdom*', a broadside printed in Edinburgh in 1718, but obviously written before the Union. Behind its unassuming and loosely textured surface it is loaded with historical precedent and association:

> Shall Monarchy be quite forgot,
>   and of it no more heard?
> Antiquity be razed out,
>   and Slav'ry put in Stead?
> Is *Scots* Mens Blood now grown so cold
>   the Valour of their Mind,
> That they can never once reflect
>   on old long sine...
> How oft have our Fore-fathers spent
> their Blood in its Defence;
> Shall we then have it stol'n away
>   by *English* Influence?
> We'll curse the Actors of the Deed,
>   when under Yoke we pine;
> Why will ye not again reflect
>   on old long sine...

Was not our Nation sometime brave,
   invincible and stout;
Conquering *Cesar* that great King,
   could not put it to Rout;
Nor not so much as Tribute get,
   for all his great Design:
These Men I think thought to maintain
   good old long sine...
The Royal *Bruce,* if now alive,
   he surely would regrate,
And blame our Grandees irefully
   of *Scotland's* wretched State;
And tell them he priz'd Monarchy,
   while he was in his Prime,
And bid them look right speedily
   to old long sine *&c.*
May not Experience teach thee well,
   in *Edward Lang-shank's* Reign,
How they pretended Good to thee,
   yet since mean'd no such Thing;
But meerly stole from us the Chair,
   we did so much esteem:
It's strange to me you should forget
   good old long sine...
Remember *William Wallace* Wight,
   and his Accomplicies,
Scotland they undertook to free,
   when it was in Distress,
Likewise Sir *James* the Black *Douglas*
   under the *Bruce's* Reign;
These men spar'd not their Blood to spill
   for old long sine, *&c.*
Why did you thy Union break
   thou had of late with *France;*
Where Honors were conferr'd on thee?
   but now, not so is thy Chance:
Thou must subject thy Neck unto
   a false proud Nation;
And more and more strive to forget
   good old long sine, *&c.*
Was it their seeming Riches that
   induced thee to sell
Thy Honors, which as never yet
   no Monarch e'er could quel?
Nor our Integrities once break,
   in all the bygone Time?
Yet now ye seem for to forget
   good old long sine...
Now mark and see what is the Cause
   of this so great a Fall:
Contempt of Faith, Falshood, Deceit,
   and Villany withal;

> But rouse your selves like *Scotish* Lads,
> and quit yourselves as Men:
> And more and more strive to maintain
> good old long sine, &c.[25]

All important political events were incorporated into the popular history and were transmuted by it, including the careers of Queen Mary, Charles I, James VII and the Old and Young Pretenders. The whole of the recent past was a battlefield which contending parties struggled to control, with the result that processes in some sense myth-producing were at work throughout the Scottish historical experience.

Ironically, it was the Jacobites themselves who destroyed the myth of King Fergus, and for urgent political reasons. This was the work of Thomas Innes of the house of Drumgask, Principal of the Scots College in Paris, and a leading contemporary Scottish historian. His *Critical Essay on the Ancient Inhabitants of the Northern Parts of Britain or Scotland* ((London 1729) was, ostensibly, a work of disinterested scholarship intended to free the early history of Scotland from error and fable. In reality, however, it was a calculated blow in the contemporary debate about the nature of kingship, and it was dedicated, privately, to the Old Pretender. Innes grasped that not only were the early kings probably spurious but that they could as easily be used to support the notion of elective monarchy as divine right. Accordingly he traced the origin of the crown to the Pictish line which was, in his view, clearly Absolute. At the same time, he argued that even reckoning only from Fergus II, son of Erch, there were sixty-three kings in lineal descent down to James VI, which still made the Scottish crown the most ancient in Europe.[26]

With this still largely mythic fabric, the destinies of the Stuarts were intricately entwined.

When the Young Chevalier landed in the wilds of Moidart in 1745 to be saluted by the poet Alasdair MacMhaighstir Alasdair as '*an àilleagan cheutach* '*shloichd áifeachdach Bhàncho*'—the beautiful jewel of the race of brave Banquo—this was no bardic extravagance, nor was it the only branch of Charles Edward's extensive family tree.[27]

For sheer concentration of kingly mystique, the Stuarts were one of the most glittering dynasties in Christendom. They were endowed by blood and marriage with a legitimacy far-flung and long descended, and wreathed in prophetic lore going back deep into the Middle Ages. Their title to the crowns of Britain was far more formidable than the mere fact of intermarriage with the Tudors. Their claim to sovereignty was derived from Fergusiana, sister of King Hungus of the Picts, and from Mordred of Lothian, heir to Uther Pendragon; from Canute and the Danish kings; from the Saxon royal family through Queen Margaret, daughter of Edward the Confessor; from the Norman kings, and from the royal line of Wales, through Banquo, thane of Lochaber, whose son Fleance married the princess Nesta, daughter of Griffith ap Llewelin.[28]

'The French wife shal beare the sonne Shal weld all Bretane to the sea' was merely one of the prophecies canvassed at the time of King James's accession to the English crown in 1603. He was hailed as 'the infant crowned in the cradle' destined to make the isle of Brutus whole. Indeed the British legendary history was carefully re-interpreted to present him as the true *Arturus Revividus*. An oracular anagram was made upon his name: 'Charles James Steuart Claims Arthur's Seat', and he was proclaimed King of Great Britain, relinquishing his separate titles.[29]

The Stuarts were well aware of the power of the legendary past and actively employed it as an inspiration to royalist sentiment. It had been the custom at the crowning of the Scottish kings to recite their lineage in the Fergusian line. This was done in the time of Alexander III, and seems to have been continued at least until the coronation of Charles I, whose ceremonial was directed by the poet William Drummond of Hawthornden.[30]

When Sir George Mackenzie of Rosehaugh, the King's Advocate, declared in his *Defence of the Antiquity of the Royal Line of Scotland* (Edinburgh 1685) that

> the Honour of the Ancient and Royal Race of our Sovereigns is the chief thing wherein we glory...nor is it one of the least Arguments which prevail with us, to hazard all for our Royal line, that we have been so long Subjects to it, and happy under it...[31]

he was expressing the feelings of generations of loyalists, feelings which were to persist in various forms for generations to come.

The loyalists argued that their opponents, by abandoning their allegiance, had not only distorted the Scottish constitution, but had flung open the door to English interventionism and betrayed the liberties 'handed down to them with the Blood and Immortal Honour of a long *Series* of Valiant Ancestours'. [32]

These, then were the main features of the Scottish world-picture at the time of the Union: the past had enormous importance and took the form of a series of heroic legends. The present was something which, at its highest, could be (and was) incorporated into this fabric by processes similarly mythogenic. The resulting complex of ideas and beliefs was the common inheritance of all Scots. For the right, however, it possessed an added force, because of the mystical aura surrounding the Stuarts and the way the dynasty was woven into the fabric of the national mythology. This was the bedrock of Jacobite thinking and found expression in poems and songs and novels throughout the eighteenth and well into the nineteenth century.

Chapter Three

'A BLOODY SWORD FOR THEE O SCOTLAND'

This chapter deals with the religious controversies of the time, and their contribution to party mythology during the later seventeenth and early eighteenth centuries.

The great obstacle to Stuart supremacy was the Presbyterian faction within the Kirk, firstly, because it held that the church should be governed by elected committees of ministers and elders, and should be therefore, in a limited sense, 'democratic', and, secondly, that the church should have primacy over the secular state, i.e. that the state should be, in a very real sense, theocratic.

The Stuarts supported the Episcopal system of church government because it echoed aristocratic ideals and kept the Kirk subordinate to the Crown. For more than a hundred and fifty years after the Reformation there was a ferocious struggle between the adherents of the rival systems, with all the familiar apparatus of ecclesiastical warfare—inquisition, deposition, excommunication, schism, and, in the last resort, naked physical violence. After 1560 a loosely hierarchical arrangement developed with titular Bishops and Superintendents administering the Church. In 1592, however, the Presbyterians led by Andrew Melville succeeded in capturing the establishment, only to be outmanoeuvered by King James who re-established Episcopacy in 1610. The hierarchy was overthrown amid the general tumult of the Civil War, and the Kirk became Presbyterian again in 1638. At the Restoration in 1660, Episcopacy was revived. At the Revolution it was once again overthrown.[1]

But this was not the end of the struggle. It continued with undiminished vigour until well into the eighteenth century. It is almost certain, for example, that if the Pretenders had been victorious in 1715 or 1745, the Episcopate would speedily have been restored.

Broadly speaking, when the Stuarts were in the ascendant, Episcopacy prevailed, and when they were not, it did not. The adherents of hierarchy in the church were closely identified with the supporters of royal supremacy in the state. In most respects, indeed, the Jacobite movement was simply an armed extension of militant Scottish Episcopalianism.

At the Revolution, the Episcopalians split. A small minority took the oaths of allegiance to King William and were officially tolerated; the rest (called 'nonjurants' because they refused the oaths), went on as a separate body owing allegiance, although covertly, to the Stuart Pretenders. This situation continued until the death of Charles Edward Stuart in 1788. The non-jurant Episcopal church acted as the ecclesiastical wing of the Jacobite party, and provided the basis of its organisation within Scotland during the first half of the eighteenth century.[2]

The protagonists of both sides were haunted by the mythic past.

Not content with ransacking the annals of the Primitive Church, they found additional fuel for controversy in the government and practice of the early church in Scotland.

The Scots had been amongst the very first to receive the Evangel; this was not in dispute, at least north of the Tweed. Like the antiquity of the state itself, this was one of the chief points of national pride. God had given Christ the uttermost ends of the earth. Scotland was well known to be the uttermost end: therefore it was subject to a special dispensation. Here, for example, is the Covenanter Alexander Shields in *A Hind let loose, or An Historical Representation of the Testimonies, Of the Church of Scotland, for the Interest of Christ* (n.p., 1687):

> It is not without reason reckoned among the peculiar prerogatives of the renouned Church of Scotland, that Christ's conquest in the conversion of that Nation, is one of the most eminent Accomplishments of Scripture Prophecies...because it was...in the acknowledgement of all, among the *uttermost parts of the Earth*, which were given to Christ for His...it is clear from Ancient Records, the Christian Faith was imbraced here, a few years after the Ascension of our Saviour, being taught by the Disciples of *John* the Apostle.[3]

The Episcopalians had problems with this, because some centuries seemed to have elapsed between the conversion of the Scots and the appearance of the first Bishop, Palladius, amongst them, and their opponents eagerly seized upon this as proof that the church had originally been Presbyterian.

But this pillage of ecclesiastical antiquities was no more free from political considerations than the debate about the historical character of the crown had been. The historical justification of Episcopacy was inextricably connected with that of the Stuart dynasty itself.

Here is Sir George Mackenzie again:

> the Presbyterians...urg'd from our Historians, that we had a Church for some years without Bishops...but...many thousands in Japan and China were converted by Presbyters before Bishops were sent there; and since it cannot be deny'd but that these who ordain'd our Presbyters were Bishops; it necessarily follows, that Episcopacy was settled in the Christian Church before we had Presbyters...it does not follow that because our Church in its infancy...was without a Bishop for some years; that therefore it was reasonable for Subjects, to enter into a Solemn League and Covenant, without, and against the consent of their Monarch; and to extirpat Episcopacy settled then by Law, and by an old prescription of 1200 years at least.[4]

The past was a glass in which men saw their own reflections darkly. Accordingly we find Alexander Shields casting about in the annals of the Culdees for authority for the doctrine of Defensive Arms and the obligation of resistance to Tyrants:

Figure 1. 'Baptism from Stonehaven Jail'. (Courtesy of Bishop of Aberdeen and Orkney, and Rev A Allan).

we have ground to conclude, they were for *War*, & did maintain the principle of resisting Tyrannie...& maintained the purity & freedom of their Ministry, independent on Pope, Prelate, or any humane Supremacy...[5]

Scots like these saw themselves as a chosen people, and their country as the cockpit of Europe. They believed that the fate of the Reformation and perhaps of Christianity itself hung upon their actions. Considered in this light, the Solemn League and Covenant was not just an episode, however important, in ecclesiastical politics, but the high-water mark in the cosmic history of man's reconciliation to God.

As a shaping force in the mental world of seventeenth and early eighteenth century Scotland its influence can hardly be overstated.

The Covenant was a treaty entered into by the Scottish Estates and the Parliament of England in 1643 to extirpate popery, prelacy, heresy, and schism, and to introduce uniformity of church government and doctrine in the three kingdoms. But its appeal was never merely political. It was a pledge by the Scots to their Creator to be redeemed through all succeeding time, a trumpet summons to Presbyterian crusade, a thing of apocalyptic significance whose implications resonated through Scottish culture for many generations. Its symbolic power was certainly not overlooked by the Royalists who burned it at the cross of Edinburgh in 1661.

In the ecclesiastical revolution which followed the Restoration, most of the parish ministers in the Whiggish South-West were deposed. The Synods of Dumfries, Galloway, Glasgow and Ayr virtually ceased to exist. Armed field-conventicling sprang up throughout the region as the persecuted remnant cried in the wilderness 'for the Covenant and down with the Bishops'.

While the hill-men (as they were called) sought to reclaim Scotland by dint of rebellion and assassination, the Government tried to harry them into compliance by fining, quartering, banishment and execution. The Covenanters became progressively more extreme. In 1684 at the town of Sanquhar they published a declaration disowning their allegiance and solemnly declaring war on the king.[6]

Alexander Shields proclaimed the doctrine of the two Covenants: one between the King and the People with God, and one between the King and the People alone. If the King was a Tyrant, then it obliged the People to uphold the first Covenant against the second and vindicate the Law against the Ruler:

> it is the interest of all mankind to know and be resolved in Conscience, whither the Government they are under be of God's Ordination or of the Devils administration; whether it be Magistracy or Tyrannie...the Constitution & Administration of the Government of the two *Royal Brothers*, [Charles II and James VII] under whose burthen the earth and we have been groaning these 27 years past hath been a compleat & Habitual Tyranny, and can no more be owned to be Magistracy then Robbery can be acknowledged to be a rightful possession...No Lyon is born King of Lyons, nor no man born King of men, nor Lord of men, nor Representative of men, nor Rulers of men...because none by nature can have those things that essentially constitute Rulers, the calling of God, nor gifts and qualifications for it, nor the election of the People.[7]

Here, then, is the radical ethos that lay at the heart of west country Whiggism in the second half of the seventeenth century.

The persecution triggered off a great revival of popular spirituality in the region. The Covenanting pamphleteer Patrick Walker called it:

> that good, ill time of persecution...a day of the power of the gospel, to the conviction and conversion of many souls, which made some to call in question if there had been a greater, since the apostles ceased out of the world, in so short a time and in so little bounds of the earth as in the south and west of Scotland...a day of great confirmations, support and comfort to the souls of his people...wherein the Lord answered them in the day of their distress, and wherein they had their Bethels, Penuels, and Mahanaims, which made them to set up stones, and write on them *Ebenezer*...[8]

A revolutionary millenarianism swept the west, and all kinds of visionary doctrines were propounded. The Stuarts were equated with the *Rex Iniquus* of the Last Days, and preparations for the Second Coming were laid accordingly.

Behind this lay an apocalyptic tradition going back to the Hebrew Books of Prophecy, and telling of a time of cosmic catastrophe in which the world would fall under the sway of a demoniacally inspired and infinitely evil power which should at last be cast down by the Saints with a destructiveness so thorough that it would purge the accumulated sin of ages and prepare the way for the New Jerusalem.[9]

The teaching of the hill preachers was shot through with apocalyptic prophecy, and on every hand the talk was of Antichrist and the imminent arrival of Gog Magog. According to Alexander Peden 'the prophet', this was to be signalled by a devastating French invasion and he cried out:

> see the Frenches marching with their armies thorow the breadth and length of the land, marching to their bridle-reins in the blood of all ranks...A bloody sword, a bloody sword, a bloody sword for thee, O Scotland...Many miles shall ye travel, and shall see nothing but desolation and ruinous wastes...The fertilest places...shall be as waste and desolate as the mountains. The woman with child shall be ript up and dashed in pieces...Oh the Monzies [*Monsieurs*], the French Monzies, see how they run, how long will they run? Lord, cut their houghs, and stay their running.[10]

In accordance with the well-established timetable of Apocalypse, a remnant of the saints was to be spared for the day of Armageddon in which the might of Antichrist was to be overthrown for ever, and in the vanguard, purified and exalted, were to be the last of the Scottish Covenanters.[11]

At a field conventicle in Clydesdale in July 1680, the famous hill preacher Richard Cameron delivered his final sermon. In it he declared:

> that he was assured the Lord would lift up a standard against Antichrist, that would go to the gates of Rome and burn it with fire; and that 'Blood' should be their sign, and 'No Quarters' their word; and earnestly wished that it might first begin in Scotland.[12]

It was a recurring preoccupation of millenarian movements that the most effective way to eliminate sin was to eliminate sinners, and in Scotland during the later seventeenth century a similar ethos developed. It was a popular theme, and much expounded, but for sheer intensity of vision, Alexander Peden was unrivalled. He foresaw the remnant rising against their oppressors in a holocaust of destruction which derived its inspiration as much from Stuart repression as from scriptural precedent. In Peden we can recognise plainly what Norman Cohn called 'the central phantasy of revolutionary eschatology'.[13] His words must constitute one of the most compelling expressions of this urge in the literature of the subject:

> O how sweet will it be to see Christ marching up in a full body, with all the trumpets sounding the triumph of the Lamb's victory, when his sword shall be made red with the blood of his enemies...Verily, I fear, the followers of the Lamb shall be forced to tread on the dead corps of wicked men ere all the play be played; the whole land shall have enough ado to shovel them into the earth; Christ will kill faster with his own hand than the kingdom will be able to bury; and many shall be buried unstraightened, and moals shall be the winding-sheet of many that look life-like in that day...blood shall be the sign of Christ's soldiers, and 'No Quarters' shall be their word; 'Death and destruction' shall be written in broad letters on our Lord's standard, a look of him will be a dead stroke to any that comes in his way.[14]

In passages like these the psychological world of the later Covenanters achieves its most vigorous expression. It was a world in which the idea of divine super-intendance became heightened into an overwhelming sense of Immanence. The laws of the natural world and the ordinary rules of perception could at any moment be suspended and a particular providence might lurk in the most trifling occurrence. The partition between the real and the invisible world was paper-thin, and the sense of evil broodingly present.

The existence of necromancy and devil-worship were seized on as inverse proofs of the existence of God. As one contemporary declared, 'No GOD, no Devil, no Spirit, no Witch' and the ethos which produced Peden the Prophet could as easily bring forth Weir the Warlock.

The pages of Presbyterian writers like Patrick Walker and Robert Wodrow teem with revenants and apparitions, visions and prophecies, spectral congregations seen on the hillsides singing the penitential psalms; open graves appearing in the earth; showers of bonnets and broadswords falling from the heavens, and ghostly companies of Highland soldiers marching and countermarching through the countryside.[15]

Such experiences had little connection with revealed religion, but had their roots deep within folk tradition. The Presbyterian movement had always been strongly populist, and in the later seventeenth century began to exhibit pronounced anti-aristocratic tendencies.

As Patrick Walker said:

> after these defections and judgments are over, ye may see the nettles grow out of the bed-chambers of noblemen and gentlemen, and their names, memorials, and posterity to perish from the earth.[16]

It was from such sources that the characteristic rhetoric of the Covenant came— a vertiginous, hypnotic compound derived from the Authorised Version of the Old Testament and the rhythmical demotic speech of the South and West, culminating in a popular preaching style which was unflaggingly satirised by the Scottish Royalists. They collected such flowers of rhetoric assiduously and in 1692 published a collection of them with the title *Scots Presbyterian Eloquence Displayed*. It was crammed with examples of the popular style of preaching richly suggestive of the popular Calvinist ethos in the closing decades of the seventeenth century. Here, for example, is one soul-refreshing gospeller on the first chapter of Job:

> The Devil comes to God one day; *God said*, now Deel, thou foul thief, whether are thou going? I am going up and down now, Lord, you have put me away from you now, I must even do for myself now. Well, well, Deel, *says God*, all the world kens that it is your fault; But do not you know that I have an honest servant they call Job? Is not he an honest man, Deel? Sorrow to his thank, *says the Deel*, you make his cup stand full even, you make his pot play well: but give him a cuff, I'll hazard he'll be as ill as I am call'd. Go Deel, *says God*, I'll yoke his honesty with you: Fell his cows, worry his sheep, do all the mischief ye can, but, for the very saul of you, touch not a hair of his tail.[17]

The Episcopalians pretended to find this hugely comic, but it is not just low-burlesque. It is hard to be unmoved by the sheer idiomatic energy of such preaching:

> Did you ever hear tell of a good God, and a cappet prophet, Sirs? The good God said, Jonah, now billy Jonah, wilt thou go to Nineveh for auld lang syne? The de'il be on my feet then, said Jonah. O Jonah, said the good God, be not ill-natured, they are my people. What care I for you or your people either, said the cappet prophet? Wherefore shall I go to be made a liar in my face? I know thou wilt have mercy on that people. Alas, alas, we bide not the tenth part of that bidding; yet when we come to you, I fear we'll find you like Ephraim, a cake unturned, *that is*, 'tis stone-hard on one side, and skitter-raw on the other.[18]

Or by the powerful combination of the cosmic and parochial in this sermon by the veteran John Semple of Carsphairn, in which he pictured himself arriving with his congregation before the judgement-seat:

> Sirs, This will be a terrible day; we'll all be there, and all of you will stand at my back. Christ will look to me, and he will say, who is that standing there...I know thou's honest John Simple; draw near John; now John, what good service have you done to me on earth? I have brought hither a company of blue bonnets for you, Lord. Blue bonnets, John! What is become of the brave hats, the silks, and the sattins, John? I'll tell I know not, Lord, they went a gait of their own. Well, honest John, thou and thy blue bonnets are welcome to me; come to my right-hand and let the devil take the hats, the silks, and the sattins.[19]

When used in the grand manner by a preacher like Alexander Peden it could achieve a harrowing power. We can see, for example, in a sermon upon the backslidings of Israel he preached in Kyle in 1682 to the text 'the plowers plowed upon my back; they made long their furrows' (Psalms, CXXIX, 3) the fervour, impetus, and relentless accumulation of familiar detail which characterised the style at its best:

Would you know who first yoked this plough? It was cursed Cain, when he drew his furrows so long and so deep, that he let out the heart-blood of his brother Abel; and all his cursed seed has and will design, desire, and endeavour to follow his cursed example: and that plough has and will gang simmer and winter, frost and fresh-weather, till the world's end; and at the sound of the last trumpet, when all are in a flame, their theats will burn, and their swingle-trees will fall to the ground; the plow-men will lose their grips of the plough, and the gade-men will throw away their gades; and then, O the yelling and skreeching that will be among all his cursed seed, clapping their hands, and crying to the hills and mountains to cover them from the face of the Lamb and of him that sits upon the throne, for their hatred of him and malice at his people.[20]

This ability to bring the cosmic and the local into powerful conjunction, or to reduce them to a set of interchangeable terms, coupled with an overwhelming sense of Immanence and a strong undercurrent of folk demonology, marks the writings of many contemporary apologists. The popular Presbyterian style and the intellectual habits it fostered is at the heart of the Whiggish contribution to the Lowland world picture in the later seventeenth and early eighteenth centuries.

Chapter Four

'*A PACK OF SATYRIC DIVELLS*'

Political song in eighteenth century Scotland is preserved in written or printed sources ranging from privately compiled manuscripts and transcripts, to published broadsides song collections and chap-books which formed the major vehicles of the popular culture of the day. From time to time it entered oral circulation and was, no doubt, shaped by non-literate tradition, but the extent to which this happened can now only be guessed at. In one respect, however, it did owe a substantial debt to oral sources, because it was here that the tunes came from, and the tunes were an important influence on the development of Jacobite song as an independent form during the eighteenth and early nineteenth centuries.

We are accustomed nowadays to song-tunes having a specific set of words, but in eighteenth century Scotland popular melodies could, and usually did, have any number of lyrics attached to them. Usually, though, one set of verses predominated, and from them the tune took its name. One great favourite with political song-writers was 'Old Highland Laddie', whose words dealt with the courtship of a Lowland girl and a bonny Highlandman. Despite the many different lyrics that were set to it over the years, the title remained stable, until the mid nineteenth century when the dominant text was displaced by a new one and the tune thereafter took its name—'Kate Dalrymple'.[1]

Judging from the surviving evidence, one of the most widely current political songs during this period was 'Killiecrankie', which celebrated in a wryly mocking style a victory by the Jacobites over government forces shortly after the Revolution of 1688-9. Many later songs exist, often widely different in character, but all set to the tune of 'Killiecrankie' or 'Old Killiecrankie',[2] as it was sometimes called. The air was a good one, pronounced by James Hogg 'among the finest of the slow strathspey kind in the kingdom',[3] and 'Gilliecrankie' became a cant name for Highlandmen generally, as we learn from a contemporary anti-Union poem '*A Pill for* Pork-Eaters: *Or* a Scot's *Lancet for an* English *Swelling*' which envisages a time when

> Insulting *England* to her Cost shall know,
> What Brave united *Scotsmen* then can do,
> When our best Troops are at thy Borders rang'd,
> Then Caledonia's Wrongs shall be reveng'd;
> Our Highlanders thy City-walls shall Greet,
> And *Gilliecrankies* rifle *Lombard-Street.*[4]

Obviously the creative stimulus came from the tune, because the words themselves, in typical broadside style, were coarsely made, rambling, sometimes even
incoherent—as the the opening section shows:

> *Clavers,* and his *Highlandmen,*
> Came down upo' the Ra' Man,
> Who being stout, gave mony a Clout,
> The Lads began to cla' then,
> With Sword and Targe into their Hand,
> Wi' which they were nae sla' Man,
> Wi' mony a fearful heavy Sigh,
> The Lads began to cla' then.
> O'er Bush, o'er Bank, o'er Ditch, o'er Stank,
> She flang amang them a' Man.
> The *Butter-box* got mony Knocks,
> Their Riggings paid for a' then.
> They got their Paikes, wi' sudden Straikes,
> Which to their Grief they sa' Man;
> Wi' Clinkum Clankum o'er their Crowns,
> The Lads began to fa' then.
> Hur skipt about, hur leapt about
> And flang amang them a' Man.
> The *English* Blades got broken Heads,
> Their Crowns were cleav'd in twa then.
> The Durk and Door made their last Hour,
> And prov'd their final Fa' Man:
> They thought the Devil had been there,
> That play'd them such a Pa' then:
> The Solemn League, and Covenant,
> Came Whigging up the Hills, Man,
> Thought Highland Trows durst not refuse
> For to subscribe their Bills then.
> In *Willie*'s Name, they thought nae ane
> Durst stop their Course at a' Man.
> But hur Nane-sell, wi mony a Knock,
> Cry'd *Furich Whiggs* awa' Man.[5]

Broadsides were the main vehicle of commercial popular song during the first
half of the eighteenth century. They were printed, usually fairly crudely, in double
columns on large sheets with decorated borders and woodcut designs. Sometimes,
although rarely, they printed music in staff notation; usually, though, they simply
indicated the tune title at the top. They were sold in urban areas by professional
street-singers and distributed throughout the country by packmen and pedlers of
the lower sort. Because of their large format and generally decorative quality they
were often pasted up in inns and other places of public resort, to form a kind of
poetic wallpaper which could be read by anybody who came along.[6]

There are broadside songs in the 'Killiecrankie' style from all the major rebellions. One example from the '45, 'The Battle Preston[pans]' is actually set to the

same tune, although it is written with considerably more dash and skill than the original, as the following excerpt may show:

> The Chevalier being void of Fear,
> Did march up *Birsle* Brae Man,
> And through *Tranent* e're he did stent,
> As fast as he could gae Man,
> While General *Cope* did Taunt and Mock,
> Wi' mony a loud Huzza Man;
> But e'er next Morn proclaim'd the Cock,
> We heard another Craw Man.
>
> The brave *Lochyel* as I heard tell,
> Led *Camerons* on in Clouds Man,
> The Morning fair and clear the Air,
> They loos'd with divelish Thuds Man,
> Down Guns they threw, and Swords they drew,
> And soon did chase them aff Man,
> On *Seaton* Crafts they bust their Chafts,
> And gar'd them run like daft, Man.
>
> The Bluff Dragoons swore Blood and 'oons
> They'd make the Rebels run Man,
> And yet they flee when them they see,
> And winna fire a Gun Man,
> They turn'd their Back, the Foot they brake
> Such Terror seis'd them a Man,
> Some wet their Cheeks, some fyl'd their Breeks,
> And some for Fear did fa Man...
>
> Some Highland Rogues, like hungry Dogs,
> Neglecting to pursue Man,
> About they fac'd, and in great haste
> Upon the Booty flew Man,
> And they as Gain for a their Pain,
> Are deckt wi Spoils of War Man,
> Phow bald can tell, phow her nane sel
> Was nee'r sae pra before Man.
>
> At the Thorn Tree, which you may see,
> Bewest the Meadow Mill Man,
> There many slain lay on the Plain,
> The Clans pursuing still Man,
> Sic unko Hacks and deadly Whacks,
> I never saw the like Man,
> Lost Hands and Heads cost them their Deads,
> That fell near *Preston* Dike Man.
>
> At Afternoon when a was done,
> I gade to see the Fray Man,
> But had I wist what after past,
> I had better stay'd away Man.
> On *Seaton* Sands, wi' nimble Hands,

A RACE at SHERIFF-MUIR,

Fairly run on the 13th of November 1715.
To the Tune of the HORSEMAN's SPORT.
Nota, The first two Lines of each Verse are to be repeated.

There's some say, That we wan, some say, That they
Some say, That nane wan at a, Min: (wan,
But one Thing I'm sure That at Sheriff-muir—
A Battle there was, which I sa - - Man.
And we ran and they ran, and they ran, and we ran,
And we ran, and they ran awa - - Man.
Brave Argyl and Bellaven, not like Frightn'd L——n,
which Rothes and Haddingtoun sa - - Man;
For the all with Wightman advanc'd on the Right Man,
while others took Flight leing ra - Men,
And we ran, and they ran &c.
Lord Roxbrugh was there in Order to share,
with Douglas who stood not in Awe - Man;
Volunteerly to ramble with Lord Loudoun Campbel,
Brave Ilay did suffer for a - - Man,
And we ran and they ran, &c.
Sir John Shaw that great Knight with Broad Sword most
On Horse back he briskly did charge - Man; (bright,
An Hero that's bold none could him withhold,
He stoutly encounter'd the Targe - Man:
And we ran and they ran, &c.
For the cowardly Whittim for Fear they should cut him,
Seeing glittering broad Sowrds with a Pa - Man,
And that in such Thrang, made Baird Edicang,
And from the brave Clans ran awa Man.
And me ran and they ran, &c.
Brave Mar and Panmure, were firm I am sure,
The Letter was kidnapt awa Man,
With brisk Men about, brave Hary retook
His Brother, and laught at them a - Man.
And we ran and they ran &c.
Brave Marishal and Lithgow and Glengary's Pith too,
Assisted by brave Loggia - Man.
And Gordon s the bright, so boly did fight,
The Red coats took Flight and awa Man
And we ran and they ran &c.
Strathmore and Clanronnald cry'd still advance Donald
Till both of these Heros did fa - Man:
For there was such Hashing and broad Swords a clashing,
Brave Forfar himself got a Cla - Man.
And we ran and they ran, &c.
Lord Perth stood the Storm, Seaforth but luke-warm,
Killyth and Strathallan not sta - Man:
And Hamilton pled, the Men were not bred,
For he had no Fancy to fa - Man,
But we ran, and they ran, &c.
Brave generous Southesk, Tillibairden was brisk,
Whose Father indeed would not draw - Man:
Into the same Yoke, which serv'd for a Cloak,
To keep the Estate 'twixt them twa - Man:
And we ran, atd they ran &c.
Lord Rollo not fear'd, Kintore and his Beard,
Pitsligo and Ogilvie a - Man
And Brothers Belfouts, they stood the first Sohw'rs,

Clackmannan and Burleigh did cla - Man:
And we ran, and they ran, &c.
But Cleppan act'd pretty, and Strowan the witty,
A Poet that pleases us a - Man:
For mine is but Ryme in Respect of what's fine,
Or what he is able to draw - Man.
Tho' we ran and they ran, &c.
For Huntly and Sinclair they both plaid the Tinclair,
With Conscienses black like a Crd - Man.
Some Angus and Fife Men, they ran for their Life Men,
And ne're a Lot's Wife there at a - Man.
And we ran and they ran &c.
Then Lowrie that Traitor, who betray'd his Master,
His King and his Country, and a - Man,
Pretending Mar might, give Orders to fight,
To the Right of the Army awa - Man,
And we ran and they ran &c.
Then Lawrie for Fear of what he might hear,
Took Drummond's best Horse and awa - Man;
Instead of going to Perth, he crossed the Firth,
Alongst Stirling Bridge and awa - Man.
And we ran and they ran &c.
To London he press'd and there he address'd,
That he behav'd best of them a - Man;
And there without Strife, got settled for Life,
An Hundred a Year to his Fa - Man,
And we ran and they ran, &c.
In Borrowstouness he resides with Disgrace,
'Till his Neck stand in Need of a Dra - Man,
And then with a Tether, he'll swing from a Ladder,
Go off the Stage with a Pa - Man.
And we ran, and they ran, &c.
Rob Roy stood Watch on a hill for to catch,
The Booty for ought that I saw - Man:
For he ne're advanc'd from the Place he was stanc'd,
Till no more to do there at a - Man,
And we ran and they ran, &c.
So we all took the Flight, and Moubry the Wright,
But Letham the Smith was a bra - Man,
For he took the Gout, which truly was wit,
By judging it Time to withdra - Man.
And we ran, and they ran, &c.
And Trumpet Marine too whose Brecks were not clean
Misfortune he happen'd to fa - Man, (throw,
By saving his Neck, his Trumpet did break,
Came off without Musick at a - Man.
And we ran, and they ran, &c.
So there such a Race was, as ne're in that Place was,
And as little Chase was at a - Men;
From other they ran without Took of Drum,
They did not make Use of a Pa - Man
And we ran, and they ran, and they ran, and we ran,
And we ran, and they ran awa - Man.

F I N I S.

> They pick'd my Pouches bare Man,
> But I wish ne'er to drie sic Fear,
> For a the Sum and mair Man.[7]

The most durable of the '15 broadsides, 'A Race at Sheriff-Muir, Fairly run on the 13th of *November* 1715', uses a different tune, 'The Horseman's Sport'. This may have been because of its Highland affinities—it is mentioned by the Jacobite poet William Meston in his political sequence 'Old Mother Grim's Tales', 'Tale VIII, A Lochaber Tale', in which two Highlandmen disputing the merits of their respective lineage are induced to settle the matter not by the sword, but by having a lice race, the notion being that the one with the best blood will have the most nimble lice, and the piper, 'Habbie, for he was at the sport,/On bagpipe play'd the horseman's sport'.[8] It may have been considered suitable, on the other hand, because the Battle of Sheriffmuir was an absurd mutual rout in which large parts of both armies fled in confusion. In any case, like 'Killiecrankie' the song is in the highest degree allusive, a vivid mosaic of names and titles which relies on a mass of social and political association for full appreciation. What can still be enjoyed, perhaps, is the pleasantly cynical tone of the common man considering the bungling incompetence of the mighty with ill-concealed glee:

> *There's some say, That we wan, some say, That they wan,*
>   *Some say, That nane wan at a Man:*
> *But one Thing I'm sure That at* Sheriff-muir
> *A Battle there was, which I sa—Man.*
>   And we ran and they ran, and they ran, and we ran,
>   And we ran, and they ran awa—Man...
> *Brave* Argyl *and* Belhaven, *not like Frightn'd* L---n,
>   *which* Rothes *and* Haddingtoun *sa—Man;*
> *For they all with* Wightman *advanc'd on the Right Man,*
>   *while others took Flight being ra—Men.*
>   *And we ran, and they ran* &c.
> Lord Roxbrugh *was there in Order to share,*
>   *with* Douglas *who stood not in Awe—Man;*
> *Volunteerly to ramble with Lord* Loudoun Campbel,
>   *Brave* Ilay *did suffer for a—Man,*
>   *And we ran and they ran,* &c...
> *Brave* Marishal *and* Lithgow *and* Glengary's *Pith too,*
>   *Assisted by brave Loggia—Man*
> *And* Gordons *the bright, so boly did fight,*
>   *The Red coats took Flight and awa Man*
>   *And we ran and they ran* &c...
> *Then* Lowrie *that Traitor, who betray'd his Master,*
>   *His King and His Country, and a Man,*
> *Pretending* Mar *might, give Orders to fight,*
>   *To the Right of the Army awa—Man,*
>   *And we ran and they ran* &c.
> *Then* Lawrie *for Fear of what he might hear,*
>   *Took* Drummond's *best Horse and awa—man:*
> *Instead of going to* Perth, *he crossed the* Firth,
>   *Alongst* Stirling *Bridge and awa—Man.*

And we ran and they ran &c.
To London h*e press'd and there he address'd,*
That he behav'd best of them a—Man;
And there without Strife, got settled for Life,
An Hundred a Year to his Fa—Man,
And we ran and they ran &c.
In Borrowstouness *he resides with Disgrace,*
Till his Neck stand in Need of a Dra—man,
And then with a Tether, he'll swing from a Ladder,
Go off the Stage with a Pa—Man...
So there such a Race was, as ne're in that Place was,
And as little Chase was at a—Man;
From other they ran without Took of Drum,
They did not make Use of a Pa—Man.
And we ran, and they ran, and they ran, and we ran,
And we ran, and they ran awa—Man.[9]

In the world of eighteenth century political verse, parody reigned supreme. Episcopalian satirists repeatedly turned to the liturgy for inspiration, partly, no doubt, because of its familiarity. but there were also more mischievous reasons. To the rigid Presbyterian anything approaching set forms of worship was quite intolerable, so that the very convention was offensive quite apart from the actual content. We can see it at work in 'Scotland and England must be now/United in one nation' a song attacking the Union and its advocates from a manuscript in the Dalhousie Muniments, which is modelled on a formal curse, and ends with a resounding 'Amen', (which it would have choked a Covenanting Whig to pronounce). The Abjuration mentioned in the text was one of several oaths required to be sworn by anybody seeking public office. There were three important ones, the oath of allegiance to the *de facto* monarch, the oath of abjuration which explicitly disowned the Pretenders, and finally an oath called the assurance which was designed to plug the loopholes in the first two, and leave as little room as possible for mental reservation, and similar special pleading. As the song acknowledges what most people did was simply to grit their teeth and lie, but the oaths remained in force throughout the eighteenth century, and could still create problems of conscience for people like Robert Burns and Lady Nairne's brothers generations later.

> Scotland and England must be now
> United in one nation
> And wee must all perjure anew
> And take the Abjuration
> The Stuarts Antient true born race
> Now wee must all give over
> And must receive into their place
> The Mongrells of Hanover
> Curst be the papists who withdrew
> Our King by their perswaision
> Curst be the covenanting Crue
> Who gave the first occassion

Curst be the wretch who seis'd his throne
And Marr'd our constitution
Curst be they all who helped on
the Cursed Revolution
Curst be the traiterous traiters who
by their perfidious knavery
Have brought our nation into
Ane everlasting slavery
Curst be the parliament that day
they gave the confirmation
And Curst for ever be all they
Who take the Abjuration

Amen[10]

Liturgical sources also provide the model for 'Our parliaments mett on a hellish design', a typically comprehensive satire on the unionists in parliament. It rages against the apostacy of the Hanover succession and links contemporary opponents with the blackest implications of the Covenant.

This is what is meant by the 'game of old fortie nine', which refers to the execution of Charles I, a particularly tender point with Jacobites and Episcopalians. The opening verses provide the general frame of reference:

Our parliaments mett on a hellish design
Gainyst God and ye true heir knaves do combyne
To play ye game over of old fortie nine
unless they repent theyl be damn'd

Some the son of a whore would have plac'd on ye throne
which makes each brave cavaleer pray sigh and groane
and dame ye whole pack who to this are prone
since without amendment they are damn'd

And cursed for ever be ye first of July
If yt Hannover come in so undulie
And those who exclud ye heir vere soli
without repentance are damnd

When thrones are disposed of by Athiest and knaves
Who their countrie have sold and to England are slaves
And ye true royal line of all just right bereaves
such cannot escape damnation...

Then follow a couple of dozen verses excoriating the adherents of the Court as a set of traitors, thieves, apostates, fools, liars, hypocrites, pedants, upstarts, fornicators, syphilitics, drunkards, cockscombs, cuckolds, rebels, deists, atheists, and blasphemers. As a synopsis of possible human aberration, it must be very nearly exhaustive:

Thow base blustring Anandale false and unjust
Unfaithfull to all and unworthie of trust
To kings and friends false slave to oaths drink and lust
ffor which sin on and be damnd

Thow Johnstoun thou span of a villaine and traitor
A varlet by birth educatione and nature
Old Scotlands base cut throat and false Englands creature
    ffor which sin on & be damnd

Thow trooker thow traiter thou false Jamme Wylie
Who endeavours to break king ffergus old Tailzie
Thy sins for damnation does call wt out failzie
    wherfor sin on and be damnd

Thou Athiest thou factious thou infidel Yester
Thy Grandfathers true heir old N. is thy master
Thy sores are beyond all physick and plaister
    Wherfor sin on and be damnd

Ye Lauderdail Loudoun and fforbes ye tall
Ye Sutherland Hynford and Glencairn ye are all
A Drucken Rebellious senseles cabal
    and unless ye repent youl be damnd[11]

Political song was based upon the wholesale pillage of existing lyrics. Stanzas were borrowed, refrains preserved unaltered, words and phrases of the parent text carried over (sometimes with scant regard to sense), themes adapted and re-made, and then re-made all over again, so that from a single starting point a whole radiating network of song could spread. From an artistic point of view, the results were often unsatisfactory. Where, however, the theme of the parent song and its offspring happened in some way to coincide, the result could be momentarily felicitous, as in the opening stanza of 'The Treaty of Union', an anonymous piece based upon Francis Sempill's classic song'The Blythsome Bridal' which had recently been published in James Watson's *Choice Collection of Comic and Serious Scots Poems Both Ancient and Modern* (Edinburgh 1706).

It may be useful to remind ourselves briefly what this song was like, because it provided a model for many others. It is a sketch of a country wedding, rejoicing in the coarseness of the common people but at the same time full of lightness and grace. Sempill (or whoever wrote it, the authorship is disputed) uses the catalogue method, a fast-moving, kaleidoscopic survey of people, and events, which ideally unites intricate word-music with driving impetuous energy. The main focus here is on food and drink, a tumbling evocative fouth of Scots delicacies which suggest, like the 'Big Rock-Candy Mountain', and other songs of this type, the ultimate vision of the good life.

> *Fy, let us a' to the bridal,*
>   *For there will be lilting there,*
> *For* JOCK'S *to be married to* MAGGIE,
>   *The lass wi' the gowden hair.*
> And there wil be langkail and porridge,
>   And bannocks of barley-meal,
> And there will be good sawt herring,
>   To relish a cogue of good ale.
>   *Fy let us,* &c.

And there will be SAWNEY the soutar,
　And WILL wi' the meikle mou:
And there will be TAM the blutter,
　With ANDREW the tinkler I trow;
And there will be bow'd-legged ROBIE,
　With thumbless KATIE'S goodman;
And there will be blue-cheeked DOWBIE,
　And LAWRIE the laird of the land.
　　Fy let us, &c.

And there will be fadges and brochen,
　With fouth of good gabbock of skate,
Powsowdie, and drammock, and crowdie,
　And caller nowtfeet in a plate.
And there will be partens and buckies,
　And whytens and spaldings enew,
And singit sheepheads, and a haggies,
　And scadlips to sup till ye spue.
　　Fy let us, &c...

Scrapt haddocks, wilks, dulse, and tangles,
　And a mill of good snishing to prie;
When weary with eating and drinking,
　We'll rise up and dance till we die.
　　Then fy let us a' to the bridal,
　　For there will be lilting there,
　　For JOCK'S *to be married to* MAGGIE,
　　The lass wi' the gowden hair. [12]

But Sempill's ease is deceptive. As the many leaden-footed imitations testify, it is not a simple technique to control.

'The Treaty of Union' issues an ironic invitation to the shotgun wedding of Scotland and England; the master of ceremonies is the arch-Whig Earl of Stair, widely, but erroneously, regarded as the real architect of the affair (for which he was afterwards known as 'The Curse of Scotland')[13]

Fy, let us all to the treaty,
　As there will be wonders there,
For Scotland's to be a bryde,
　And married be the Earle of Stair.

The vigour of the opening verse is not, however, sustained. The rest of the song has a rough, improvisatory quality, the words at times barely singable to the beautiful original air:

There's Queensberry, Seafield, and Marr,
　And Morton comes in by the by;
There's Lothian, Leven, and Weems,
　And Sutherland, frequently dry.

There's Ormistone, and Tilliecoutry,
    And Smollett for the town of Dumbarton;
There's Arniston, and Carnwath,
    Put in by his uncle, Lord Wharton.

There's young Grant, and young Pennycook,
    Hugh Montgomerie, and David Dalrymple;
And there is one who will shortly bear bouk
    Prestongrange, that indeed is not simple.[14]

The ability of the parent text to colour the structure and tone of politically inspired derivitaves, is of central importance to the development of later Jacobite song.

We can see the beginning of this process in a broadside 'An excellent New Song Entituled, the New way of the Broom of Cowden Knows', which was published shortly after the '15. One surviving manuscript version bears the note 'Said to be done by my Lord Duffos when he left Scotland anno 1716',[15] but whether this is accurate or not is anybody's guess. A Whig riposte was set to the tune at about the same time, and the root-song was used at least once again during the '45, as the basis for 'Lord Balmerino's Lament'.[16]

The old seduction song of 'The Broom of Cowdenknows' can be traced back to the early seventeenth century where it appears in a list of songs as 'The lovely Northerne Lasse, Who in the Ditty, here complaining, shewes What harme she got milking her Daddies Ewes. To a pleasant Scotch tune, called, The broom of Cowdon knowes'. An early version is published by W Chappell & J W Ebsworth in the *Roxburghe Ballads* (Hertford, 1871-97). It is set in the borders and tells of the narrator's betrayal by a false shepherd lad:

Through Liddersdale as lately I went,
    I musing on did passe,
I heard a Maid was discontent—
    she sigh'd and said, 'Alas!

All maids that ever deceived was,
    beare a part of these my woes,
For once I was a bonny Lasse,
    When I milkt my dadyes Ewes.
With O, the broome, the bonny broome,
    the broome of Cowdon knowes,
Faine would I be in the North Countrey,
    to milke my dadyes Ewes.' [17]

Allan Ramsay published a version in *The Tea-Table Miscellany*, during the 1720s, although the text had obviously been in existence for several years. It features a sentimental banishment scene in which the narrator bids farewell to her home and familiar surroundings and re-affirms confidence in her lover:

Hard fate that I should banish'd be,
    Gang heavily and mourn,
Because I lov'd the kindest Swain

That ever yet was born.
O the Broom &c.

My Doggie and my little Kit
    That held my wee Soup Whey,
My Plaidy, Broach and crooked Stick,
    May now ly useless by.
O the Broom, &c.

Adieu, ye *Cowdenknows,* adieu,
    Farewel a' Pleasures there,
Ye Gods restore to me my Swain,
    Is a' I crave or care.[18]

    'The New way of the Broom of Cowden Knows' is the personal lament of a male Jacobite on the eve of exile for the cause. Its debt to the Ramsay version is obvious and shows how closely its creator followed his probable original:

Hard Fate that I should banisht be
    And Rebell called with Scorn,
For serving of a Lovely Prince,
    As e'er yet was Born,
O the Broom the Bonny Broom
    The Broom of Cowding knows
I wish his Frinds had Stayed at home
    Miking there Dadys Ewes.

My trustie Targe and good Claymore
    Must now ly useless by:
My Pleding Trows that heretofore
    I wore so Cheerfully.
    O the Broom the Bonny Broom

Aduie old *Albain* I say,
    Farewell all pleasures there,
Till I come back to my own Land,
    which I hope to see once more
    O the Broom &c...[19]

    There follows a coda, clearly added later, which optimistically surveys the European prospects of the cause:

But since the *French* doth take our part
    my fears Dispelled be
I hope few months will end our smart
    And we our Friends shall see
    O! the Broom, &c.

The Noble *Sweed* our Friend appears
    The Christian King also,
The King of Spain *Britan* not fears
    That he will them o're thro
    O the Broom, &c.

And the song ends with a robust vision of restoration:

> Well meet our Friends with Noble Heart,
> Attired with Armour clear
> Who him opose shall feel our Darts,
> Like Old *Scot* Men of Weir,
> *O the Broom, &c.*

> Then happay Days and Pace well have
> Content in every place,
> Ashamed all the Rouges shall be,
> And Honest Men shall have Place
> O *the Broom, the bonny Broom*
> *The Broom of* Cowden-Knows,
> *I wish his Friends had stayed at home*
> *a Milking of the Ewes.*

As well as the twin themes of exile and restoration, the Jacobite songwriter has imported from the original its subjective lyricism—which focuses attention upon the emotions of the singer rather than on public affairs—and its pervasive ambience of love and regret. Present here in embryonic form, therefore, as early as 1715 are the major ingredients of the later Jacobite lyric.

The process was to be repeated again and again as the century advanced. As Jacobite songwriters increasingly plundered the central canon of Scottish love song, the ambience of love increasingly invaded what had started as a purely political convention. Starting life as satirical parody, the Jacobite song gradually developed into a lyric of sentiment and established itself as an independent form.

Figure 3. 'Prince Charles Edward Stuart'—Whig Caricature. (Courtesy of the
National Portrait Gallery of Scotland).

Figure 4. 'Prince Charles Edward Stuart at Holyrood Palace' by John Pettie. (Courtesy of The Registrar, Royal Collection).

Chapter Five

'CHARLES AND HIS HELLISH BAND'

During the first half of the eighteenth century many contemporaries considered Scotland as basically two different countries, Highland and Lowland, with different cultural values, manners, language and dress. Made roads, modern communications, air travel and a host of other changes—like extensive drainage and the disappearance of the great bogs—have blurred our appreciation of the Grampian mountains as a great geographical barrier. Beyond the Highland boundary fault lay a country almost unknown in the south. Few southerners went there, and those who did usually made their wills before setting out. Into considerable areas the Reformation had never penetrated. The people worshipped sticks and stones, or so the Society in Scotland for the Propagation of Christian Knowledge affected to believe, and they lived under a complex socio-legal system, a local compromise between feudality and the old kindred network, which was riven by conflict and productive of almost constant turbulence.[1]

Above all the inhabitants spoke a different language. There was, apparently, no border culture where the peculiarities of each society blended and were ameliorated. Neighbours living at opposite ends of a single township could be mutually unintelligible. The differences were stark and excited the imagination. Daniel Defoe (who considered himself an expert after his spell in Edinburgh as an English spy at the time of the Union) accused cartographers of indiscriminatingly filling up the Highlands with mountains, in the same way that they peopled darkest Africa with lions and elephants.[2]

To certain parts of the Lowland mind the Highlands were equally a *tabula rasa* upon which could be projected whatever was most feared. Paganism, cannibalism, lycanthropy—anything could be attributed to the inhabitants of these barbarous parts. Ethnic hatred thickened the atmosphere on both sides of the Highland line. The Gaels cherished a memory, accurate enough perhaps, that their ancestors had formerly possessed the more fertile parts of the country before their dispossession by the mongrel Lowlanders. Some of them, indeed, denied that they were Scots, refusing even to share a common identity with the contemptible Saxons of the plains.[3]

The *Gaidhealtachd* was extremely significant from a military point of view, however, because of the large numbers of fighting men it contained, and the prevailing system of land tenure, which meant that when the lairds came 'out' their people were compelled to follow them. It was thither, accordingly, that

Charles Edward Stuart bent his steps, arriving in Moidart with a handful of companions in the spring of 1745.[4]

What happened next is well known. The government forces under General Sir John Cope thrust rashly into the hills, were outmanoeuvred, because of the superior mobility of Highland foot (heavily equipped infantry of the line could march as little as ten miles a day; Highlanders could do thirty or forty at a push), and within a fortnight Charles Edward was in Edinburgh. Cope shipped his force back to Dunbar and marched to the relief of the capital, only to be surprised and routed at Prestonpans, almost within sight of the city.[5]

The unimaginable had happened. The serenely confident Whig establishment, self-styled bulwark of 'British liberties', had collapsed like a house of cards. The Auld Stewarts were back again with a vengeance and Edinburgh was in the hands of what many had been conditioned to regard as a heathenish and barbaric rabble.

As one would expect, both sides rapidly accomodated these startling events to their mythic world-picture. The Whigs made enormous play with the fact that the Prince was a Catholic, brought up in Italy as a pensioner of the Vatican. A typical Whiggish broadside of the time, '*The Original and Conduct of the Young* Pretender' gives more than half of its thirty verses to a summary of Stuart iniquity stretching back deep into the seventeenth century, and refurbishing all the old party taunts, such as the Old Pretender being an illegitimate foundling smuggled into his mother's bed in a warming-pan, and so on. The Grass-Market is referred to as the place of common execution in Edinburgh, and to many Whigs the proverbial phrase 'to justify God in the Grassmarket' had evil enough associations:

> All loyal *Scots* within our Land,
>   You're warned to beware
> Of *Charles* and his hellish Band,
> And all such hellish Ware...
>
> His Father, none of royal Race,
>   Was a Brick-Maker's Son,
> Which you may ken, if search the Case
>   Anent the Warming-Pan.
>
> She that some nam'd his Grand-Mother,
>   A Prostitute most base,
> Was deem'd to be a common Whore,
>   That none her Lust could please.
>
> All that profest the Name of God
>   To them she Spite did bear,
> Brought here a Swarm, as in a Cloud,
>   Of Rome's most loathsome Ware.
>
> *Grass-Market* sure can Witness bear,
>   How they the Saints did hang.
> They headed, han'g and quarter'd there,
>   By Order of her Gang...[6]

Then at the Revolution, James is deposed for his cruelties and the male line of the Stuarts debarred from the crown:

> And ever since, unto this Hour,
>   No Man of *Stuart's* Race
> Durst ever venture, to be sure,
>   On Throne to shew his Face.
>
> Although that *Charlie's* Father came
>   Here in the year *Fifteen*,
> With Band of Robbers, thieving Gang,
>   And in our Land was seen.
>
> Our men in Armour did appear,
>   Did skelp their Buttocks bare,
> At *Preston* and at *Sheriff-Muir*,
>   In both these places, where.
>
> Our gallant Generals Conduct had
>   Under great *George* then King;
> Some Traitors and some Rebels did
>   Then high on Gallows hing.

The narrator now turns his attention to Charles Edward and the Highland army. He draws on the historical caricature already implanted in the audience's mind to evoke a chilling picture of the Chevalier as a ghoulish predator and his followers as unclean spirits, scarcely within the pale of humanity:

> Now in our Day this Bird of Prey,
>   Son of *James* bigot great,
> From's Nest at *Rome* has flown away,
>   Come here, as if in State;
>
> Thieves and Rogues come at his Back,
>   These *Amorites* from North,
> A bare-ars'd nasty Lousy Pack
>   Come o'er the Water of *Forth*...

The power of these images lies in their alluding not so much to inhabitants of the natural world, as to the fabulous beast-men of Hebrew prephecy. Indeed the verse beginning 'Now in our Day...' probably has in the background a specific text—Revelation xviii, 2: 'Babylon the great is fallen, is fallen, and become the habitation of devils...and a cage of every unclean and hateful bird', obviously suggesting to a theologically minded Whiggish audience a parallel to the recent fall of Edinburgh. It would, moreover, recall the traditional equation of Babylon with Rome and so identify the mother of abominations with the Prince's grandmother 'drunken with the blood of the saints' in Edinburgh. The writers reliance upon a tissue of loose biblical allusion gives the song a unity over and above the temporal progression of the narrative and at the same time claims kindred for the Whigs with the victorious forces in cosmic history. For here, exulting in property, consumed by ethnic hatred, and deeply imbroiled in the bloody martyrology of the Solemn League and Covenant is militant Scottish Whiggism in its most distinctive popular form.

The writers vision is bounded by the narrow circuit of the kirk, the custom-house, and the gallows. He understands the threat to religion very well, but treats secular affairs with an undiluted materialism. In his eyes the Highlanders' main offence is not Popery but peculation:

> These Locusts fell, as come from Hell,
> They on the Booty flew,
> Syne rich was made the scurvy Blade,
> And all his nasty Crew.

> To steal and reave is all they want,
> For that they've ta'en the Way;
> Only of Honesty they're scant,
> That does not match their Play.

With a single voice Whig songwriters condemn the Highland army as a band of thieves and its leader as the greatest thief of all. One contemporary broadside 'The Rebels bold March into England, with their shameful Retreat', pursues the theme through more than thirty verses:

> They rob'd and plunder'd a' the Gate,
> Through Dub and Mire they plasht it out;
> Their Head of Robbers with them gae,
> Out o'er the Hills and far away...

> O Charlie, what's the Matter, Man,
> Since ye're Head of the thieving Clan,
> That to St. James ye did nae gae,
> To take the British Crown away?

> Strange! Man, what made you turn your Back,
> Ye neither Thieves nor Rogues did lack,
> To steal, and reave, and run away,
> To you as Master of the Play?...

> For from your least to highest Clan,
> None can produce one honest Man,
> But Thieves and Rogues to skelp the Brae,
> Out o'er the Hills and far away.

> You scurvy Lowns, with Buttocks bare,
> That robs and plunders every where,
> And of the same you get your Fa',
> As Chief of Rogues among them a'.

> In England, as you rang'd about,
> To steal and reave, was very stout;
> But when it came to fighting Play,
> Ye're o'er the Hills and far away...[7]

This clamour about robbery and plunder appears to have relatively little basis in fact.[8] It may owe something of its origin, however, to the mechanical application of scripture to politics, and derive in part from an opportunistic reading of the parable of The Good Shepherd. To a Whig, King George would be the Shepherd,

An Excellent SONG on the prefent Times, by a Country *Hind.*

To the Tune of Killycranky.

I.

IN this auld Year, whofe End is near,
 Dark Providence is frowning,
Some native *Scots,* they act like Sots,
 Their King they are difowning.
For *James* the Eight they boldly fight
 Againft their native Nation,
They do intend at once to end
 Our glorious Reformation.

II.

That Baftard Brood, who fhed the Blood
 Of our bold brave Forebeers,
Is now once more arriv'd on Shore,
 Which mony a ane admires :
But this poor Trafh, whofe Love to Cafh
 Will make them fell their Nation,
With *France* and *Rome* do now prefume
 To make a new Relation.

III.

From the cold North, ftraight to the *Forth,*
 The *Highland* Clans advanced,
On *Sabbath*-Day made their Pipes play,
 And merrily they danced.
With fingle Pumps they made clean Jumps,
 Like Lambs among the Heather,
With Buttocks bare they did not care
 Neither for Wind nor Weather.

IV.

Still South they come, with Pipe and Drum,
 With their Prince or Pretender ;
Whate'er he be, he may well fee.
 He is no fmall Offender.
Inftead of Laws his Sword he draws,
 And acts with great Oppreffion,
Folks Goods he takes, and his he makes,
 And thinks it no Tranfgreffion.

V.

When Men fhould fleep, abroad they creep,
 In order for to plunder,   (Gear,
With Gun, Sword, Spear, they kill Folks
 And drive their Flocks afunder.
Like a wild Hawk, their Prey they take,
 And greedily they flay them,
To be foon fu', they finge the Woo',
 And take nae Time to flay them.

VI.

Some called Lairds, gae to Stack-Yards,
 The Stacks they caufe fome draw them,
For ftolen Horfe, the Sheaves by Force
 Upon the Ground they ftraw them.
To their Club-Law, both great and fma'
 Muft quickly yield Subjection,
Thus their new King does Slav'ry bring,
 Inftead of fafe Protection.

VII.

His Troops they fteal the good Oatmeal,
 And in cauld Water fteer it,
Then like to Fifh plunge in the Difh,
 And from their Kits they clear it.
Thus their Cauld-Steer, they think brave
     (Cheer,
They fnuff and crack right canty ; .
They rant and roar becaufe great Store
 Of Victuals they have Plenty.

VIII.

Through Town and Stead they ran with
       (Speed,
 And put Men in Diforder,
The Salt-Beef they fteal all away,
 And Mutton in our Border.
Of Rich and Poor they keep the Door,
 And make themfelves the Porter,
The Butter Pigs of all the Whigs
 They knead like Dough and Morter.

IX.

Are grave wife *Scots* now blinded Sots ?
 Or are they fo forgetful
Of former Kings, whofe wicked Reigns
 Were cruel and deceitful ?
Their Subjects they did bafely flay,
 Contrair to Law and Reafon,
Their Faithfulnefs was thought no lefs
 Than Error, Guilt and Treafon.

X.

A King like this, O who will blefs ?
 Or what Prieft will pray for him ?
I hope none wife will venture Lives
 In order to reftore him.
Of Tyranny and Cruelty
 We have a bad Example,
And I do fear, if *James* were here,
 The Stock prove like the Sample.

XI.

Bees-Skeps they cut with Bayonet,
 Wherever they can find them,
And tho' the Bees fting their bare Thighs,
 They skip and never mind them ;
The Honey fweet with Greed they eat,
 Tho' through their Meggs it droppeth,
And thus like Tar their Fingers are,
 No Filth nor Dirt them ftoppeth.

XII.

Thus may we fee how mightily
 Our Neighbours are opprefled,
Our native Land with cruel Hand
 Is very fore diftrefled.
Religion, Laws and Liberties,
 Are now all in great Danger,
If that we yield or quit the Field
 To an *Italian* Stranger.

XIII.

But I do hear that *Ligonier,*
 Is South with a great Army,
And the bold Duke of *Cumberland*
 Is in Purfuit of *Charlie.*
And tho' they're rude, yet for their Blood,
 His Troops they dare not face them,
But from them fcoups, with their bare
      (Doups,
As if the De'il did chafe them.

XIV.

May Sea and Land, with Heart and Hand,
 Fight for our King *Hanover,*
Whofe gentle Reign great Peace doth bring,
 All his Dominions over.
And if we fall by Sword or Ball,
 For Truth and Peace contending,
Our Death will crown us with Renown,
 And that's a happy Ending.

F I N I S.

Charles Edward the Thief, the Sheep the people of Britain, and the Door of the
Sheepfold the Act of Succession. The Thief,

> entereth not by the door into the sheepfold, but climbeth up some other way, [by
> Moidart, perhaps?] the same is a thief and a robber. But him that entereth in by the
> door is the shepherd of the sheep...and the sheep follow him; for they know his voice.
> And a stranger will they not follow, but will flee from him: for they know not the
> voice of strangers...The thief cometh not, but for to steal, and to kill, and to destroy.[9]

Returning to '*The Original and Conduct of the Young* Pretender' we discover
another preoccupation perhaps not so noticeable at first, namely an acute awareness
of the physical presence of the Highlanders. There is repeated reference to the
unpleasantness of their persons. Again and again the writer insists that they are
'nasty' and 'lousy', using the words so often as to suggest a depth of repugnance
which he is otherwise unable to articulate. The writer of 'An Excellent Song on
the present Times, by a Country *Hind*', sees Lowland Scotland as a land flowing
with milk and honey wantonly plundered by the hungry northern hordes. His
distaste at their savage exuberance of appetite amounts almost to physical nausea:

> His troops they steal the good Oatmeal,
>   And in cold Water steer it,
> Then like to Fish plunge in the Dish,
>   And from their Kits they clear it.
> Thus their Cauld-Steer, they think brave Cheer,
>   They snuff and crack right canty;
> They rant and roar because great Store
>   Of Victuals they have Plenty.
>
> Through Town and Stead they run with Speed,
>   And put Men in Disorder,
> The Salt-Beef they steal all away,
>   And Mutton in our Border.
> Of Rich and Poor they keep the Door,
>   And make themselves the Porter,
> The Butter Pigs of all the Whigs
>   They knead like Dough and Morter...
>
> Bees-Skeps they cut with Bayonet,
>   Wherever they can find them,
> And tho' the Bees sting their bare Thighs,
>   They skip and never mind them;
> The Honey sweet with Greed they eat,
>   Tho' through their Meggs is droppeth,
> thus like Tar their Fingers are,
>   No Filth nor Dirt them stoppeth.[10]

This is a recurrent feature of contemporary Whig songs. In ' *A Poem on the
Rebellion, &c. To the Tune of* William *of* Plymouth', for example, the writer, after
several fairly ordinary verses about robbing and stealing, suddenly succumbs to
an apparently quite genuine fit of ethnic hysteria:

> New Cesses, new Tartans, new Shoes, and new Brogues,
> In Haste must be ready for these *Highland* Rogues,
> Most part whereof seemed like Swine or like Stirks,
> Polluting our Lodgings, defiling our Kirks.[11]

The sudden irruption of a gentile horde delivered a severe check to the confidence of the Presbyterian ascendency in the Lowlands. In this nightmarish situation, 'there were moments when nothing seemed impossible; and, to say the truth, it was not easy to forecast, or imagine, any thing more unlikely, than what had already happened'. Some lost their apprehension for the succession in fears for the Reformation itself.

The heterodox Highlandmen lay beyond the reach of the Kirk's penitential system and as they did not seem to acknowledge any form of the moral law, Presbyterian terrors were amplified by a rich awareness of the antinomian alternatives. The Gaels had already given ample evidence of unnatural behaviour:

> From the cold North, straight to the *Forth*,
>   The *Highland* Clans advanced,
> On *Sabbath*-Day made their Pipes play,
>   And merrily they danced.
> With single Pumps they made clean Jumps,
>   Like Lambs among the Heather,
> With Buttocks bare they did not care
>   Neither for Wind nor Weather.
>
> Still South they come, with Pipe and Drum,
>   With their Prince or Pretender;
> Whate'er he be, he may well see,
>   He is no small Offender.
> Instead of Laws his Sword he draws,
>   And acts with great Oppression,
> Folks Goods he takes, and his he makes,
>   And thinks it no Transgression.
>
> When Men should sleep, abroad they creep,
>   In order for to plunder,
> With Gun, Sword, Spear, they kill Folks Gear,
>   And drive their Flocks asunder...
> To their Club-Law, both great and sma'
>   Must quickly yield Subjection,
> Thus their new King does Slav'ry bring,
>   Instead of safe Protection.[12]

The Highland occupation was a standing reproach to the ethnic supremacism of the Lowlands. If any liberal attitude had hitherto been discernible in the general response of southern Lowlanders to the people of the Highlands, it had been an attempt to exercise moral tutelage from a distance, as part of a long-standing campaign to induce conformity with Lowland standards in language, education and public order. Now the lion had swallowed the lion-tamer; the roles were reversed, and the Lowland establishment found it deeply degrading. Here, for example, is the Presbyterian minister and minor Enlightenment *littérateur* Alexander Carlyle, who had gone to assist the surgeons after the battle of Prestonpans, and got a view of the conquering clans at close quarters:

> It was...not long before we arrived at Cockenzie, where I had an opportunity of seeing this victorious army. In general they were of low stature and dirty, and of a contemptible appearance...This...confirmed me in the prepossession that nothing but the weakest and most unaccountable bad conduct on our part could have possibly given them the victory. God forbid that Britain should ever again be in danger of being overrun by such a despicable enemy.[13]

But there was, if possible, a still darker side to Whig fears. If the Highlanders were indeed exempt from the moral law, then quite horrific theological possibilities opened up. Instead of being a dynastic squabble, which was a reasonably familiar idea, or a super *creach*—perhaps more familiar still—the rebellion could be seen as a desperate encounter in the cosmic struggle between God and Antichrist and the field of Prestonpans a precursor of Armageddon. While the Jacobites gave thanks to a beneficent Providence for their unexpected victory, the Whigs turned to gloomy visions of the Apocalypse.

Throughout the Christian era, men had applied the prophecies concerning Antichrist to the great political upheavals of their day. So now the sensitivity of the Presybterian mind to the reality of the invisible world induced serious eschatological speculation about the '45. The words of Ezekiel must have had an ominous ring:

> Therefore, son of man, prophesy and say unto Gog, Thus saith the Lord God...thou shalt come from thy place out of the north parts, thou, and many people with thee, all of them riding upon horses, a great company and a mighty army: and thou shalt come up against my people of Israel, as a cloud to cover the land; it shall be in the latter days.[14]

The frequent use of prophecy bears tribute to the vitality of the mythogenic world-picture at this period. The Jacobites often used the scriptures in a similar way, and they drew, too, upon a rich vein of secular prophecy which had long circulated amongst the common people in popular printed form and was associated with such names as Merlin, and Thomas the Rhymer. It was a point of honour amongst them to style their victory 'Gladsmuir' rather than 'Prestonpans', although that village lay some distance off, to make it square with numerous prophecies that there would one day be an apocalyptic battle fought there. Thus, from 'The Prophecie of Bertlington', reprinted by David Laing in his *Collection of Ancient Scottish Prophecies, in Alliterative Verse* (Edinburgh 1833):

> On Glaidsmoore shall the battle be
> It shall not be Gladsmoore by the sey,
> It shal be Gladsmoore where ever it be.[15]

The contemporary currency of these prophecies is attested by the popular poet Dougal Graham in his metrical 'History of the Rebellion':

> The place old Rhymer told long before,
> 'That between Seaton and the sea,
> 'A dreadful morning there should be,
> 'Meet in the morning lighted by the moon,
> 'The lion his wound here, heal shall not soon'.
> In Thomas' book of this you'll read,
> Mention'd by both Merlin and Bead.[16]

In this kind of atmosphere it was easy for the Whigs to identify Charles Edward with the figure of Antichrist. The ground had in any case been prepared by generations of Whig pamphleteers assiduously equating the pretensions of the Stuarts with those of the Pope and the Devil. The Reformers had long ago identified Antichrist with the office of the Papacy itself, and the arrival in Scotland of a Catholic prince hot-foot from Rome would naturally bring the Revelation of St John with its magniloquent denunciation of the great whore sitting on many waters drunken with the blood of the saints and martyrs vividly before the mind.[17]

And the Whigs found a slaughtered saint readily enough to hand, in the person of Colonel James Gardiner, cavalry officer, kirk elder and leading Edinburgh evangelical. On the day of Prestonpans his men turned and ran and Gardiner was killed trying vainly to rally the few still fighting on.[18]

He was instantly assimilated to the Whig martyrology as witnessed by the broadside 'Elegy On the Memory of the Honourable Colonel James Gardiner, who was cruelly murdered by the Antichristian Mob near Tranent, Sept.21, 1745'. The 'Elegy' leans heavily on the Authorised Version and its imagery is loaded with biblical allusion drawn, in the main, from the book of Revelation, but it is very largely preoccupied by local events. It is informed by the same kind of dualism that we saw in the sermons of the hill preachers, the same startling combinations of the sacred and profane, the cosmic and parochial. In a sense two battles are going on simultaneously. The first, obviously, is the actual engagement at Prestonpans with its very human ambience of heroism and treachery:

> Our Men in Armour did appear,
>   As being fill'd with Hope
> Of Victory, and free of Fear,
>   Till sold by Traitor Cope...
>
> Dragoons they fled with greatest Speed,
>   Him left to stand alone,
> And in his Time of greatest Need
>   With him sure was not one.[19]

The second is a conflict of apocalyptic forces of which the human protagonists are merely the agents. The descent of the Jacobite army is described in the following terms:

> From Rome a Limb of Antichrist,
>   Join'd with a Hellish Band
> Of Highland Thieves, came here in haste,
>   God's Laws for to withstand.

To introduce the Man of Sin
It sure was their intent,
'Gainst God their Battle did begin
Hard by the Town Tranent.

The identification of the Chevalier with the cause of Antichrist is meant to be taken literally, as the writer's systematic use of St John's vision of 'The Last Things' indicates:

This dear Saint's Blood sure cries aloud,
And will Vengeance down
On Steuart's Cause, and on their Laws,
And them with Vengeance Crown.

(I saw under the altar the souls of them that were slain for the word of God, and for the testimony which they held; and they cried out with a loud voice, saying, How long, O Lord, holy and true, dost thou not judge and avenge our blood...Revelations vi, 9,10)

They surely shall have Blood to drink,
Who dares to draw a Sword,
To fight, oppose, and so to think,
'Gainst Him that's God the Lord.

(they have shed the blood of the saints and prophets and thou hast given them blood to drink; Revelations xvi,6).

Gardiner is exalted among the martyrs 'under the altar' and assured of a place in the first resurrection. By thus placing his hero's death in the familiar eschatological framework, the writer is free to concentrate upon his beatification—which he does at considerable length—and remain true to his fundamentally didactic purpose. Charles Edward and the clans are meantime abandoned to a fate so obvious that it need only be suggested.

The mythogenic Covenanting world-picture survives in traditional form and apparently full vitality in southern Lowland Scotland until at least the middle of the eighteenth century. When we turn to the Jacobites, however, we discover the royalist myth transformed by the absorption of new elements from contemporary popular culture. King Fergus and the early Stuarts fade into the background and the picture is dominated by a striking new mythic creation, 'Bonny Prince Charlie'. And we can watch this process happening step-by-step in popular political songs during the '45 and the years immediately following it.

The Characters
Introduction

WHEN Israel first provock'd the Liveing Lord
God Scourg'd their Sins with famine plague & Sword
They still rebell'd God in his wrath did Sting
No thunder bolts amongst them but a King
A George like King was heavens severst Rod
The utmost fury of an incens'd God
God in his wrath sent Saul to punish Jewry
And George to England in a greater fury
For George in Sin as far exceeded Saul
As Bishop Burnet did the great Saint Paul

Characters

1
Shame fall my Eyn if ever I have seen
  Such a parcell of Rogues in a Nation
For the Campbell and the Graham are equaly to blame
  Seduc'd by a strong Infatuation
The Squadrone and the Why are upish & look big
  And designe for to ride us at pleasure
For to lead us by the nose is what they do propose
  And Enhance to themselves all our Treasure

2
The Dalrymples come in play tho' they've Sold us all away
  And basely betray'd this poor Nation
On Justus levy no stuff for this Country they'le oppress
  Haveing no Sort of Commiseration
No Nation ever had a sett of men so bad
  That feed on its vitals like Vultures
Bargeny & Glenco & the Union doth Show
  That to Country & Crown they are Traitors

3
Lord Annandale must rule tho' he's but a very tool
  Hath deceiv'd every man that did trust him
To promise he'l not Slak & to break will be as quick
  Queen him money you cannot disgust him
Ti happen'd on a day that us Cavaliers did say
  And drink to their health in a Brimmer
But now he's turn'd his Coat & again has Chang'd his note
  And acted the part of a Trimmer

4
Little Rothes now may huff & all the Cadies cuff
  Sonny Black must resolve to knock under
Belhaven has of late found out his Fathers was a Cheat
  And his Speech on the Union a Blunder
And Haddington that Saint may row row & rant
  He's a prop to the Kirk in this Nation
And Ormeston will bring all the Torries in a bang
  And every man thats against Reformation

5
Mr Baillie with his songs & Roxburghs Eloquence
  must find out a designd Assasination
If their Plotts are not well laid Mr Johnston will them Aid
  He's Expert in that nice Occupation
Tho David Baillies dead honest Hersland's in his Stead
  His Grace can make use of such Creatures
Can teach them how to Sweer against whom & what to Swear
  And prove whom He will to be Traitors

Chapter Six

'LADDIE WI' THE TARTAN PLAIDIE'

We saw in the previous chapter how Whig songwriters displayed a deep-rooted antipathy to Highlanders and to some of the more obvious manifestations of Highland culture. But this was not a new tendency: it was merely the contemporary application of a long tradition of anti-Highland satire going back deep into the Middle Ages. Even in such early pieces as William Dunbar's 'Dance of the Sevin Deidly Synnis', and Sir Richard Holland's 'Book of the Howlat' the lines of opposition are already defined: Highlandmen are proud, obstinate, boastful, treacherous, violent, fickle, cowardly, and ragged; they speak very loudly in a barbarous language that nobody can understand, and there are altogether too many of them.

Dunbar's riotous *Walpurgisnacht* of sin and debauchery actually comes to its climax in an infernal Highland games (there are, naturally, a great many Highlandmen in Hell). The resulting racket and confusion is more than even the Devil can stand so he banishes them to the depths of the Pit:

> Then cryd Mahoun for a Heleand padyane;
> Syne ran a feynd to feche Makfadyane,
> Far northwart in a nuke;
> Be he the correnoch had done schout,
> Erschemen so gadderit him abowt,
> In Hell grit rowme thay tuke.
> Thae tarmegantis, with tag and tatter,
> Full lowd in Ersche begowth to clatter,
> And roup lyk revin and ruke:
> The Devill sa devit wes with thair yell,
> That in the depest pot of hell
> He smorit thame with smuke.[1]

The Holland piece has a similar flavour. A typical mediaeval parliament of the birds is suddenly disrupted by a reiving, ranting, swaggering Highland bard loudly demanding food and drink and dazing the auditors with a pyrotechnic display of unintelligable celtic lore:

> Sae come the Ruke, with a rerd and rane roch,
> A bard out of Ireland, with 'Banachadee'.
> Said: 'Gluntow guk dynydrach, hala mischy doch—
> Rax her a rug of the roast, or sho shall ryme thee.

Mich macmory ach mach mountir moch loch—
Set her doun, give her a drink, what deil ails thee?
O dermyn, O Donall, O Dochardy droch.
Thir are the Ireland kingis of the Irishery:—
O Knewlyn, O Connochar, O Gregor MacGrane.
   The Shennachy, the Clarsach,
   The Ben shene, the Ballach,
   The Crekery, the Corach,
      Sho kennis them ilkane'.[2]

This satiric tradition had once, no doubt, been the common possession of all Lowlanders, but increasing reliance by the Jacobites upon Highland troops was beginning to make it by the end of the seventeenth century a distinctly Whiggish preoccupation. The most developed example from the period is probably the racy Hudibrastic '*Mock* Poem, Upon the EXPEDITION Of the Highland-host: *Who came to destroy the* Western Shires, in *Winter* 1678', by William Cleland, an educated west country Whig who was killed commanding the Cameronian regiment in the skirmishing after Killiecrankie. The 'Highland Host' of the title was a force of Highland militia which the government quartered in the Westland to keep the locals quiet and generally make a nuisance of themselves, and the poem deals with the usual things southern Lowlanders disliked about Highlandmen, their acquisitiveness, revolting personal habits, outlandish dress, and apparently insatiable sexual appetite. It is too long to be quoted in its entirety, but the following extracts give some idea of its flavour:

Nought like Religion they retain,
Of moral Honestie they're clean.
In nothing they're accounted sharp,
Except in Bag-pipe, and in Harpe.
For a misobliging word,
She'll durk her neighbour ov'r the boord,
And then she'll flee like fire from flint,
She'll scarcely ward the second dint;
If any ask her of her thrift,
Forsooth her nain sell lives by thift...
They durk our Tennants, shame our Wives

And we're in hazard of our Lives,
They plunder horse, and them they loaden,
With Coverings, Blankets, sheets and Plaidin
With Hooding gray, and worsted Stufs,
They sell our Tongs for locks of snuff.
They take our Cultors and our soaks,

And from our doors they pull the locks...
Amongst the rest of their Trespasses
They're oft imployed in chaseing Lasses,
It is too evident a token,
Of this when Maidens bakes are broken
Yea tho they touch them not at all,
They'r like to starve for very cald

For when they sit their plaids do hang by,
Ye'l see from Navels down each thing fy,
Such sights the Lasses cannot bide,
So they must starve in a backside,
And here an instance *I* shall tell,
Of what to one of them befell:
This red-shank from no good pretence,
Pursued the Lass ben to the spence
And aiming at some naughtie deed,
Pull'd up his plaid and ran with speed,
She with a fleshcruik in her hand,
Advised him a back to stand,
But he presuming for to strugle,
Occasioned a huble buble
The story it is something od
She with the Flesh-cruik gript his cod,
So held and rag'd and made him squil
And ay cry out the Deu'l the Deu'l,
But getting of away he flees,
While blood was spreading down his Thighs
For several dayes he keept his Bed
And when he got up he strid led
From either hands they get small thanks
Who are the Authors of such pranks.[3]

The predilection of Highlandmen for acts of sudden violence, and their comic incompetence when it came to the bit, crop up repeatedly in contemporary poetry. Here, for example, is the Edinburgh poet Alexander Pennecuik's 'Curse on the Clan M'Phersone, occasioned by the news of Glenbucket his being murdered by them', which exhibits the moral outrage characteristic of an ingrained Lowland attitude. Glenbucket was the Gordons' factor in Badenoch, and had aroused the wrath of the local people by his evictions. They decided to do away with him while he was ill in bed but the canny Glenbucket had a sword handy and kept his assailants at bay. The reports of his death proved premature, but they inspired Pennecuik in the meantime to the following bloodthirsty couplets which view proscription as the only feasible bridle for these wild Highlandmen:

May that curs'd clan up by the roots be plucked
Whose impious hands have killed the good Glenbucket;
Villainy far worse than Infidel or Turk,
To hack his body with your bloody durk,
A fatal way to make his physick work.
Rob Roy and you fight 'gainst the noblest names,
The generous Gordons and the gallant Grahames.
Perpetual clouds thro' your black clan shall ring;
Traitors 'gainst God, and Rebells 'gainst your King,
Until you feel the law's severest rigour,
And be extinguished like the base M'Gregor.[4]

The public execution of Gaels for various misdemeanours provided an irresistable temptation to Lowland songwriters to exercise their sense of ethnic superiority, and there are a number of examples of the Highland 'goodnight' in the style of the popular gallows literature of the time, full of satiric humour. The writer of 'The Highland Man's Lament, For the Death of *Donald Bayn*, alias *M'evan Vanifranck*, who was Execute in the *Grass Market* of *Edinburgh*, on *Wednesday* the 9th Day of *January* 1723' seizes the opportunity to poke fun at the Highlanders' uncouth pastimes and quaint English usage:

> *Donald* and her, for mony a Day,
> Eat Kebbecks, and drank Huskiebae;
> And syne took up te Trumps to play,
>   *M'ferson's* Rant.
> We liv'd as blyth as the Lord *Gray*,
>   or Laird of *Grant*.
>
> Pe sure, her nane sell never saw,
> Te' Man tat valued less te Law,
> For he gae Folk, cald Coals to blaw,
>   which gard them groan.
> And when he carried all away,
>   cry'd Pockmohon.[5]

The singer bewails Donald's demise as a serious blow to the moral fabric of the Highlands. Donald is not a good man, of course, at least not as goodness is commonly understood; on the contrary, his death will cause all kinds of villainy to come unstuck. The account of his exploits, which make up the body of the poem, is one long catalogue of spoliation and slaughter, recounted with unblushing, indeed enthusiastic approval. To the narrator, violence, depredation and bloodshed are perfectly normal even desirable things, and the mock elegy form enables his creator to exploit the irony of this moral inversion at great length, and with considerable humour:

> Te like of this did ne're befal us,
> *Tonald* as stout as *William Wallace*,
> Was guarded by, te *Southland* Fallows,
>   her Heart will plead.
> For his pare Arse to grace the Gallows,
>   and now he's tead...
>
> *M'cleods, M'tonalds* and *M'panes*,
> And a te M's tat kend him anes,
> Hing toun te Head, and mak great Mains,
>   we Cronohs sair,
> For *Tonald's* gean Pelow te Stanes,
>   we ill cou'd spare.
>
> Te *Clans* will make te firy fery,
> Frae *Fokoburs* to *Inverary*,
> And frae *Glenshiels* doun to *Glengary*,
>   for *Tonald Bayn*,

> I fear te Plots will a' miscarry,
> sin *Tonald's* gane.

This, then, was the standard Whiggish Scot's view of his Highland compatriot on the eve of the '45: on the one hand he was regarded as a species of vermin fit merely for extermination, while on the other he was seen as a relatively harmless buffoon, a proper object of raillery and satire and figuring in a comic role in many Lowland songs.

Amongst the Jacobites, however, a rather different view prevailed.

In Robert Chambers's 'Jacobite Papers' in the National Library of Scotland there is a song preserved which begins 'Come let uss go drink boyes/a health unto our king'. The manuscript has been damaged and some of the text lost, but enough remains to show the writer drawing a vigorous parallel between the rebellion of 1715 and the Wars of Independence, regarding the struggle to restore the Stuarts as a war of national liberation under a native prince, and looking to Jacobite victory as a means of ending English domination.

Since the Civil Wars of the mid seventeenth century the practice of arms had been in slow decline in the Lowlands. By the early eighteenth century Highland support had become indispensable for anybody wishing to wage private war in Scotland. The succession crisis, moreover, cut across the ethnic bounds of Scottish society, and through much of the north Gael and Saxon found themselves on the same side. To a considerable body of Lowland opinion, therefore, the promise of Highland arms was sufficient to transform the Gaels from barbarous aliens into heroes and patriots, the potential deliverers of their country:

> our king they doth despise him
> becaus of Scotish blood,
> [?——————————]
> his title still is good,
> but let our brunswick sceptre stand boyes
> weell all dye on the field boyes
> for wee will never yeild boyes
> to serve a forin brood.
>
> Let the brave loyal Clans
> the Stuarts ancient race
> restoar with sword in hand [?————]
> and all there foes displace
> the union overturn boyes
> which makes our nation m[?ourn boyes]
> like bruce at bonick burn [?boyes]
> the english home weell Ch[?ase][6]

The idea appeared again very strongly at the time of the '45, especially in the triumphant aftermath of Prestonpans, when the deeds of the clans were saluted by loyalists of every hue. If they could so easily subdue all Scotland, what could they not do? The writer of the panegyric 'To His Royal Highness, Charles, Prince of *Wales*, Regent of the Kingdoms of *Scotland, England,France* and *Ireland, &c.*' beginning 'Hail Glorious Youth! the Wonder of the Age,/The future Subject of th' Historian's Page;' comparing the Prince's achievement with the exploits of the Swedish hero Gustavus Vasa, saw the Highlanders as the agents of Providence and their victory as evidence of the divine purpose working through history:

> Thus glorious *Vasa* work'd in *Swedish* Mines;
> Thus helpless saw his Enemy's Designs;
> Till rouz'd, his hardy *Highlanders* arose,
> And pour'd Destruction on their foreign Foes.
>
> Thus soon, Great Sir, thy honest Cause procur'd,
> A Loyal Race ne'er swore, or ne'er abjur'd;
> A Set of Men, the Terror and the Dread
> Of the detested *Hanoverian* Breed;
> A Set of Men, whose Worth was scarcely known;
> A Set of Men th' *Usurper* did disown:
> Disown'd indeed! reserv'd for some great Blow;
> Some Hangman Work, like loyal good *Glencoe*.
>
> These are the Few whom Heaven and Fate reserve,
> From further Slav'ry *Scotia* to preserve;
> To aid their Prince, and set him on his Throne;
> Strike Tyrants dead; make *James* be King alone:
> These are the hardy Sons the Gods decree
> To set three Nations from *Usurpers* free.
>
> Proceed, Great Warriors, worthy Men proceed,
> And latest Ages shall the Annal read;
> How hardy loyal *Highlanders* alone
> Restor'd the *Stewarts*, and set them on the Throne![7]

In themselves these tendencies are relatively unremarkable, but the link with Highland militarism gradually produced amongst Jacobites an openness to other aspects of the Highland ethos that could be mediated through Lowland vernacular culture. And out of this nexus there emerged, during the first half of the eighteenth century, one of the most remarkable developments in the history of Scottish popular culture: the amatory symbol of the Bonny Highland Laddie.

The Highlandman begins to appear in popular literature as an object of sexual curiousity from about the end of the seventeenth century onwards. By an odd quirk of cultural history, one of the earliest examples which can be dated firmly is English. In *The Earl of Mar marr'd*, a 'Tragi-Comical Farce' produced in London in 1716, and obviously inspired by the events of the previous winter, we find the Prologue addressing the following remarks to the ladies in the audience:

> *Tall* Highlanders—*(ah Ladies!) Lusty Fellowes,*
> *'Tis pitty Men like these—deserve the Gallows.*
> *Had they but cast their Plads, and travell'd hither,*
> *To taste the Softness of our milder Weather;*
> *I mean without their Arms, and warlike Geer,*
> *They might have found—a better Service here.*[8]

There can be no doubt that the pause in the middle of the last line is intended to convey heavy sexual innuendo. The ladies are expected to *admire* Highlanders, and although at this stage there is little curiousity about the details of Highland dress, sophisticated southern women were obviously expected to be intrigued by the man inside it. That is, the curious arms and attire do not blur the perception of the writer and, presumably his audience, that the Highlander is essentially a man. Immune in London from the threat of his military organisation, they could probably afford to be detached. And yet the new interest finds expression in Lowland Scotland as well, and in the first half of the century the amatory symbol of the Bonny Highland laddie is defined and elaborated—not in plays indeed, but in broadside ballads and popular songs of varying degrees of 'politeness'.

The earliest Highland Laddie song which can be dated reasonably accurately appears in *The Tea-Table Miscellany* with words by Allan Ramsay himself. The most prominent feature of the song—and one it shares in greater or less measure with most of the rest of the group—is its contrast between the voluptuous simplicity of Highland life and the artificiality and luxury of the Lowlands. The singer is a susceptible Low-country lass who considers and rejects in turn country laird and burgh-town beau in favour of her lusty Highland laddie, preferring the more ardent, if spartan, style of Highland wooing to the insipidities of sassenach dalliance:

> The Lawland Lads think they are fine,
>   But O they're vain and idly gaudy!
> How much unlike that gracefu' Mein,
>   And manly Looks of my Highland Laddie?...
>
> A painted Room and Silken Bed,
>   May please a Lawland Laird and Lady;
> But I can kiss and be as glad
>   Behind a Bush in's Highland Plaidy.
>
> *O my bonny, bonny Highland Laddie,*
> *My handsome charming Highland Laddie:*
> *May Heaven still guard, and Love reward*
> *Our Lawland Lass and her Highland Laddie.* [9]

As this was an influential song, often reprinted, it may be useful to summarise the picture of the Highlander it presents. We learn he has a 'gracefu' Mein', 'manly Looks', wears a blue bonnet and belted plaid, and has an amorous disposition. In short, the only things which distinguish him from countless other brisk young gallants in contemporary love-song are his clothes, which symbolise, although in the discretest fashion, his sexual attractiveness.

These erotic overtones receive more explicit treatment in a broadside from the Rosebery Collection entitled 'The New way, of the Bonny Highland Laddie. *To its own Proper Tune &c.*' In this version there is a 'Butter-Box' amongst the rejected lovers. This was a slang term for a Dutchman, current at the time of the Revolution and suggests that the song may considerably antedate the one in the *Tea-Table Miscellany*. In Ramsay's version, the Lowland lassie escapes into an idealised world of rustic love, but the Highlands are by no means a scented garden for the heroine of the Rosebery ballad. Despite rejecting her southern background, she carries its commercial values with her, and although ruefully consoling herself with the prospect of boundless sensual gratification, she is still disconcerted to discover that gentility in the Highlands is not based upon money. This is not revealed, however, until the end of the song, which opens with her 'adieu' to the south and the Lowland ethos:

> *I Crossed* Forth, *I crossed* Tay,
>   *I left* Dundee, *and* Edinborrow,
> *I saw nothing there worth my Stay,*
>   *and so I bad them all Good-morrow.*

> O my bonny, bonny Highland Laddie,
>   O my bonny, bonny Highland Laddie,
> When I am sick and like to dye,
>   Thou'lt row me in thy Highland Pladie.[10]

'Sickness' and 'death' are, of course, periphrases for desire and consummation. During the next two centuries literally hundreds of song heroines would be thus 'row'd', and the phrase became one of the commonest sexual metaphors in Scottish popular poetry.

On her way into the hills, the singer meets the Highland Laddie, vigorous and ready, whose direct style of courtship offers exactly the kind of escape from restraint she had in mind. We may note that not only the garments but the military equipment of the Highlander are pressed into service as bawdy metaphors:

> *For on the* Cairnamount *I spy'd,*
>   *in careless Dress a Highland Laddie,*
> *Who briskly said wer't thou my Bride,*
>   *I'd row thee in my Highland Pladie,*
>   O my bonny, bonny, &c.

> *No* Butter-Box *he seem'd to be,*
>   *no* English-Fop, *nor Lowland Laddie,*
> *But by his mein he was well known,*
>   *to be some Gentie Highland Laddie.*
>   O my bonny, bonny, &c.

> *His Quiver hang down by his Thigh,*
>   *his Mein did show his Bow was ready,*
> *A thousand Darts flew from his Eye,*
>   *and all fell down before his Lady.*
>   O my bonny, bonny, &c.

The next verse closely resembles the concluding stanza of Ramsay's song, but here the cash fails to materialise and the promise of high life dissolves. There are still the pleasures of the 'Highland Pladie', however, and all it implies:

> *It's Silken Rooms and Pearled Beds,*
>   *and laced Shoes fit for a Lady;*
> *But he can do't as wantonly,*
>   *in Highland Trews and belted Plade*

O my bonny, bonny, &c.

But when we came to Stirling *Town,*
he promise'd to make me a Lady,
But all the Tocher that I got,
he row'd me in his Highland Pladie.

There are many songs at this time which celebrate the love of a Highland man and a Lowland woman. Apart from the Bonny Highland Laddie group itself, 'Lizie Balie' was perhaps the most widely current. It appears in printed song-collections in an abbreviated form as a rule which has Lizie forsake her dragoon lover to follow Duncan Grahame. In the fuller broadside version used here, 'Bonny *Lizie Balie*. A New Song very much in Request', the Highlandman accosts the heroine with the now-familiar proposition:

My bonny *Lizie Balie*
I'll row thee in my Pladie,
If thou will go along with me
and be my Highland Lady.[11]

Lizie says that she cannot milk a cow, or speak Gaelic, but the Highlandman overcomes her objections and despite family opposition she gives up all for love and Duncan Grahame. Here the renunciation of alternative suitors assumes a formally repetitive pattern strongly reminiscent of the traditional ballad, and Duncan's plaid and trews once again suggest his personal attractiveness:

She would not have a Low-land Laird,
he wears the high-heel'd Shoes.
[?But] she will Marry *Duncan Grahame*
for *Duncan* wears his Trews:
She would not have a Gentleman,
a Farmer in *Kilsyth*,
But she would have the Highland-man,
he lives into *Monteith*:
She would not have the Low-land man
nor yet the English Laddie,
But she would have the Highland man,
to row her in his Pladie.

The hardships of Highland courtship are emphasised also in this song, and the heroine's sacrifices are presented in an elaborately patterned fashion similar to the passage above:

Now She's cast off her silken Gowns
that she wear'd in the Lowland,
And she's up to the Highland Hills
to wear Gowns of Tartain.
And she's cast off her high-heel'd shoes
was made of the gilded Leather,
And she's up to *Gilliecrankie*

> to go among the Heather.
> And she's cast off her high-heel'd Shoes
> and put on a pair of laigh ones,
> And she's away with *Duncan Grahame*
> to go among the Brachans.

A view of Highland life emerges from these songs which, while being arduous in various ways, has decided compensations, and these are expressed metaphorically in terms of Highland dress. They show the Bonny Highland Laddie at the centre of an established popular love fantasy which becomes increasingly prominent with successive Highland rebellions. Although the Bonny Highland Laddie is basically an erotic figure, he owes his popularity—indeed his very existence—to the spread of Jacobite sentiment in the Lowlands and is an early and important example of the cultural change the movement was to bring about.

As we have seen, however, his neighbours did not consider the Highlandman's talents to stop short at mere gallantry. The descent of Charles Edward Stuart in 1745 with a predominantly Highland army presented Whig satirists with a glorious opportunity to identify him with the Comic Gael of popular tradition, and transform him into a typical brigand-figure at the head of a cateran band.

'O Brother *Sandie*, hear ye the news', printed in '*A Collection of Loyal Songs. For the Use of the Revolution Club*' (Edinburgh 1748), uses the device to develop a series of pointed contrasts between the backwardness and poverty of the Highlands and the wealth and power of the south. The Prince embodies the classic Highland vice of arbitrary violence and by donning the plaid (which he did frequently, both during and after the campaign) and openly espousing the Gaelic cause forfeits the support of the rest of the kingdom. Against barbarian invasion the writer opposes the whole weight of civilised society, maintaining throughout a tone of easy superiority which seems to indicate a date of composition some time before the battle of Prestonpans:

> O Brother *Sandie*, hear ye the news?
> *Lilli Bullero, Bullen a la.*
> An army's just coming without any shoes.
> *Lilli Bullero, Bullen a la.*
>
> *To arms, to arms, brave boys to arms;*
> *A true* British *cause for your courage doth call;*
> *Court, country and city, against a banditti.*
> *Lilli Bullero, Bullen a la.*
>
> The *Pope* sends us over a bonny young lad,
> *Lilli Bullero, Bullen a la.*
> Who, to court *British* favour, wears a *Highland* plaid
> *Lilli Bullero, Bullen a la.*
> *To arms, to arms, &c.*[12]

Another song from the same collection—'With masses and pardons for ages to come,/With thousands of crosses, the blessings of Rome', personifies the Prince as fly-by-night 'Young *Tartan*', the leader of a breekless band of cut-throat

Highlandmen who show a light pair of heels as soon as the Duke of Cumberland arrives on the scene.[13]

The volume also includes a piece beginning 'When you came over first frae *France,*/Bonny Laddie, highland laddie', which treats the rebellion as a dance in which the Prince and his partners are swept unceremoniously off the floor. It has a different structure from the group of Highland Laddie songs discussed earlier, the four line verse being replaced by an octave in which verse and refrain line alternate. It has a formidable list of later variants and is the second main root-song in the group.

'When you came over first frae *France*', has a curious significance. It is one of the earliest examples of the direct identification of Charles Edward Stuart with the erotic figure of the Bonny Highland Ladddie.[14]

Although it is an obvious parody, no earlier version appears to have been preserved. It clearly existed: even the Duke of Cumberland knew it—and sang it. A crowd had gathered on the outskirts of Edinburgh to see him off during the closing stages of the rebellion, and as he mounted he turned and, in a rare moment of humour, cried ' "Shall we not have one song?" and then...as he galloped off he broke into the old Scots melody, "Will you play me fair, Highland Laddie, Highland Laddie?" '[15]

A version is printed in a near contemporary Jacobite volume entitled *A Collection of Loyal Songs, Poems, etc.* (n.p., 1750), with the title 'Highland Laddie'. It has a simple scenario in which the heroine agrees to postpone the wedding while her Highland sweetheart is fighting for the cause, and ends in a characteristic blending of amatory and political themes, in which the Pretender, presumably, wins the crown and the Highlander gets the girl. The union of the lovers is a part of, indeed a consequence of, a larger political consumation:

> If thou'lt play me fair Play,
> *Bonny Laddie, Highland Laddie.*
> Another Year for thee I'll stay,
> *Bonny Laddie,* &c.
> For a' the Lasses hereabouts,
> *Bonny Laddie,* &c.
> Marry none but *Geordi's* Louts.
> *Bonny Laddie,* &c.
> The Time shall come when their bad Choice,
> *Bonny Laddie,* &c.
> They will repent, and we rejoice:
> *Bonny Laddie,* &c.
> I'd take thee in thy highland Trews
> *Bonny Laddie,* &c.
> Before the Rogues that wear their Blues.
> *Bonny Laddie,* &c.
>
> Our Torments from no Cause do spring,
> *Bonny Laddie,* &c.
> But fighting for our lawful King;
> *Bonny Laddie,* &c.
> Our King's Reward will come in Time,

Bonny Laddie, &c.
And constant *Jenny* shall be thine,
Bonny Laddie, &c...[16]

That fusion of politics with love and Highland gallantry which was to distinguish the whole subsequent course of Jacobite song is already in place before the end of the Rebellion.

The 'love-interest' of the '45 which has such an influence upon later songwriters, has at least some basis in fact. One contemporary wrote:

> the rebells' successes at Edinburgh and Prestonpans soon changed the scene. All Jacobites, how prudent so ever, became mad; all doubtfull people became Jacobites, and all bankrupts became heroes, and talked of nothing but hereditary rights and victory; and what was more grievous to men of gallantry, and, if you will believe me, much more mischievous to the publick, all the fine ladys, if you will except one or two, became passionatly fond of the young adventurer, and used all their arts and industry for him in the most intemperate manner.[17]

The route of the rebellion was punctuated by balls, and it sometimes seems that every ford and crossing had its complement of ladies waiting 'to pree his royal highness's mou'.' By the spring of 1746, the links between love and gallantry and the Jacobite cause were already firmly implanted in the popular mind. For example, the writer of the song 'Drummossie' breaks off his narrative to scoff at the modish 'Jacobite-chic' in the person of 'Colonel' Anne Mackintosh who had raised the clan for the Prince:

> Of all the Rebel Beauties here,
>   There's one I will not name, Man,
> Who there did head five hundred Men,
>   For which she's much to blame, Man.
>   *Up and run awa'*, Charlie,
>   *Make haste and run awa'*, Charlie,
>   *Duke* William *he is at your Heels,*
>   *Dragoons and Foot, and a'*, Charlie.
>
> No *Bathsheba*, nor *Venus* fair,
>   Could e'er so well appear, Man,
> As she did in her Feelabeg
>   Before the *Chevalier*, Man.
>   *Up and run*, &c.[18]

While Whig songwriters used the disreputable side of the Highland Laddie tradition, their opponents asserted its more attractive features. They retained at first the basic love-song conventions and merely altered their setting, allowing the Highland Laddies and Lowland Lassies to remain in the foreground. Before long, however, Charles Edward was himself identified with the central male character. Both of the root-songs show this change, and readers familiar with the songs of Burns, Hogg and Lady Nairne, will find the result rather interesting:

The bonniest lad that e'er I saw,
Bonny laddie, highland laddie,
Wore a plaid and was fu' braw,
Bonny laddie, highland laddie;
On his head a bonnet blue,
Bonny laddie, &c.
His royal heart was firm and true,
Bonny laddie, &c.[19]

The song comes from *The True Loyalist; or Chevalier's Favourite: Being a Collection of Elegant Songs, never before printed,* a small Jacobite miscellany published in 1779. No earlier version has been recovered. As James rather than Charles is envisaged succeeding to the crown, however, the song can hardly be later than 1766, the year of the former's death. The narrative does not continue beyond the battle of Prestonpans and the jubilant tone gives no hint of the disasters that followed. There is no sign of retrospective composition or subsequent reworking. The song is obviously contemporary with the events it describes:

But when the Hero did appear,
Bonny laddie, highland laddie,
C-pe and his men were seiz'd wi' fear;
Bonny laddie, highland laddie;
Then he boldly drew his sword,
Bonny laddie, &c.
And he gave his Royal word;
Bonny laddie, &c.

That from the field he would not fly,
Bonny laddie, highland laddie,
But with his friends would live or die:
Bonny laddie, highland laddie;
I hope to see him mount the th--ne
Bonny laddie, &c.
G----e, and all his foes, begone.
Bonny laddie, &c.

Here's a health to J---s our K--g,
Bonny laddie, highland laddie,
God send him soon o'er us to r--gn,
Bonny laddie, highland laddie;
For then we a' fu' glad will be,
Bonny laddie, &c.
When we his Majesty do see.
Bonny laddie, &c.

The True Loyalist also prints 'Pr--ce C-----s is come o'er from France' a song of fourteen verses on the campaign up to Prestonpans, which exploits Highland dress symbolism even more fully. The parent song is the Ramsay lyric discussed earlier and its love ambience is strongly present in its descendant which attributes the rising solely to the personal charms of a Highland prince:

Pr--ce C-----s is come o'er from France,
  In Scotland to proclaim his dadie;
May the heav'ns pow'r preserve and keep
  That worthy P—-ce in's highland plaidie.

O my bonny, bonny highland laddie,
My handsome, charming, highland laddie,
  May heav'n reward, and him still guard
When surrounded with foes in's highland plaidie.

First when he came to view our land,
  The graceful looks of that young laddie,
Made a' our true Scots hearts to warm,
  And choose to wear the highland plaidie.
    O my bonny, &c.[20]

Considering the song as a whole, the Prince's role is relatively unaffected by the eroticism of the prototype and its variants, but the prominence of the Highland dress motif can hardly be overstated. The plaid takes on an imaginative existence of its own, but with its usual meaning reversed. To be 'row'd in a Highland plaidie' here signifies not love, but death:

But when G---die heard the news,
  That he was come before his daddie,
He thirty-thousand pounds wou'd give
  To catch him in his highland plaidie.
    O my bonny, &c.

He sent John C-pe straight to the North,
  With a' his army fierce and ready,
For to devour that worthy P---ce
  And catch him in his highland plaidie.
    O my bonny, &c...

Our worthy P---ce says to his men,
  For God's sake, haste, and make you ready,
And gratify C-pe's fond desire
  He hath to see me in my plaidie.
    O my bonny, &c...

John C-pe cries then unto his men,
  For God's sake, haste and make you ready;
And let each man fly as he can,
  For fear he catch you in his plaidie.
    O my bonny, &c.

Some rode on horse, some ran on foot,
  And some, wi' fear, their heads turn'd giddy;
And some cry'd, Oh! and some, Woe's me!
  That e'er I saw a highland plaidie.
    O my bonny, &c.

When C-pe was then a great way off,
  He said, Since I was a young babie,

I never met with such a fright,
As when I saw him in's highland plaidie.
O my bonny, &c.

We see the same pattern in 'Though Geordie reigns in Jamie's Stead', which seems to date from just after the '45. In the opening verses the Prince appears as the very incarnation of Highland arms:

He's far beyond *Dumblain* the Night,
Whom I love weell for a' that;
He wears a Pistol by his Side that makes me blyth
for a' that,
The Highland Coat, the Philabeg, the Tartan Hose,
and a' that,
And tho' he's o'er the Seas the Night,
He'll soon be here for a' that.
For a' that, and a' that,
And thrice as muckle a' that;
He's far beyond the Seas the Night,
Yet he'll be here for a' that.

He wears a Broadsword by his Side,
And weell he kens to draw that,
The Target and the Highland Plaid,
The Shoulder-belt and a' that;
A Bonnet bound with Ribbons blue,
The White Cockade, and a' that,
And tho' beyond the Seas the Night,
Yet he'll be here for a' that.
And a' that, etc.[21]

The Jacobites remained inveterately opposed to the Union and all it stood for, as a song from the '45, 'Come, all brave Scotsmen, and rejoice/With a loud Acclamation;' written just after the fall of Edinburgh, forcefully reminds us:

Come, all brave *Scotsmen*, and rejoice
With a loud Acclamation;
Since Charles is come over the Main
Into our Scottish Nation.

Let Hills, and Dales, and Mountains great,
And every Wood and Spring,
Extend your Voices to the Clouds
For Joy of Stewart our King.

Ye Nightingales and Lav'rocks too,
And every Bird that sing,
Make haste and leave your doleful Notes,
And Royal Stewart sing.

All Beasts that go upon all Four,
Go leap and dance around;

Sung by a party of Gentlemen the night before they embarked for France 1746

This night let's carouse be merry & dine
And drink a health to young Charles our Prince
And swear we will never return home from France
But along with our Royal bright Laddie
The Stars they proclaim that a King he must be
By Heaven appointed to set us all free
To banish Usurpers a Whig Committee
And favour the Cause of our Laddie
At our present condition let's never repine
For fate in all cases must have it own time
If banished our Country it not for a crime
But for favouring the Cause of our Laddie.

> Because that the curst Union's broke,
> And fallen to the Ground.[22]

In 'A Song. Since royal P---ce C-----s is come to this land', this is carried a stage further. Here, Highland dress is deliberately propounded as a symbol of Jacobite triumph, and also, perhaps, of something larger—of national revival:

> Since royal P---ce C-----s is come to this land,
> To fight for his country, his sword in his hand;
> He's put on his plaid, and also his trouze,
> To honour the Scots, give the English their dues.
> *And weel may he bruik his highland trouze,*
> *And weel may he bruik his highland trouze,*
> *My heart did rejoice when they told me the news,*
> *And weel may he bruik his highland trouze.*[23]

When this nationalistic urge was fused with the colourful panoplay of Highland militarism, the result was very similar to the romantic conflation of tartanry and Toryism re-stated during the Napoleonic Wars and given durable expression in so many songs, poems and novels at that time. The crucial bonding of Highlandry with Jacobitism and love by contemporary songwriters made this available to the creators of national myth and symbol within five years of the Rebellion.

With the passage of time the presentation of the Stuart prince in popular song became increasingly affected by material from non-political sources. Simply by describing his return the writer had already placed Charles Edward in a fictional situation, and it was but a short step from that to other kinds of invention as the last song to be considered here, 'Lewis Gordon', may show:

> Oh! send me Lewis Gordon hame,
> And the Lad I dare not name;
> Altho' his back be at the wa',
> Here's to him that's far awa.
>
> *Hech hey! my Highland-man,*
> *My handsome charming Highland-man.*
> *Weel wou'd I my true love ken*
> *Among ten thousand Highlandmen.*
>
> Oh! to see his tartan-trews,
> Bonnet blue, and laigh-heel'd shoes,
> Philabeg aboon his knee,
> And that's the Lad that I'll go wi'.
> *Hech hey! &c.*
>
> The Lovely Lad I now do sing,
> Is fitted for to be a King:
> For on his breast he wears a star,
> You'd take him for the god of war.
> *Hech hey! &c.*

> Oh! to see this Princely One
> Seated on a royal throne;
> Our griefs wou'd then a' disappear,
> We'd celebrate the jub'lee-year.
> *Hech hey!* &c.[24]

The principal features of Jacobite song up to 1745 are here substantially displaced. The prospect of restoration, at least to a kingdom of this world, has all but been relinquished, along with the traditional air of political immediacy and robust masculine enterprise; gone too are the conquerors and lawgivers who had formerly been the centre of party panegyric. In their place we find an empire of the affections at once grand and remote; an ardour so personal and intense that it can only be expressed by a woman (and it is notable how many later Jacobite songs do have a female narrator); and a prince who has so far entered the domain of folklore that it is considered unlucky even to name him.

Party songwriters portrayed the Prince as a glamorous Highlander decked in tartans of state because the song-group from which they borrowed dealt with glamorous Highlanders and used their clothes in an explicitly symbolic way. It would seem reasonable, for example, to expect Ramsay's lyric of Highland courtship to have lost in the course of adaptation everything except the tune, the stanzaform and the dress-motif; but the first three lines of the refrain are transferred practically intact into its political descendant 'Pr--ce C-----s is come o'er from France', and transferred with them wholesale are the qualities usually associated with the Bonny Highlandman figure—youth, personal beauty, sexual energy, and the other implications of 'the tartan plaidie'. Here we find a popular tradition almost entirely literate in character achieving the kind of creative transformation usually thought specific to oral cultures. In 'Lewis Gordon' politics are pushed into the background by the amorous preoccupation of the singer; he is addressed not so much as a statesman and conqueror, but as a lover and gallant. 'Warlike Charles' turns into 'Bonny Prince Charlie'.

Chapter Seven

'TO REASSUME TH' IMPERIAL SWORD'

By 1750 Jacobite song had acquired everything necessary to its existence as an independent type, its association with glamorous Highlandry, love-ambience, and sentimental focus upon exile and loss.

What happened next? Very little. A number of Jacobite airs crept into Scottish music collections, and the general song anthologies printed one or two older pieces like 'Killiecrankie' and 'A Race at Sheriffmuir'. But the 1760s and 1770s produced only a handful of new songs, most of them trivial. A contemporary might well have written off the form as a dead end, as dead as the movement which had produced it.[1]

And to all outward appearances Jacobitism really was finished. The '45 was a bolt from the blue, a last brilliant, or despairing, throw which caught the Government and the party alike absolutely cold. But now effective steps were taken to make sure that it could not threaten the Hanoverian state again. The Highlands were disarmed and the military tenures which made it possible to raise Highland armies abolished. The estates of active Jacobites were confiscated and for the first time serious steps were taken against the Episcopal church in Scotland and its numbers drastically declined. The Prince wandered erratically about the Continent one jump ahead of the British secret service, drinking too much and quarrelling with everybody about him. Real party commitment survived (Episcopalians, for example, considered him as their head until his death in 1788), but few continued to regard the restoration of the Stuarts as a realistic proposition.[2]

And yet it was precisely during these years in the generation after the '45 that the movement itself began to be accommodated to the vision of the heroic past so that it could eventually become the common cultural possession of all Scots.

One can see this beginning to happen in one of the most important song collections of the period, David Herd's *Ancient and Modern Scottish Songs, Heroic Ballads, Etc. Collected from Memory, Tradition and Ancient Authors*, published in two editions in Edinburgh in 1769 and 1776. Herd printed only a handful of older Jacobite songs, perhaps an indication that it was still risky to do this kind of thing at all. The point is that he explicitly classified them as a species of traditional ballad, placing them in his section of 'Heroic Ballads and Fragments' side by side with 'Johnie Armstrang', 'Sir Patrick Spence' and 'Chevy-Chace' as near-contemporary specimens of high antiquity. The collection was also agressively national in its outlook. The general anthologies of the period usually contained a mixture of Scottish, English and Irish material; but Herd was determined to print

Scottish songs and Scottish songs *only*. This marked a decisive break with the past and gave authoritative impetus to the nascent concept of 'national song' with Jacobite balladry enshrined at the very heart of it.[3]

There were other qualities latent in Jacobitism which made it attractive to a later generation of Scots moved by the first stirrings of Romantic nationalism, not least its aptness as a focus for anti-Union sentiment and as a symbol, therefore, for Scottish cultural and political distinctiveness. The tendency to associate Jacobitism triumphant with the idea of national revival has already been noted. We see it, for example in William Hamilton of Bangour's celebratory ode on the battle of Prestonpans which sees the genius of Scotland arise phoenix-like from the ashes of political compromise and military defeat:

> As over Gladsmuir's bloodstain'd field,
>   Scotia, imperial goddess flew,
> Her lifted spear and radiant shield,
>   Conspicuous blazing to the view;
> Her visage lately clouded with despair,
> Now reassum'd its first majestic air...
>
> Loud as the trumpet rolls its sound,
>   Her voice the Power celestial rais'd,
> While her victorious sons around,
>   In silent joy and wonder gaz'd.
> The sacred Muses heard th'immortal lay,
> And thus to earth the notes of fame convey.
>
> ' 'Tis done, my sons! 'Tis nobly done!
>   'Victorious over tyrant power:
> 'How quick the race of fame was run!
>   'The work of ages in one hour!
> 'Slow creeps th' oppressive weight of slavish reigns,
> 'One glorious moment rose, and burst your chains.
>
> 'But late, forlorn, dejected, pale,
>   'A prey to each insulting foe,
> 'I sought the grove and gloomy vale,
>   'To vent in solitude my woe.
> 'Now to my hand the balance fair restor'd,
> 'Once more I wield on high th' imperial sword.'[4]

In the same way, many Scots who were by no means committed Jacobites regarded Culloden as a national disaster. In 1746 Tobias Smollett published 'The Tears of Scotland', the poem that was to establish his literary reputation, surveying the aftermath of the rebellion from an explicitly nationalistic point of view:

> Mourn, hapless Caledonia, mourn
> Thy banish'd peace, thy laurels torn!
> Thy sons, for valour long renown'd,
> Lie slaughtered on their native ground.
> Thy hospitable roofs no more
> Invite the stranger to the door;

In smoky ruins sunk they lie,
The monuments of cruelty...

What boots it then, in every clime,
Through the wide-spreading waste of time,
Thy martial glory, crown'd with praise,
Still shone with undiminish'd blaze?
Thy towering spirit now is broke,
Thy neck is bended to the yoke:
What foreign arms could never quell,
By civil rage and rancour fell...

Whilst the warm blood bedews my veins,
And unimpair'd remembrance reigns,
Resentment of my country's fate
Within my filial breast shall beat;
And, spite of her insulting foe,
My sympathizing verse shall flow.
Mourn, hapless Caledonia, mourn
Thy banish'd peace, thy laurels torn![5]

It was reasoning like this, consolidated and amplified during the generation after the '45 which made it possible for somebody like Robert Burns to be a Whig and a Jacobite at the same time. When he contemplated British politics Burns did so as a perfectly sincere Foxite Whig. But when he turned to Scottish affairs, and particularly to patriotic themes, his attitude grew naturally from the rhetoric of later Jacobitism and its nationalistic offshoots.[6]

The final important changes to occur during these years were the gradual recognition of Highlanders as being within the pale of the national Scottish identity and the gradual acceptance by Lowland Scots of Highland kilts and tartans as a source of national emblem.

When the '45 ended and the Highlanders returned to their straths and glens, they left behind in the memory of their tartans a new and powerful political symbol. Party strife in Edinburgh was for a time dominated by a war of tartans in which all kinds of unlikely objects appeared swathed in the stuff. The Whigs used it with satirical mockery, the Tories with disgruntled patriotism. In the end, though, the Whigs won. They produced the public hangman decked in their own colours; an argument which seemed to be, in the circumstances, unanswerable. In England, Tory members sported tartan waistcoats in the Commons, as a pointed reminder to the establishment of what a close run thing the '45 had been. The Whigs counter-attacked in a ballad called 'Plaid Hunting' to the old political tune of 'Packington's Pound', trying to shame the English right out of their foppery by contrasting their timorous inaction during the rebellion with the genuine courage and self-sacrifice of the Highlanders whose conduct, by implication, entitled them alone to their distinctive martial dress:

And ye *Highlanders* brave, in despite of the laws,
Who adventur'd your all in defense of the cause;
Your contempt for these pageants must surely express
Who deserted your cause, tho' they mimick your dress;

> While each honest man
> Will do what he can,
> To bring to confusion these Apes of the clan;
> And their principles treat with due detestation,
> And hiss the plaid waistcoats quite out of the nation.[7]

Its abundance of fighting men had long been recognised as one of the few usable resources of the Highlands and acute Lowland minds had for some time been speculating how to exploit it. In 1739 accordingly, the Independent Companies of the Highland Watch were regimented as the 43rd (later 42nd) of foot: destined for renown in many a song and story under their more familiar names: the Black Watch, the Royal Highland Regiment, 'The Gallant Forty-Twa'.

The men believed that they had been raised for home service only, and were greatly disconcerted when, as a result of increasing British involvement in the War of the Austrian Succession, they were marched south to embark for Flanders in 1743. They mutinied in London. A party tried to slip back to Scotland, but it was intercepted and the ringleaders were executed. As may be imagined, this aroused considerable public interest. A contemporary pamphlet entitled *A Short History of the Highland Regiment* recorded the astonishment caused by the kilted Gaels in the English capital:

> When the *Highlanders* walk'd the streets here, every body must be sensible that there was more staring at them than ever was seen at the *Morocco* embassador's attendance, or even at the *Indian* chiefs...The amazement expressed by our mob was not greater than the surprize of these poor creatures; and if we thought their dress and language barbarous, they had just the same opinion of our manners; nor will I pretend to decide which was most in the right.[8]

But astonishment soon changed to respect as news was received of the regiment's conduct at Fontenoy. Even the French were impressed. One soldier wrote:

> The British behaved well...and could be exceeded in ardour by none but our officers, who animated the troops by their example, *when the Highland furies rushed in upon us with more violence than ever did a sea driven by a tempest*...we gained the victory; but may I never see such another.[9]

Fifty batallions of Highland troops were raised during the next two generations. Quebec, Ticonderoga and Seringapatam established their reputation for military valour and Highlandmen began to be assimilated into the heroic national mythology. Their gallantry in the imperial service enabled even the staunchest Whig to accept them as the latter-day standard-bearers of the ancient military ideals of the Scots, and they played a key role in the continuous redefinition of national stereotypes in the century following the Union.[10]

As Highland soldiers gained acceptance as the guardians and restorers of national military glory, the image of Scotland itself began to change. It came to be considered, even by Lowland Scots, as essentially a Highland country, evolving over the next generation or so into the 'land of the mountain and the flood' which peers out at us so curiously now from a thousand Victorian prints. We can see this beginning in one of the most famous contemporary songs celebrating Highland regimental gallantry, 'The Garb of Old Gaul'. It has a marvellous tune, a cocky little *march militaire* from the pen of one of the leading Scottish amateur musicians of the age. The authorship of the words is disputed, but according to one account, they were composed about the time of Fontenoy, and 'Major Reid [of the 42nd, later General John Reid, founder of the Reid Chair of Music at the University of Edinburgh] set them to music of his own composition...' The version printed in the general song collections, however, appears to date from nearer the middle of the 1760s.[11]

The song celebrates the martial qualities of the Gael, reviving the old Fergusian boast that even the Romans, the most warlike race of the ancient world, had failed to conquer Scotland, owing to the prowess of the Highlanders, and the virtues of their hardy way of life. But the revolution in political perspective is its most remarkable quality. While Charles Edward's army was viewed by the Whig establishment as the vanguard of popery and slavery, Highland soldiers appear here as the bulwark of British Liberties, an amazing reversal in just twenty years:

> In the garb of old Gaul, and the fire of old Rome,
> From the heath-cover'd mountains of Scotia we come,
> Where the Romans endeavour'd our country to gain,
> But our ancestors fought, and they fought not in vain.
> Such our love of liberty, our country and our cause,
> Like our ancestors of old, we'll stand by freedom's laws;
> We'll boldly fight like heroes bright, for honour and applause,
> And defy the French and Spaniards to alter our laws.
>
> No effeminate customs our sinews embrace,
> No luxurious tables enervate our race;
> Our loud-sounding pipe bears the true martial strain,
> So do we the old Scottish valour retain.
> Such our love of liberty, &c...

This apparently simple song gathers together the threads of centuries of political myth-making: the heroic loyalist ideal enshrined in the story of King Fergus with its notion of warlike valour shielding political liberty and independence; the idea of superior Scots hardihood and vigour seen at its highest in a Highland setting, which percolates down by various routes from the Bonny Highland Laddie tradition; and finally a spirit of nationalistic assertiveness which derives its outlook from the popular traditions of the Scottish right and advances the imperial ambitions of the Hanoverian establishment by appropriating the rhetoric of the Jacobite cause.

Chapter Eight

'THE DESPERATE RELICS OF A GALLANT NATION'

'It has long been a just and general Complaint, that among all the Music-Books of Scots Songs that have been hitherto offered to the Public, not one, nor even all of them put together, can be said to have merited the name of what may be called A Complete Collection'.[1] Thus begins the preface of *The Scots Musical Museum*. What its publisher, a music engraver called James Johnson, actually envisaged was a modest compilation of two volumes, but his plans were transformed by an introduction early in 1787 to Robert Burns.

Johnson explained his project and solicited contributions. Burns leapt at the idea. 'There is a work going on in Edinburgh, just now, which claims your best assistance' he wrote that Autumn to another fine songwriter, the Rev. John Skinner, Episcopalian Dean of Aberdeen, 'An Engraver in this town has set about collecting and publishing all the Scotch songs, with the Music, that can be found...I have been absolutely crazed about it, collecting old stanzas, and every information remaining, respecting their origin, authors, &c.'[2]

For five years he threw all his energies into collecting, editing and composing songs for the *Museum*, which ultimately swelled to six volumes. Although the first was almost ready to go to press in the spring of 1787, Burns was the moving force behind the next four, and the final volume was in an advanced state of preparation when he died in July 1796.

His influence on the collection was deep and pervasive; and nowhere was this more evident than in the songs of the Jacobite movement. He printed nearly thirty of them, far more than any previous general collector. Two-thirds of them were written by Burns himself, and all but three appear in the volumes over which he had direct control.

At first sight, this aspect of his work creates serious problems. On the one hand, he was by far the most prolific and accomplished Jacobite songwriter to appear in Scotland between the Revolution of 1688-9 and the end of the eighteenth century. On the other hand, his songs were composed nearly fifty years after the defeat of the party which inspired them, and there are many things in his background— especially his regional background—which seem highly incompatible with such activity. It is difficult to reconcile the appearance of a major Jacobite poet in the south-west heartland of old Scottish Whiggism at the end of the eighteenth century with any of our conventional views of Scottish literature and history.

We are not helped towards a solution by the poet's attitude towards the British politics of his time, which, on the surface seem to be guided by a labyrinthine tortuousness. Until his appointment to the Excise in 1789, he broadly supported the Tory government, as his poems indicate; but in public he associated himself with the Whig Opposition especially people like James, Earl of Glencairn and Henry Erskine, the Dean of Faculty. In 1789 he was appointed to the Excise under the protection of Robert Graham of Fintry, an ally of Henry Dundas, the master of the Tory machine in Scotland. He became a minor official dependent for his daily bread on the good offices of the ruling party. It was precisely at this point that he began to gravitate ideologically towards the Whigs, ending up as a supporter of the Foxite left. This, in turn, coincided with his most active phase as a writer of Jacobite songs, as an apparent advocate of high hereditary right, and absolutist monarchism in the grand style.[3]

Nor are we assisted by the traditional bi-focalism of Scots politics at this period. The Scots had been involved in general British politics since the time of the Union, after centuries of more or less separate development, and party labels like 'Whig' and 'Tory' were, by Burns's time, only beginning to indicate similar things on both sides of the border. Through his friendship with the Earl of Glencairn, Burns gained *entrée* to the inner circles of British Whiggism, which was predominantly English in character, aristocratic in flavour, and secular in outlook.[4]

But Scottish Whiggism was a very different thing, and retained strong ecclesiastical overtones; indeed even at this period, it may still be considered the party of the Church of Scotland. It had come into being during the later seventeenth century as an offshoot of the Covenant, and following the triumph of Presbyterianism in 1688-9, had dominated the public life of the country. To this kind of Whiggism, the poet was violently opposed, the more so, perhaps, because it was strongly entrenched in the part of the country in which he grew up. The religious flavour of the South-West remained in many respects austere and old fashioned. By the time of Burns's early manhood, for example, it was one of the few areas in Scotland to retain the stool of repentance in regular use. His rejection of its ethos as a mature man is documented in a score of ecclesiastical satires and in many of his letters; some writers, indeed, have fixed upon it as the principal theme of his intellectual life.[5]

By the same token, he was immersed in old-style Scots Whiggism from infancy. 'Burns Country' lies squarely within that tract of ground hallowed in Presbyterian memory by the sufferings of the persecuted remnant. Drumclog, Airds Moss, and Bothwell Brig all lie within a few miles of his native parish. Peden the prophet had been schoolmaster of Tarbolton. In the centre of Mauchline itself stood a tablet commemorating the execution of people taken in field-conventicles by Graham of Claverhouse and Grierson of Lag.[6]

His early childhood was dominated by his mother, Agnes Broun, a powerful and vivid personality from whom he would have absorbed much Covenanting lore. Her grandfather had been shot at Airds Moss. It was from his mother and the women about her that he was first exposed to folk-tradition and, one may guess, to an imperfectly literate and highly localised version of popular Presbyterian spirituality. We can see something of this mental world in the writings of Robert Wodrow, minister of Eastwood in Renfrewshire earlier in the century. These give

Figure 8. Robert Burns by Alexander Nasmyth. (Courtesy of the Gallery of Modern Art).

a vivid picture of the Presbyterian sensitivity to the invisible world and how the sons and daughters of the persecuted remnant lived in an obsessively inward mental environment teeming with prophecy and visions, ghouls and revenants, thought transfer, and foreknowledge.[7]

The mature Burns rejected the ethos root and branch, and came to despise the canting, credulous and hypocritical cast of mind it tended to produce. His letters are strewn with derogatory references to Whiggism in the Scottish sense, and it is clear that he used the term as a form of expletive.[8]

There was an alternative world-view readily enough to hand, however, and as strongly represented in Burns's own family tradition.

Just after the '45, the poet's father, William Burnes, migrated from the North-East, first to Edinburgh, and later to Ayrshire, bearing with him a certificate attesting that he had taken no part in 'the late wicked rebellion'. He sprang from a long line of Episcopalian tenant farmers in the Braes of Glenbervie in the hinterland of Stonehaven. His mother was Isabella Keith of Criggie on the estate of Fetteresso which belonged to the Earls Marischal to whom her father, James Keith, was a 'familiar servitor'. The last Earl Marischal was one of the most important Jacobites in Scotland, 'out' in the '15 and again in the '19 for which he suffered forfeiture and banishment.[9]

Why William Burnes became a Presbyterian and settled in one of the most Whiggish parts of the country, must remain in the realms of speculation. What is certain is that his son liked, in the right kind of company, to make much of his Jacobite ancestry.

He stated to the antiquary Ramsay of Ochtertyre that his people had been plundered and driven out during the '15 and that he himself was a Jacobite upon that account. It was still, of course, perfectly possible to be one. During Burns's early manhood Charles Edward Stuart was still alive, and was only in his sixties when he died in the Winter of 1788. The succession passed to the Prince's brother Henry Benedict, Cardinal Duke of York, and after his death in 1807, to the King of Sardinia who was offered the allegiance of the surviving Scottish Jacobites.

According to Ochtertyre Burns claimed one of his forefathers had been gardener to the Earl Marischal at Inverurie (an obvious slip; probably it should be Inverugie) and had shared in the fate of his patron.[10]

The poet left two other accounts of his family's involvement in the Jacobite movement. In one, sent to the writer Dr John Moore in 1787 he merely noted: 'My Fathers rented land of the noble Kieths of Marshal, and had the honor to share their fate'. But for Lady Winifred Maxwell Constable, grand-daughter of the famous Jacobite Earl of Nithsdale, he had a more elaborate version, comparing the fate of his own ancestors with that of the Jacobite leaders, and saluting her as a common sufferer 'in a Cause where even to be unfortunate is glorious, the Cause of Heroic Loyalty!' He continued:

> Though my Fathers had not illustrious Honors and vast Properties to hazard in the contest; though they left their humble cottages only to add so many units more to the unnoted crowd that followed their Leaders; yet, what they could they did, and what they had they lost: with unshaken firmness and unconcealed Political Attachments, they shook hands with Ruin for what they esteemed the cause of their King and their Country.[11]

Generations of Burnes's farmed in the adjoining estates of Feteresso and Inch-breck and worshipped at the Episcopalian chapel of Drumlithie, burned by Cumberland in 1746. The area was strongly Jacobite. The Earl Marischal entertained the Old Pretender at Fetteresso during the '15, and nearby lay the fortress of Dunnottar which was used as a Jacobite prison during the rebellion with the poet William Meston as governor. Many people from the district went over the hill to to join the standard at Braemar, and likely enough some of the sprawling tribe of Burnses would have been amongst them, especially if they were dependants of the Earl Marischal.[12]

Burns made contact with the leading Edinburgh Episcopalians during his first visit to the capital in the winter of 1786 and moved familiarly thereafter among the well-heeled members of Old St Pauls. The chapel lay in Carrubbers Close and had housed the congregation of St Giles ejected with Bishop Rose at the Revolution. It was strongly Jacobite in flavour even at this late period, and there was hardly a Jacobite of consequence during the eighteenth and early nineteenth century from the Chevalier's secretary Murray of Broughton to the songwriter Lady Nairne, who was not connected with it; people like Thomas Ruddiman, James Murray of Abercairney, the Earl and Countess of Seaforth, the Duke of Perth, the Oliphants of Gask, Sir Robert Strange, the Threiplands of Fingask, even Provost Archibald Stewart who surrendered Edinburgh to the Jacobite army in 1745. Burns knew the then minister, Dr Webster, and the solicitor James Steuart, son-in-law of Thomas Ruddiman, whose house at Cleland's Garden on the outskirts of the city was used as the meeting place for the annual celebrations of the Chevalier's birthday. The last one took place on 31 December 1787; amongst those present were Lady Nairne's father and *aide de camp* to the Prince, Laurence Oliphant; Robert Burns was invited and responded with a Jacobite poem of his own composition and a note saying 'Burn the above verses when you have read them, as any little sense that is in them is rather heretical, and do me the justice to believe me sincere in my grateful remembrances of the many civilities you have honoured me with since I came to Edinburgh'. These were not sentimental dabblers but the hard core of the party in Scotland and the poet was clearly *persona grata* amongst them. Burns continued to be acceptable in the highest Scots Tory circles, as we can see by his election to the Royal Company of Archers in 1792. [13]

What probably aroused their interest in him was the glowing Scottish patriotism of the Kilmarnock edition, and above all his explicit enthusiasm for the heroic Scottish past, which would have indicated to them pretty clearly the underlying drift of his politics.

Burns's Jacobitism was perfectly genuine, as genuine as his patriotism, and intimately connected with it.

In his Highland tour in the Autumn of 1787, he collected Jacobite songs, and left the following lines 'Written by Somebody in the Window of an inn at Stirling on seeing the Royal Palace in ruins'. They are bitterly anti-Hanoverian in sentiment:

> Here Stewarts once in triumph reign'd,
> And laws for Scotland's weal ordain'd;
> But now unroof'd their Palace stands,
> Their sceptre's fall'n to other hands;

> Fallen indeed, and to the earth,
> Whence grovelling reptiles take their birth.—
> A Race outlandish fill their throne;
> An idiot race, to honor lost;
> Who know them best despise them most.[14]

He wrote to the Earl of Buchan in February 1787:

> Your Lordship touches the darling chord of my heart when you advise me to fire my
> Muse at Scottish story and Scottish scenes.—I wish for nothing more than to make
> a leisurely Pilgrimage through my native country; to sit and muse on those once hard-
> contended fields, where Caledonia, rejoicing, saw her bloody lion borne through
> broken ranks to victory and fame; and catching the inspiration, to pour the deathless
> Names in Song.—[15]

He visited the grave of Robert the Bruce at Dunfermline Abbey, and knelt and
kissed the stones. At Stirling he knelt again at the tomb of Sir John the Graham,
the companion of Wallace, and 'said a fervent prayer for old Caledonia over the
hole in a blue whin-stone, where Robert de Bruce fixed his royal Standard on the
banks of Bannockburn'.[16] More characteristic still, perhaps, was his visit to the
patriotic Mrs Catherine Bruce of Clackmannan, of which his travelling companion
Dr James Adair left the following account:

> This venerable dame, with characteristical dignity, informed me, on my observing
> that I believed she was descended from the family of Robert Bruce, that Robert Bruce
> was spring from her family...She was in possession of the hero's helmet and two-
> handed sword, with which she conferred on Burns and myself the honour of knight-
> hood, remarking, that she had a better right to confer that title than *some people*... the
> old lady's political tenets were as Jacobitical as the poet's, a conformity which con-
> tributed not a little to the cordiality of our reception and entertainment.—She gave
> as her first toast after dinner, *Awa' Uncos*, or Away with the Strangers—Who these
> strangers were, you will readily understand.[17]

The Winter of 1788/9 marked the centenary of the Glorious Revolution, and
Burns was so disgusted by the party rancour and meanness of spirit the celebrations
called forth that he wrote to the *Edinburgh Evening Courant* in defence of the
Stuarts. The letter was anonymous, but even so it was a risky thing to do. In the
published version he adopted the stance of a broad friend to Revolution principles
pleading for historical relativism, and arguing that the Stuarts contended for no
more than conventional kingly rights in their time, as the Tudors had done in
theirs. He ended with a strong appeal to patriotic sentiment, urging his readers to
consider the Stuarts as erring parents of the national family (a significant concept,
as we shall see), whose failings ought to be decently forgotten rather than trumpeted
abroad:

> The Stuarts have been condemned and laughed at for the folly and impracticability
> of their attempts, in 1715 and 1745. That they failed, I bless my God most fervently;
> but cannot join in the ridicule against them...let every man, who has a tear for the
> many miseries incident to humanity, feel for a family, illustrious as any in Europe,

and unfortunate beyond historic precedent; and let every Briton, and particularly every Scotsman, who ever looked with reverential pity on the dotage of a parent, cast a veil over the fatal mistakes of the Kings of his forefathers.[18]

This, of course, was for public consumption. His private sentiments were much more extreme, as we see in the furious, indeed scarcely even coherent, letter he sent shortly afterwards to his friend Mrs Frances Dunlop concerning his piece in the *Courant:*

> If you have an opportunity of seeing the Edinr evening Courant of Saturday the 22d of November, you will see a piece of my Politics, signed A Briton.—Heaven forgive me for dissimulation in that Paragraph! I too, Madam, am just now Revolution-mad, but it is not the tarantula-frenzy of insulting Whiggism, like an ass's Colt capering over the generous hound breathing his last; mine is the madness of an enraged Scorpion shut up in a thumb-phial; the indignant groans and bloodshot glances of ruined Right, gagged on the pillory of Derision to gratify the idiot insolence of [us]urpation—[19]

Burns's Jacobite songs themselves are the most convincing evidence of the importance of the creed to his creative personality and its centrality to his world-view.

The immediately striking thing about them is their astonishing range and virtuosity. There are highly wrought art-songs springing from the cult of sensibility like 'Strathallan's Lament' and 'The Chevalier's Lament'; straightforward party songs delivered 'in character' like 'Awa whigs awa'; Highland Laddie songs like 'The White Cockade'; pieces inspired by the broadside style like 'The Battle of Sherramoor'; songs of simple pathos like 'There'll never be peace till Jamie comes hame'; songs of caustic exchange like 'Killiecrankie'; imitations of the high ballad style like 'The Lovely Lass o' Inverness'; Jacobite love-songs like 'It was a' for our rightfu' King'; swaggering songs of local patriotism like 'Kenmure's on and awa''; and songs inspired by the folk and street traditions like 'Charlie he's my darling'.[20]

His earliest exercises in the form, 'Strathallan's Lament', 'O'er the water to Charlie', and 'Up and warn a' Willie', appear in the second volume of *The Scots Musical Museum* published in March 1788 and show a typical blend of fresh composition and brilliantly opportunistic borrowing from the past. 'Strathallan's Lament' was written in 1787 and set to a melancholy pastoral air from the pen of Burns's schoolmaster friend Allan Masterton who also wrote the tune for 'Willie brew'd a peck o' maut'. The poet noted 'As he and I were both sprouts of Jacobitism, we agreed to dedicate the words and air to that cause'.[21] With regard to content the song is an obvious piece of mythologising: Viscount Strathallan was actually killed at Culloden, but here he is shown skulking in the Highlands after the battle and indulging his woe in a wild romantic setting. If the result appears to be a fairly unremarkable exercise in the 'pathetick' and sublime, we must remember that in the context of Jacobite song it is, in fact, highly innovative and unconventional: we see an historical pseudo-event from the rebellions taken up years later and transformed by the application of a modish contemporary aesthetic:

Thickest night, surround my dwelling!
Howling tempests, o'er me rave!
Turbid torrents, wintry swelling,
Roaring by my lonely cave
Chrystal streamlets gently flowing,
Busy haunts of base mankind,
Western breezes softly blowing,
Suit not my distracted mind.

In the cause of Right engaged,
Wrongs injurious to redress,
Honor's war we strongly waged,
But the heavens deny'd success:
Ruin's wheel has driven o'er us,
Not a hope that dare attend,
The wide world is all before us—
But a world without a friend![22]

The piece is, no doubt, overwrought. But it establishes, at a stroke, many of the characteristics of the later Jacobite song, including the wild landscapes, the preoccupation with defeat, and the pervasive ambience of exile and loss. There is, even more obviously, a dramatic shift in focus away from the dynasty, in favour of a new concentration on what Jacobitism meant for the people of Scotland who were involved in it. Very apparent too, and also new, is the strongly subjective tone, the inner/outer parallelism which recruits the forces of nature to symbolise the spiritual reaction of the singer to the consequences of defeat. The probable source for the song emphasises even more the novelty of the perspective. In *The True Loyalist*, which Burns knew and used, there is—'A Song. Tune, *The Highland King*'. which begins 'Blow ye bleak winds around my head,/No storm nor tempest do I hear'.[23] It has similar soliloquising in a wild landscape but the focus of attention is wholly on Prince Charles Edward: the singer prays that the Prince be preserved by heaven and emerge purged and strengthened by his experiences.

The cult of sentiment informs at least one other Jacobite song by Burns, 'The Chevalier's Lament', which although it does actually concentrate on the Prince, does so in a rather interesting way. Once again nature imagery emphasises the psychological condition of the central character, although here it is used as a foil to the predominant mood:

The small birds rejoice in the green leaves returning,
The murmuring streamlet winds clear thro' the vale;
The primroses blow in the dews of the morning,
And wild-scented cowslips bedeck the green dale:
But what can give pleasure, or what can seem fair,
When the lingering moments are numbered by Care?
No birds sweetly singing, nor flowers gayly springing,
Can sooth the sad bosom of joyless Despair.

The deed that I dared, could it merit their malice,
A King and a Father to place on his throne;
His right are these hills, and his right are these vallies,
Where wild beasts find shelter but I can find none:

> But 'tis not my sufferings, thus wretched, forlorn,
> My brave, gallant friends, 'tis your ruin I mourn;
> Your faith proved so loyal in hot, bloody trial,
> Alas, can I make it no sweeter return![24]

Once one recognises the aesthetic perspective, there is nothing particularly unusual about this. The significant point is that just as in the *Courant* letter, rebellion is seen to flow not from political ambition but filial piety, i.e. it is treated in domestic rather than dynastic terms.

Natural imagery is also used to heighten 'Awa whigs awa' an apparently straightforward exercise in party songwriting. No earlier complete version has been recovered, although there is a cognate fragment in David Herd's MSS. with the refrain 'Awa, whigs, awa!/Awa, whigs, awa!/ Ye're but a pack o' lazy loons,/Ye'll do nae good aval!',[25] but what we have here seems to be almost entirely by Burns. Yet in terms of its content, the song could have been written almost at any point during the century, a telling indication of his knowledge of the convention. Particularly interesting is the reference to the theme of 'Guid Auld Lang Syne' ('Our ancient crown's fa'n in the dust...') and his equation of the Stuart monarchy with national independence and well-being. Lurking perceptibly in the background, too, is the old communitarian ideal of Scotland as the 'Land o' cakes and brither Scots', and it is ultimately this that the Whigs are blamed for destoying:

> Awa whigs awa,
> Awa whigs awa,
> Ye're but a pack o' traitor louns,
> Ye'll do nae guid at a'.
>
> Our thrissles flourish'd fresh and fair,
> And bonie bloom'd our roses;
> But whigs cam like a frost in June,
> An' wither'd a' our posies.
>   Chos. Awa whigs &c.
>
> Our ancient crown's fa'n in the dust;
> Deil blin' them wi' the stoure o't,
> An' write their names in his black beuk
> Wha gae the Whigs the power o't!
>   Chos. Awa whigs &c.
>
> Our sad decay in church and state
> Surpasses my descriving:
> The whigs cam o'er us for a curse,
> And we hae done wi' thriving.
>   Chos. Awa whigs &c.
>
> Grim Vengeance lang has taen a nap,
> But we may see him wauken:
> Gude help the day when royal heads
> Are huntit like a maukin.
>
> Awa whigs awa,
> Awa whigs awa,

Ye're but a pack o' traitor louns,
Ye'll do nae guid at a'.[26]

On the surface 'O'er the water to Charlie', is a very different kind of song: a vernacular lyric apparently straightforward in its expression of Jacobite fervour and of beguiling simplicity when compared with the elaborately formal Strathallan's and Chevalier's Laments. The roots of the song go back to the '45. A tune with this title was published by Robert Bremner in his *Collection of Scots Reels or Country Dances* 1757-9), and there are two cognate versions with words in *The True Loyalist*.[27] The first of these, 'The K--g he has been long from home,/The P---ce he has sent over', apparently dates from the early stages of the rebellion and deals with the Whigs' preparations to defend Edinburgh, with a verse on Prestonpans tagged on to the end. It is a simple affair, urging Jacobites to seize their chance, and violently anti-Presbyterian in tone. Burns discards the text completely, using only the refrain:

O'er the water, o'er the sea,
O'er the water to C---lie,
Go the world as it will,
We'll hazard our lives for C---lie.[28]

The second song, 'Over the Water to C---lie' comes from the aftermath of the rebellion, and deals with the vengeance of the Edinburgh Whigs and the trials of the Jacobite prisoners at Carlisle. Although otherwise undistinguished, it does show considerable warmth of personal feeling towards the Prince, and it is this which seems to have fired Burns's imagination:

When C---lie came to Edinburgh-town,
And a' his friends about him,
How pleas'd was I for to go down,
I cou'd not be merry without him.
But since that o'er the seas he's gone,
The other side landed fairly,
I'd freely quit wi' a' that I have,
To get over the water to C---lie.[29]

Burns matches the rhythmical impetus of the superb original tune with subtly varied repetition and an unobtrusive pattern of alliteration and internal rhyme to produce a heady evocation of Jacobite exile with a distinctly millenarian flavour. 'O'er the water to Charlie' is a vision of joyous pilgrimage to a better land in which the messianic pull of the Chevalier is balanced by the thoughts and feelings of his ordinary followers and political rhetoric counterpointed by a delicate particularity, even down to the name of the boatman.

Come boat me o'er, come row me o'er,
Come boat me o'er to Charlie;
I'll gie John Ross anither bawbee
To boat me o'er to Charlie.—

We'll o'er the water, we'll o'er the sea,
  We'll o'er the water to Charlie;
Come weal, come woe, we'll gather and go,
  And live or die wi' Charlie.—

I lo'e weel my Charlie's name,
  Tho' some there be abhor him:
But O, to see auld Nick gaun hame,
  And Charlie's faes before him!

I swear and vow by moon and stars,
  And sun that shines so early!
If I had twenty thousand lives,
  I'd die as aft for Charlie.—[30]

Volume three of the *Museum* contains his brilliant re-working of the Sheriffmuir broadside '*Dialogue between Will Lick-Ladle and Tom Clean-Cogue*'.[31] The original is a fairly leaden affair in which two countrymen debate the outcome of the battle with typical broadside prolixity. It is transformed in Burns's hands into a genuinely humorous exchange full of comic exaggeration and knock-about technical display. The almost indecently complicated verse form was probably suggested by the melodic pattern of the original tune, that 'vain carnal spring, called the Cameronian Rant' with its two extra bars mischievously slipped into the second measure. Despite the intricate structure, however, Burns sustains a narrative of breathless pace, a headlong torrent of alliteration, assonance and internal rhyme:

O cam ye here the fight to shun,
  Or herd the sheep wi' me, man,
Or were ye at the Sherra-moor,
  Or did the battle see, man.
I saw the battle sair and teuch,
And reekin-red ran mony a sheugh,
My heart for fear gae sough for sough,
To hear the thuds, and see the cluds
O' Clans frae woods, in tartan duds,
  Wha glaum'd at kingdoms three, man.
    Chos. la la la, &c.

The red-coat lads wi' black cockauds
  To meet them were na slaw, man,
They rush'd, and push'd, and blude outgush'd,
  And mony a bouk did fa', man:
The great Argyle led on his files,
I wat they glanc'd for twenty miles,
They hough'd the Clans like nine-pin kyles,
They hack'd and hash'd while braid swords clash'd,
And thro' they dash'd, and how'd and smash'd,
Till fey men di'd awa, man.
    Chos. la la la, &c.

But had ye seen the philibegs
  And skyrin tartan trews, man,
When in the teeth they dar'd our Whigs,
  And covenant Trueblues, man;

In lines extended lang and large,
When baiginets o'erpower'd the targe,
And thousands hasten'd to the charge;
Wi' Highland wrath they frae the sheath
Drew blades o' death, till out o' breath
They fled like frighted dows, man.
 Chos. la la la, &c.

O how deil Tam can that be true,
 The chace gaed frae the north, man;
I saw mysel, they did pursue
 The horse-men back to Forth, man;
And at Dunblane in my ain sight
They took the brig wi' a' their might,
And straught to Stirling wing'd their flight,
But, cursed lot! the gates were shut
And mony a huntit, poor Red-coat
For fear amaist did swarf, man.
 Chos. la la la, &c.

My sister Kate cam up the gate
 Wi' crowdie unto me, man;
She swoor she saw some rebels run
 To Perth and to Dundee, man:
Their left-hand General had nae skill;
The Angus lads had nae gude will,
That day their neebour's blude to spill;
For fear by foes that they should lose
Their cogs o' brose, they scar'd at blows
And hameward fast did flee, man.
 Chos. la la la, &c.

They've lost some gallant gentlemen
 Amang the Highland clans, man;
I fear my Lord Panmuir is slain,
 Or in his en'mies hands, man:
Now wad ye sing this double flight,
Some fell for wrang and some for right,
And mony bade the warld gudenight;
Sae pell and mell, wi' muskets knell
How Tories fell, and Whigs to h-ll
Flew off in frighted bands, man.
 Chos. la la la, &c.[32]

This amazing verbal *tour de force* has many admirable qualities: the effortlessly sustained illusion of eye-witness contemporaneity (we have to force ourselves to remember that the events described happened more than thirty years before the poet was born); the concentration upon the common man and the human fallibility of the participants; the way in which the conventionally heroic is both indulged and debunked throughout.

This essentially reductive technique is seen at its clearest in the fifth verse, where the timely retreat of the Angus lads is attributed not only to the absence of military appetite, but to the presence of an appetite of a ridiculously different kind. Despite the dreadful strokes and rivers of blood, the overall effect is deeply comic.

Burns's power of characterisation produces a picture rooted in everyday realities, where the epic and mundane are ludicrously entangled and the proverbial cast of common speech is wielded with ruthlessly deflationary effect. 'The Battle of Sherramoor' is a burlesque of the conventionally heroic, which, in its refusal to consider men in the mass, dehumanised by uniforms or warlike array is fundamentally humane.

Burns was the first to perceive the artistic possibilities latent in Jacobite tradition. He noted 'When Political combustion ceases to be the object of Princes & Patriots, it then...becomes the lawful prey of Historians & Poets', and he brought to the task a wealth of resources derived from painstaking study of both art and popular poetry.[33] Yet the best of his songs are those which, superficially at least, are the simplest, and none more so than 'Charlie he's my darling' with its teasing echoes of street and childrens songs and haunting bitter-sweet tune.

The song takes its emotional colouring from the narrator, a young woman who recounts in a sweetly indulgent tone a romantic adventure of the Chevalier. Discounting the conjunction which falls on a passing note, the refrain is made up of just seven words; and not content with allowing heavy metrical stress to fall on the word 'darling', Burns repeats it four times, giving the lines an almost incantatory quality, and something too, perhaps, of the inspired inconsequentiality of a nursery rhyme:

> An', Charlie he's my darling, my darling, my darling,
> Charlie he's my darling, the young Chevalier.—[34]

The opening verse establishes the fairy-tale ambience with a mixture of carefully placed vagueness and detail, and the same apparent capriciousness about what is revealed and what withheld that marks the best folk tales. Neither the time, the place, nor the speaker, are brought into clear focus; but we are told, with great emphasis, that it all happened on a Monday, in Winter.

The song unfolds as a highly episodic piece of Highland gallantry set in a lightly sketched dramatic framework: the Chevalier is out to see the sights, sees a handsome lass, pursues his suit, sets her on his knee, and then...

> 'Twas on a monday morning,
>   Right early in the year,
> That Charlie cam to our town,
>   The young Chevalier.—
>   An Charlie &c.
>
> As he was walking up the street.
>   The city for to view,
> O there he spied a bonie lass
>   The window looking thro'.—
>   An Charlie &c.

Sae light's he jimped up the stair,
And tirled at the pin;
And wha sae ready as hersel
To let the laddie in.—
An Charlie &c.

He set his Jenny on his knee,
All in his Highland dress;
For brawlie weel he ken'd the way
To please a bonie lass.—
An Charlie &c.

But 'Charlie is my darling' is not a bawdy song. This reaction is forestalled in the consummate final verse with its coquettish adolescent terror of Charlie, half bogyman, half boy-next-door, brilliantly encapsulating the mixture of reality and dream which gives the song its power:

It's up yon hethery mountain,
And down yon scroggy glen,
We daur na gang a-milking,
For Charlie and his men.—
An Charlie &c.

Burns is the complete master of convention here, taking what he needs from his popular printed sources without letting them determine the final shape of the song. He taps a wealth of association derived from traditional balladry and the Bonny Highland Laddie group without being indebted to either for the ultimate result; for while the song is rooted in the popular tradition, it achieves its success by baffling the expectations that tradition creates. The almost incidental revelation in the second last verse that Charlie is a 'Charming Highlandman' casts a rich retrospective significance over the earlier part of the song, arousing a robust anticipation of bawdry which is then mischievously frustrated. It is the creative tension between the song and its sources which gives it its attractively elliptical quality.

The conventional perspective is again apparently discarded in 'Ye Jacobites by name' one of Burns's best party songs, which deals with the human misery lurking behind political slogans and begins with a bold challenge to the legitimists:

Ye Jacobites by name, give an ear, give an ear;
Ye Jacobites by name, give an ear;
Ye Jacobites by name
Your fautes I will proclaim,
Your doctrines I maun blame,
You shall hear.—[35]

This sounds like a Whig song, but it is not. The singer's strictures are framed in humanitarian terms, and form a grim exposé of the suffering and misery glossed over by the glib formulae of political theory. Divine Right however exalted is shown to be like other kinds of state power, ultimately based upon brute force;

and lurking behind the fashionable cant about 'the just war' are the tragic realities
of murder and parricide:

> What is Right, and what is Wrang, by the law, by the law?
> What is Right, and what is Wrang, by the law?
> What is Right, and what is Wrang?
> A short Sword, and a lang,
> A weak arm, and a strang
> For to draw.—
>
> What makes heroic strife, fam'd afar, fam'd afar?
> What makes heroic strife, fam'd afar?
> What makes heroic strife?
> To whet th'Assasin's knife,
> Or hunt a Parent's life
> Wi' bludie war.—

The song could easily have ended at this point, as a straightforward condemnation of the Jacobites' willingness to plunge the nation into civil war for the
sake of a theory. As in so many of his better songs, however, Burns does not
present the argument simply, but places it in a dramatic context which allows the
true point of view to develop. Here he waits until the last moment before revealing
that the singer is himself a Jacobite, an ironical twist that lifts the song at a stroke
from the level of party strife to that of enduring general statement.

> Then let your schemes alone, in the State, in the State,
> Then let your schemes alone in the State,
> Then let your schemes alone,
> Adore the rising sun,
> And leave a Man undone
> To his fate.—

The singer speaks from direct personal experience, from the vantage point of a
political commitment which has destroyed him, to the Jacobites 'by name', the
meddlers, adventurers, and foolish partisans blinded by their own propaganda. At
no point does he lose sight of what ideology means in human terms: abstractions
like right and wrong are irrelevant; in real life justice is meted out by the sword-
length, and the weak are at the mercy of the strong. These soi-disant patriots are
urged in a bitter coda to pursue self-interest within the established order of things.

And so political disillusionment is given perhaps its definitive statement in a
'goodnight' ballad of extraordinary directness and power. Burns looks beyond
Jacobitism here, at war and the ordering of states, seeing with deadly clarity the
violence upon which they are founded.

This song may reflect Burns's actual convictions. The tortuous complexity of
his politics may conceal a very simple fact: maybe he didn't believe much in any
of it, and assumed and discarded party labels largely in order to survive. He was,
after all, a devious, proud and vulnerable man with many hostages to fortune,
struggling to make his way without wealth, position, or political influence in the
corrupt and authoritarian *ancien régime* of late-eighteenth-century Scotland. He

experienced and survived, (just) a major political purge as the government machine, reacting to the spread of French Revolutionary doctrines, attempted to eliminate its opponents in Scotland during the 1790s. The repressive, and vindictive nature of the British state was not a thing which existed for Burns in the realm of theory: he experienced it at first hand.[36]

Yet when he contemplated his own country, Scotland, he showed the same burning patriotism from start to finish; he gloried in its past, tirelessly collected and publicised its folk and literary traditions, and eagerly assumed the mantle of national poet, 'Caledonia's Bard, Brother Burns'. It was the one consistent strand in his public life and the dominating theme of his art.

By the same token, Jacobitism was the only political principle consistently present throughout his creative life. In his mind the two were closely linked. His great hymn to liberty, 'Scots wha hae', the nearest thing we have to a national anthem, was inspired by the Jacobite rebellions.[37] When he sent the impressario George Thomson a copy of the song, Burns stated: 'the accidental recollection of that glorious struggle for Freedom, associated with the glowing ideas of some other struggles of the same nature, *not quite so ancient*, roused my rhyming Mania'.[38] This has sometimes been taken as a reference to the French Revolution, but how a song which celebrates the traditional theme of heroic independence under a line of native kings could be construed as an essay in republicanism is less than clear. A letter Burns sent to the Earl of Buchan along with another copy of the song, shows that 'Scots wha hae' was inspired first and foremost by nationalistic fervour:

> Independent of my enthusiasm as a Scotchman, I have rarely met with any thing in History which interests my feelings as a Man, equally with the story of Bannockburn.—
>
> On the one hand, a cruel but able Usurper, leading on the finest army in Europe, to extinguish the last spark of Freedom among a greatly-daring and greatly injured People; on the other hand, the desperate relics of a gallant Nation, devoting themselves to rescue their bleeding Country, or to perish with her.—
> Liberty! Thou art a prize truly & indeed invaluable!—for never canst thou be too dearly bought![39]

The word 'Usurper' also featured prominently in the song. To an eighteenth century Scot, this had only one connotation, and it directly links the Wars of Independence with the Jacobite risings as heroic national struggles. It is not revolutionary libertarianism, but Scottish independence that is celebrated here.

Burns's career is not a collection of paradoxes. If we consider it in a European rather than in a narrowly British context, its coherence becomes at once apparent. Here we have a major poet consciously drawing his inspiration from popular tradition, in music, song, poetry, folklore, and language, in a classic example of bourgeois nationalism in the high Romantic manner.

The leading theorist of cultural nationalism was the German philosopher J G Herder who, in turn, owed much to the writers of the Scottish Enlightenment. Herder rejected the established idea of the state as a mere administrative unit made up of individuals united only by their loyalty to the crown. He drew a distinction between the *Rechtsstaat,* that is the state in its institutional form , and the *Kulturstaat*, or nation, defined as a sense of collective identity based on a common cultural tradition. He pointed to people's awareness of belonging to a shared heritage of folk and popular tradition, literature, and above all, language. These elements together constituted the *Volksgeist*, or spirit of the people. The educated classes, in Herder's view, were fatally compromised by their involvement in insecure and petty bureaucratic systems which made them fearful, subservient, and corrupt (as in the Scotland of Henry Dundas; and, perhaps, periods not quite so ancient). The vital core of the nation was the folk, the lower stratum of society, artisans, tradesmen and farmers, people, in short, like Robert Burns. From them all cultural virtue flowed. They were the means by which the *Volk* reproduced itself from generation to generation and they did it by inheriting and then creatively reproducing folklore and popular literature in their distinctive language. The nation was like an extended family (an idea which appears in many of Burns's Jacobite songs), and if it managed to maintain its cultural traditions, it could exist, as Scotland did, without the apparatus of a state.[40]

The preservation and renewal of the *Kulturstaat* was Robert Burns's lifework.

And he was not alone in this enterprise. There was a great efflorescence of cultural nationalism in Scotland during the late eighteenth and early nineteenth centuries, with key indicators like popular song collecting and publishing reaching an all time high. One thinks of Scott's *Minstrelsy of the Scottish Border* (1802-3), *Remains of Nithsdale and Galloway Song* (1810), Gilchrist's *Collection of Scottish Ballads, Tales and Songs* (1814), Alexander Campbell's *Albyn's Anthology Or a Select Collection of the Melodies & Vocal Poetry Peculiar to Scotland and the Isles* (1816), Struthers's *Harp of Caledonia: a Collection of Songs, Ancient and Modern...With an Essay on Scottish Song Writers* (1819), Hogg's *Jacobite Relics of Scotland; being The Songs, Airs, and Legends, of the Adherents to the House of Stuart* (1819-21), R A Smith's *The Scotish Minstrel, A Selection from the Vocal Melodies of Scotland, Ancient and Modern* (?1824-8), Allan *Cunningham's The Songs of Scotland, Ancient and Modern; with an Introduction and Notes, Historical and Critical, and Characters of the Lyric Poets* (1825) and Peter Buchan's *Ancient Ballads of the North of Scotland* (1828). This was also the first great period of Scottish imaginative prose, with writers like Scott, Hogg, Galt and host of lesser figures drawing their inspiration from folk and popular tradition.

This movement has received less attention than it deserves. There has in the past been too much emphasis on those sections of the Scottish intelligentsia which consciously sought to accomodate themselves to a 'British' cultural environment in the post-Union period, and not enough on the forces which resisted English cultural hegemony. The absence of an obvious political programme has encouraged the assumption that there was no nationalism in Scotland at this period, although following Herder's model one would not necessarily expect to find one—many Continental romanticists had no political programme as such; they regarded culture as the cutting edge of the national struggle; once that battle had been won, the politics followed as a matter of course.[41]

In any case, it was as a national symbol that Burns presented Jacobitism in his poems and songs, and he was able to prevail upon generations of his countrymen subsequently to accept it as such, because for the first time there was a nation in the modern sense for him to present it as a part of. He was the connecting link between the old Scottish world-picture and the new. He effectively mythologised Jacobitism by accommodating it to the heroic legendary past in a way that was entirely traditional. But he was also the leading representative in Scotland of the new age of national consciousness sweeping Europe in the early Romantic period. He generalised the anti-union element in Jacobitism into a symbol of Scottish cultural and historical distinctiveness in contradistinction to the 'British' and assimilationist ethos of the Whigs. He was able to implant his version of the Jacobite tradition at the heart of the evolving Scottish national identity, because that identity was in very considerable measure his own creation.

Chapter Nine

'THE STRAINS OF OUR COUNTRY UNSHACKLED AND STRONG'

In the twenty years that elapsed between the death of Burns and the publication of Hogg's *Jacobite Relics of Scotland* a substantial contribution was made to the body of later Jacobite song by a number of writers, and a succession of collectors and editors were working towards a definition of National Song in which Jacobite material was to occupy a central place.

Following the publication of the *Museum*, the general collections showed an increasing tendency towards national exclusiveness, and the idea that popular culture was an important element in the formation of national identity began to influence editorial selection and creep into editorial prefaces. We have already noted John Struthers's remarks in *The Harp of Caledonia*, a classic expression of bourgeois cultural nationalism based upon the pre-eminence of Scottish popular tradition a generation into the revival. Struthers traced the formative links between national character and popular song, seeing the latter as the source of that patriotism for which, he said, Scotsmen were so renowned, 'and of which every country knows something that has ever heard her warpipes play, or seen her tartans wave...'[1]

This view of Scotland as an essentially Celtic country echoes repeatedly through the nineteenth century literature. It would have astonished an average Lowlander of even a generation before.

Highland dress and Highland culture had for centuries provided an inexhaustible source of derision and contempt. Now, in the opening decades of the nineteenth century we find Lowland Scots triumphantly embracing these symbols in a mood of exhilarating national revival.[2]

Scotland which, like any part of the Hapsburg Empire, had been a culturally and linguistically diverse aggregate of peoples united only by a common monarchy, achieved in the opening years of the nineteenth century a unified national consciousness.

For the first time Highlanders and Lowlanders were prepared to regard themselves as part of a single national consciousness with a collective public symbolism.

This was marked in the Lowlands by new interest in the Gaelic ethos and new openness to the possibility of forging a homogeneous culture drawing from both strands of Scottish tradition.

To understand this state of affairs it is necessary to retrace our steps a little and consider the changing attitude towards the Gael, especially as revealed in the

Bonny Highland Laddie group of songs and its offshoots. These continued to be composed in significant numbers throughout the second half of the eighteenth century, and to reflect changing social and political circumstances.[3]

But the really interesting development comes with the military songs of the Revolutionary and Napoleonic wars. The successors of 'The Garb of Old Gaul' show the warlike traditions of the Gael realigned to depict the French as the natural enemies, as in 'The Gathering of the Clans', a swaggering re-interpretation of 'The Campbells are Coming' with its catalogue of Highland clans taking the field to demolish Napoleon:

> The king, he calls his men, his men;
> The king, he calls his men, his men;
> Rouse every clan, rise every man,
> In tower, and town, and glen, and glen.
>   The French are coming, oho! oho!
>   The French are coming, oho! oho!
>   Up wi' the Campbells,—hurra the Macdonalds,
>   Come out and beat the foe, the foe...
>
> The Gordons are forth afield, afield;
> The Gordons are forth afield, afield;
> The Murrays and Grahames have quitted their hames,
> At the sound of the spear and shield, and shield.
>   The French are coming, &c...
>
> Arranged and arrayed, advance! advance!
> Arranged and arrayed, advance! advance!
> The land of the Thanes, in freedom disdains
> The boasts and the bands of France, of France
>   The French are coming, &c...[4]

James Hogg's 'Donald M'Donald' was written at this time 'in utter indignation at the threatened invasion from France'.[5] It is placed in the mouth of a typical Highland soldier, at least as conceived by Hogg, and likewise shows the extent to which Scottish military traditions had succumbed to the mystique of the latter-day clansmen of the Highland regiments of the line. The piece is also haunted, as many of these things were, by the spectre of the '45 when Highland militarism had served a very different cause. The typical way round the problem was to generalise dynastic loyalty to the Stuarts into an expression of abstract monarchist legitimism and then transfer it lock stock and barrel to the house of Hanover, which is basically what Hogg does here:

> What though we befriendit young Charlie?—
>   To tell it I dinna think shame;
> Poor lad, he cam to us but barely,
>   An' recon'd our mountains his hame.
> 'Twas true that our reason forbade us;
>   But tenderness carried the day;—
> Had Geordie come friendless amang us,
>   Wi' him we had a' gane away.

> Sword an' buckler an' a',
> Buckler an' sword an' a';
> Now for George we'll encounter the devil,
> Wi' sword an' buckler an' a'!

Hogg gleefully anticipates the fate of the French when they land in the Highlands, and presents Bonaparte as a hapless Johnny Cope type figure:

> Wad Bonaparte land at Fort-William,
>   Auld Europe nae langer should grane;
> I laugh when I think how we'd gall him,
>   Wi' bullet, wi' steel, an' wi' stane;
> Wi' rocks o' the Nevis and Garny
> We'd rattle him off frae our shore,
> Or lull him to sleep in a cairny,
>   An' sing him—Lochaber no more!
>   Stanes an' bullets an' a',
>   Bullets an' stanes an' a';
>   We'll finish the Corsican callan
>   Wi' stanes an' bullets an' a'![6]

By the summer of 1815, real Highland laddies stood higher in public regard than at any time before, or possibly since. The battalions entering Paris with the Allied armies were the wonder of the city, and when they returned they were feted throughout the country. As they approached Edinburgh, excitement reached fever pitch. Here is James Anton, quartermaster sergeant of the Black Watch:

> We rested one night in Haddington and proceeded next day for Edinburgh...At Portobello an immense concourse of people were assembled to meet and welcome us. At Piershill the metropolis seemed to pour out the streams of its population to congragulate us on our approach, and to welcome us to its arms. Advance seemed impracticable, from the density of the surrounding multitude: from this a guard of cavalry, with its band of music, preceded us. Thus accompanied, we entered the city amidst the loud cheering and congratulations of friends; while over our heads, from a thousand windows, waved as manny banners, plaided scarfs, or other symbols of courtly greetings.
>
> We entered the castle, proud of the most distinguished reception that ever a regiment had met with from a grateful country.[7]

Highland dress had become a glamorous new national symbol whose freshness was yearly renewed on the battlefields of Europe. Great ladies affected the lofty plumed bonnets and short military coats of the Highland regiments, and long before 1822, Highland dress received the ultimate seal of establishment approval. It was worn by Prince George in 1789 at a masquerade ball at which he 'received the appelation of the Royal Highland Laddie'.[8]

The triumphal entry of the Black Watch into Edinburgh marked the high-point of more than a generation of quickening enthusiasm for certain aspects of Highland culture. *Ossian* opened the floodgates, and a greedy public were regularly regaled with volumes of Highland tours, accounts of Highland manners, and disquisitions upon Highland antiquities. In 1784 the Highland Society of Scotland was founded, numbering the cream of Edinburgh society amongst its members. It appointed a committee to enquire into the authenticity of *Ossian*, supervised the publication of a Gaelic dictionary, and most important in this context, sponsored the expeditions of Alexander Campbell to collect Gaelic song in the Highlands, which resulted in the publication in 1816 of *Albyn's Anthology*, bringing for the first time before a general public examples of genuine Gaelic Jacobite songs in the original tongue and in translation.[9]

Alasdair MacMhaighstir Alasdair's '*Oran do an gairir, am Breacan Uallach*' gives an example of Campbell's approach. The main text is reproduced in Gaelic, with an 'imitation' by the editor which tries to recapture something of the *blas* of the original:

> *Hei the home-made sable wool cloth!*
> *Hei the home-made Highland plaiden!*
> *Sassanachs may boast their broad cloth,*
> *While we brook our Highland plaiden.*

> The Highland plaid so noble,
> On shoulder, or under arm put,
> Well becomes the hero
> In peace or in heat of battle...

> My sword for Royal Charlie,
> I drew 'gainst the red-coat rebels;
> With gun, dag, dirk, and target,
> I fought for my exiled monarch...

> The joyous days are coming,
> When, smiling shall peace and plenty
> Welcome back poor Charlie:
> The clans then shall wear the tartan.[10]

A number of modern pieces by Hogg, Scott and John Wilson were included. Scott contributed three songs on Highland subjects, set to *piobaireachd* melodies: 'The MacGregors' Gathering', 'Pibroch of Donuil Dubh' and 'Lament—(*Cha till suinn tuille*)'.[11] In this year too was published Captain Simon Fraser's magnificent collection of *Airs and Melodies peculiar to the Highlands of Scotland and the Isles* (Edinburgh 1816) which contained more than two hundred tunes and became a standard work in the popular instrumental tradition during the nineteenth and twentieth centuries.

The first phase of Jacobitism as a dynastic movement was now at a close. Various social and political forces gradually weakened its hold in surviving loyalist families, but it received its death-blow from the French Revolution.

Detestation of 'French principles' united all who saw themselves as guardians of the established social order, regardless of ordinary political differences. Lady Nairne's family, the Oliphants of Gask, are a typical example of this. Her grandfather had been 'out' in both major rebellions and her father had been aide de camp to the Young Chevalier. The Oliphant children were given a thoroughly Jacobite upbringing whose principal object was 'to keep them loyal'; they were not permitted to refer to the reigning dynasty by name and even in their prayer-books, the Hanoverian title was blotted out and that of the Stuarts inscribed in its place.[12] The Revolution destroyed this ethos absolutely and at once. In the words of her biographer Charles Rogers:

> A new order of things was about to extinguish those sentiments of Jacobitism which lingered in certain families. Portentous national perils were looming on every side. The frantic reformers of France, flushed with success in overturning a throne and uprooting a dynasty, had invited the people of Great Britain to revolt and to destroy. Among the artisans of Scotland the toast in many taverns was, 'Damnation to the King, and success to the friends of the People!' Demagogues everywhere sought to inflame the minds of the peasantry. The upholders of Government were called on to unite in the preservation of order. The militia was embodied. The young Laird of Gask joined the Perthshire Light Dragoons, and served for three years, much to the detriment of his estate.[13]

The spectre of Republicanism rendered the traditional opposition of Hanoverian and Stuart obsolete at a stroke. By 1816, Alexander Campbell could write that

> the immediate offspring of the true Jacobite families are at this moment the most zealous and loyal supporters of the illustrious house of Brunswick.[14]

It was in such an atmosphere that the public rehabilitation of the movement could take place. In 1802, John Home published his long-awaited *History of the Rebellion*. The appearance of *Waverley* in 1814 swept aside the lingering aura of prohibition and Jacobitism 'at once became the fashion'.[15] In the next few years a number of works profiting from the wave of enthusiasm created by Scott's novel vied for public attention.[16]

Although it would be an exaggeration to say that under the influence of his novels 'the whole nation...went over the water to Charlie',[17] Scott was identified by contemporaries as the instigator of an historically-minded Toryism which saw no paradox in decking the new legitimism with the garments of the old. Jacobitism was thus revived as a component in an aggressive counter-revolutionary movement determined to enhance the power of the British state by presenting the Hanoverians as a focus of kingly mystique, even if this meant appropriating the traditions of their dynastic rivals. Just how serious this was in political terms can be gauged from the horrified reaction of contemporary Whigs:

> Through some odd process of *servile* logic, it should seem, that in restoring the claims of the Stuarts by the courtesy of romance, the house of Brunswick are more firmly seated in point of fact...In any other view, we cannot possibly conceive how Sir Walter imagines 'he has done something to revive the declining spirit of loyalty' by these novels. His loyalty is founded on *would-be* treason: he props the actual throne by the shadow of rebellion.[18]

Such, then, was the background against which in October 1817 James Hogg, the Ettrick Shepherd, received a letter from Col. David Stewart of Garth:

My dear sir,
   Will you be surprised to learn that there are a number of members of the Highland Society of London such Jacobites, and of these some branches of the Royal Family, that they are very desirous of collecting all the old Jacobite songs with their original words, and seem very sensible of the beauty of the one, and the wit and humour of the other—Now as I am strongly suspected of being a Jacobite in theory whatever I may be in practice, I am desired to enquire where a person can be found who is able and willing to collect, arrange, and publish a collection of all the songs and words which were sung by both sides, Whigs and Tories, during the rebellions of 1715 and 45...
   The object of the Society is to make a collection of both party's for which encouragement will be given say one hundred pounds or more to the person who undertakes the work with all encouragement and assistance in the first instance in making the necessary research, and afterwards in promoting the sale of the work.
   Now as I am sometimes a Jacobite in theory, particularly when I think of my grandmothers stories of the forty five, and being particularly anxious to see all this music now so scattered all collected so that it may be seen in one view, and as I have the happiness to know you I am sure I cannot more effectually promote the views of the Society than by stating this circumstance to you...may I hope that you will give it consideration and favour me with your opinion, and whether or not you will undertake this work, and say if you think it possible to make a small collection...[19]

To Hogg whose financial affairs were in a state of permanent crisis, the proposal must have seemed a godsend and he unhesitatingly agreed. In 1817 he was well into middle life with a long and chequered literary career behind him. He had assisted Scott with the *Minstrelsy*, enjoyed an extensive literary acquaintance, and was steeped in the traditional culture of the Borders. In some ways he was a most imaginative choice. Hogg knew more about Scottish song than anybody then living and his susceptibility to the Highlands and the romantic connotations of Jacobitism was a matter of record. On the other hand he was a creative writer rather than an antiquarian, a mercurial, ebullient individualist who was anything but a committee man, and this was to be rather a drawback when it emerged what kind of collection the Society really had in mind...[20]

Nevertheless, he began with great gusto, collecting books and manuscripts, building up a network of correspondents, and securing the active cooperation of Scott. In the enthusiasm of the chase he gaily ignored Stewart's precept about size. Within a year he was writing to the publisher, Blackwood 'I...have got plenty of songs at least six times more than I can publish' and when the first volume appeared in 1819, he was found to have got no further than the beginning of the '15.[21]

The format of the *Jacobite Relics* was based on Ritson's *Scotish Songs*, which had established the academic standard in the field. Each item was numbered, its title printed in black-letter, and the melody given in staff-notation immediately above the text. There were appendices of Whig songs, Jacobite songs to which no tune could be assigned, and a large collection of notes. The whole was prefixed by a set of dedicatory verses and a prose 'Introduction'.[22]

The lines 'To the Most Noble and Honourable President and Members of the Highland Society of London' are of considerable interest. They compare the threat

Figure 9. James Hogg by William Nicholson. (Courtesy of the Gallery of Modern Art).

to the British crown with the destruction of the Stuart monarchy, and attempt, as Scott had done, to divert a separate and fundamentally incompatible tradition of hereditary loyalty into support for the Hanoverians and the aristocratic principle in government:

> When kings were degraded, to ruffians a prey,
> Or driven from the thrones of their fathers away,
> Who then could sit silent? Alas for the while,
> That now there are myriads, the worst of the vile,
> Whose highest ambition is bent to defame
> All greatness and sovereignty, order and name!...
> Ah! woe to the nation, its honours fall low,
> When mendicant meddlers dare Majesty brow,
> And turn up the snout of derision and scorn
> At those who to honour or titles are born![23]

Of course Hogg has to turn a blind eye to the fact that the 'ruffians' who drove out the Stuarts were the immediate forbears of the current dynasty.

At the same time he is eloquent in his appraisal of the cultural power of the Jacobite song tradition. Upon the eclipse of the Stuarts,

> Then flowed the wild strains to the rock and the wood,
> Of the fall of the mighty, the Royal, and good;
> So plaintive and sweet, all were moved by the tone,
> From the child of the cot to the prince on the throne...
> These strains, which a Shepherd has travailled to save,
> With joy he consigns to the sons of the brave:
> He lov'd them when fancy was ardent and young,
> Even then of the clans of the Highlands he sung...
> For his Whiggish heart, with its Covenant tie,
> Was knit to the Highlands, he could not tell why—
> Was knit to the cause they espoused to their cost,
> And grieved that the name of the Stuart was lost![24]

He went on to ascribe the Jacobite songs to the Gaels themselves. Such, at any rate, appears to be the intention of the following lines:

> And now, Noble Highlanders, sons of the North,
> That land of blue mountains, and birth-place of worth,
> These strains that were chanted o'er many a wild heath,
> These strains of your fathers, to you I bequeath;

Highland Jacobites composed party songs of course; but they used Gaelic, like Alasdair MacMhaighstir Alasdair, or, following Struan Robertson, standard English. Scottish Jacobite song as popularly understood (and as collected by the Ettrick Shepherd), was overwhelmingly Lowland in origin and language. Hogg's is a telling slip, however, for it confirms how deep the popular association of Jacobitism with the Highlands had become.

In his prose Introduction, Hogg advances the claim of Jacobite songs to serious consideration as a group. He surveys previous publications in the field, ponders the general failure to preserve the old songs in view of their importance to the political biographer and constitutional historian, and turning to the nature of the form itself, decisively overturns the categories which had been accepted by popular-song scholars for more than a generation. He is the first to distinguish political song from the traditional historical ballad on the one hand, and art-song from folk song upon the other. 'These songs' he writes,

> are...a species of composition entirely by themselves. They have no affinity with our ancient ballads of heroism and romance; and one part of them far less with the mellow strains of our pastoral and lyric muses. Their general character is that of a rude energetic humour, that bids defiance to all opposition, in arms, sentiments, or rules of song-writing. They are the unmasked effusions of a bold and primitve race, who hated and despised the overturning innovations that prevailed in church and state, and held the abettors of these as...beings too base to be spoken of with any degree of patience or forbearance. Such is their prevailing feature.[25]

He was also on the verge of making another important distinction, between the controversial and the later lyrical Jacobite songs; but for a number of reasons he seems deliberately to avoid doing this.

In the dedicatory verses he characterises the songs as 'plaintive and sweet'; but in the Introduction he draws attention to their 'rude energetic humour', claiming that 'one part of them [have no affinity with] the mellow strains of our pastoral and lyric muses'. He remarks, in a discussion of previous collectors, that one had

> added a number of beautiful [songs] to the list; and though some of these are evidently of modern manufacture, yet have they been copied with avidity into many subsequent collections.[26]

Similarly,

> This song ['The Waes of Scotland'] is copied from Cromek's work, [Remains of Nithsdale and Galloway Song (Lond., 1810)] where it first appeared. I am afraid it is not very ancient, as it bears strong marks of the hand of the ingenious Allan Cunninghame...I do not, however, take it on me to say the song is modern; but any one acquainted with Cunninghame's poetry will easily mark the strong resemblance.[27]

He is referring here to one of the most spectacular literary frauds of the century, in which his friend Allan Cunningham a young Dumfries stone-mason, passed off on the dilettantish English collector Robert Hartley Cromek a whole volume of spurious songs, a fact well known in Scottish literary circles.[28] The most obvious explanation of his coyness on the subject is that he considered the inclusion of modern material to violate his commission as a serious antiquary binding him to preserve contemporary pieces and reject later imitations as of no historical value. Yet he admitted 'Waes me for Prince Charlie' without a qualm, remarking that

> This sweet little Jacobite song is said to have been written by a Mr William Glen, about Glasgow. I have seen a poem on the death of the princess Charlotte, and some

small pieces of merit in periodical works, by a Mr Glen, of that country. Whether or not these are by the same I have not been able to learn.[29]

Although he felt it important that his material should be considered the genuine effusions of the age, he overrode any criteria that might exclude a piece he liked. Having indicated an ambiguity in the relationship between the earlier and later Jacobite songs he cheerfully declined to resolve it.

He could be casual to a degree about the dates of songs. 'Over the Seas and far awa':

> Is an older song than these among which it is here placed; but there are so many of them of a general nature, that it is impossible to decide in what reign they had their origin; nor does it signify aught to know, for they suit one equally as well as another.[30]

'The Thistle of Scotland':

> is a modern song, and the only one that is in the volume, to my knowledge. It had no right to be here, for it is a national, not a Jacobite song; but I inserted it out of a whim, to vary the theme a little.[31]

He printed 'The Bonny Moorhen' which obviously refers to the Young Chevalier, in volume one, and of 'The Whigs of Fife', blithely confessed that

> The date of this rude rough song is quite uncertain. I meant to have published it in the first volume, and that near the beginning, as one of the most ancient...but this, with several others, fell aside about the printing office, and were never missed, till found this year among the return manuscripts.[32]

Manifestly English ballads were printed in the main body of the text, along with songs like 'Marilla' and 'A South-Sea Ballad' which had no connection with the Jacobite movement at all.[33]

Hogg's enormities were lightly committed and cheerfully confessed. 'Perfidious Britain', he announced,

> is a middling good old song...I do not always understand what the bard means; but as he seems to have been an ingenious though passionate writer, I take it for granted that he knew perfectly well himself what he would have been at, so I have not altered a word from the manuscript, which is in the hand-writing of an amanuensis of Mr Scott's, the most incorrect transcriber, perhaps, that ever tried the business.[34]

But it is important not to be misled by the breezy candour of his manner. It is well known, for example, that he passed off his own 'Donald Macgillavry' as a relic of outstanding merit and undoubted authenticity and there are almost certainly more of his own compositions included in the collection and never subsequently avowed. He liked to minimise the extent of his reliance upon printed material and the battery of privately-owned MSS. cited in the Introduction helped draw a veil over his sources, virtually giving him a free hand (when he chose to exercise it) with his texts. He appropriated whole sections of notes from Ritson, usually without acknowledgement. Indeed were it not unfair to treat Hogg so severely, this catalogue of 'horrible and awefu'' could be extended considerably. But he was not, and did not pretend to be, a pedantically serious scholar. His cavalier flourishes as an editor were the exception rather than the rule (for the collection contains much painstaking and accurate work) and they give the *Relics* an energy and charm rare in literature of this type.[35] And quite apart from editorial apparatus, his own contribution to the songs is as lively and accomplished as the volumes can show.

'Donald Macgillavry' was published in the first series of the *Relics* with a highly appreciative note. 'This', proclaimed Hogg, 'is one of the best songs that ever was made...a capital old song, and very popular'. He then preceeded upon an inquiry, as solemn as it was specious, into the historical background, unearthing several apparently genuine Macgillavrys—John M'Gillavry, executed at Preston in 1716, a Colonel M'Gillavry of the MacIntosh regiment in the '45—suggesting that 'a bard connected with that associated clan may have written it'. But the note is designed to do more than put a gloss of authenticity upon the song. Its delightful wrong-headedness seems intended (as do various of the other notes in the *Relics*) as a skit on the unsmiling pedantry apt then as now to afflict popular-song studies. Its author was, after all, one of the most masterly parodists in the country:

> The Clan-Macgillavry is only a subordinate one, so that the name seems taken to represent the whole of the Scottish clans by a comical patronymic, that could not give offence to anyone, nor yet render any clan particularly obnoxious to the other party, by the song being sung in mixed assemblies. It may, however, have been written in allusion to that particular clan, small as it was, as we see Macgillavry of Drumglass mentioned in some copies of the *Chevalier's Muster-Roll*.[36]

Hogg may simply have wanted to make his own contribution to what was very much a living tradition. It is not impossible, however, that a deeper game was afoot and that the Shepherd, well aware that 'Donald Macgillavry' was one of his best pieces, something a reviewer of the *Relics* was almost bound to notice, may have falsified its credentials in this way in order to ensnare the distinguished critic Francis Jeffrey. A few years before, Walter Scott, smarting from a slighting review of *Marmion*, had tried a similar manoeuvre, causing *The Bridal of Triermain* to be issued anonymously just a week or two after *Rokeby* hoping, in vain, to embarrass the *Edinburgh Review*.[37]

If 'Donald Macgillavry' was indeed a literary ambush, Jeffrey walked right into it. In the 1831 edition of his *Songs*, Hogg jubliantly recorded this famous victory. The piece had been

> originally published in the Jacobite Relics, without any notice of its being an original composition; an ommission which entrapped the Edinburgh Review into a high but unintentional compliment to the author. After reviewing the Relics in a style of most determined animosity, and protesting over and over again that I was devoid of all taste and discrimination, the tirade concluded in these terms: 'That we may not close this article without a specimen of the good songs which the book contains, we shall select the one which, for sly, characteristic Scotch humour, seems to us the best, though we

doubt if any of our English readers will relish it'. The opportunity of retaliating upon the reviewer's want of sagacity was too tempting to be lost; and the authorship of the song was immediately avowed in a letter to the Editor of Blackwood's Magazine. 'After all', said this avowal, 'between ourselves, Donald M'Gillavry, which he has selected as the best specimen of the true old Jacobite song, and as remarkably above its fellows for "sly, characteristic Scotch humour", is no other than a trifle of my own, which I put in to fill up a page!'[38]

Jeffrey was not mistaken in one respect, however; 'Donald Macgillavry' is one of the best things in the collection, set to a lilting 6/8 in a minor key ideally suited to the repetition and word-play packed into the stanzas, and issuing an exuberant summons to resentful Gaeldom to deliver the nation from the thraldom of Whiggery. The hero is one of the legion of Comic Gaels and has various conventional features; but Hogg treats him sympathetically, identifying with him in a way unthinkable a generation before. His Highlandman is not a clownish barbarian, but a formidable character with a decisive political role:

> Donald's gane up the hill hard and hungry;
> Donald comes down the hill wild an' angry;
> Donald will clear the gouk's nest cleverly.
> Here's to the king an' Donald Macgillavry.
> Come like a weigh-bauk, Donald Macgillavry,
> Come like a weigh-bauk, Donald Macgillavry;
> Balance them fair, and balance them cleverly,
> Off wi' the counterfeit, Donald Macgillavry.[39]

Successive verses elaborate the pattern established in the first. The initial four lines enlarge upon the Highlandman's fury, and then he is invoked in various forms, as a weaver, tailor, cobbler, and so on, and this takes up the rest of the the octave:

> Donald's run o'er the hill but his tether, man,
> As he were wud, or stang'd wi' an ether, man;
> When he comes back, there's some will look merrily:
> Here's to King James and Donald Macgillavry.
> Come like a weaver, Donald Macgillavry,
> Come like a weaver, Donald Macgillavry,
> Pack on your back, an elwand sae cleverly;
> Gie them full measure, my Donald Macgillavry.

This wealth of trade-simile does not exhaust Hogg's resources. The injustices suffered by the protean hero are transformed by the same profusely inventive intelligence. Donald's grievance is the traditional Jacobite one against 'Cess and Press, and Presbytery'. But these prosaic concepts are translated in four brilliantly alliterative lines into fresh and highly concrete terms:

> Donald has foughten wi' reif and roguery;
> Donald has dinner'd wi' banes an' beggary...

and

> Donald was mumpit wi' mirds and mockery;
> Donald was blindit wi' blads o' property...

thus:

> Donald has foughten wi' reif and roguery;
> Donald has dinner'd wi' banes and beggery:
> Better it were for Whigs and Whiggery
> Meeting the devil than Donald Macgillavry.
> Come like a tailor, Donald Macgillavry,
> Come like a tailor, Donald Macgillavry;
> Push about, in and out, thimble them cleverly
> Here's to King James and Donald Macgillavry!
>
> Donald's the callan that brooks nae tangleness;
> Whigging, and prigging, and a' newfangleness,
> They maun be gane: he winna be baukit, man;
> He maun hae justice, or faith he'll tak it, man.
> Come like a cobler, Donald Macgillavry,
> Come like a cobler, Donald Macgillavry;
> Beat them, and bore them, and lingel them cleverly.
> Up wi' King James and Donald Macgillavry!
>
> Donald was mumpit wi' mirds and mockery;
> Donald was blindid wi' blads o' property;
> Arles ran high, but makings war naething, man;
> Lord, how Donald is flyting an' fretting, man.
> Come like the devil, Donald Macgillavry,
> Come like the devil, Donald Macgillavry;
> Skelp them an' scaud them that prov'd sae unbritherly.
> Up wi' King James an' Donald Macgillavry!

Hogg summarises a world of abstract social and political concept—all the inequalities and injustice of the mercantile civilisation of Whig Scotland—by means of a fecund supply of images drawn, ironically, from commerce itself. This in part is what gives the song that energy which Jeffrey mistook for authenticity. One of the sources of its excellence lies in the balance struck between the comic impulse of the convention and the seriousness of the theme. Another lies in its deft interplay with the tune.

The air is heptachordal in the Aeolian mode with a phrase pattern which would seem to indicate a triplet-and-refrain type text to coincide with its apparently tripartite organisation, although it is actually binary in form. Hogg partially satisfies this impulse with refrain lines at the middle and end of his stanza, and in the third verse fulfils it almost exactly with the near-rhymes 'roguery, beggery, Whiggery'; but elsewhere he carefully avoids establishing it as the dominant pattern. The melody itself is highly organised and economical, with a haunting motif based upon the interplay of tonic, dominant and flattened seventh. These intervals are strongly emphasised and Hogg takes advantage of their almost incantatory quality to invoke the Highlandman in appropriate form. The resulting texture of balance and contrast reveals him as a sensitive craftsman responsive to the underlying character of the melody and subtly reflecting its tensions in his lines.

The increasing accessibility and prestige of Gaelic song influenced the Shepherd as well as Scott. Highland correspondents supplied a considerable body of material for the *Relics*; not songs as such, for Hogg had no Gaelic, but translations into English prose which he then turned back into verse. In a note to 'Maclean's Welcome', his most successful venture in this field, he explained his procedure:

> these songs from the Gaelic were mostly sent to me by different hands, translated simply into English prose, and have all been versified by me...they are rather *imitations from the Gaelic* than anything else. To have versified the short sentences from the Gaelic literally, was impossible. I trust, however, that those acquainted with the originals will confess that they have lost nothing in going through my hands exclusive of the Gaelic idioms...which must all vanish in any translation whatsoever. Yet even in these abrupt Highland Ossianic sentences, there seems to be something of the raw material and spirit of poetry, for I never got any notes of words so easily turned into songs.[40]

From such a prose fragment he created 'Maclean's Welcome' which weaves around the reception devised for the Prince's return a voluptuous fabric of assonance and alliteration, hypnotic repetition and double rhyme. The text is made up of four verses with the refrain

> Come o'er the stream, Charlie, dear Charlie, brave Charlie,
> Come o'er the stream, Charlie, and dine with Maclean;
> And though you be weary, we'll make your heart cheery,
> And welcome our Charlie and his loyal train.[41]

incorporated into each stanza. Hogg ignores for a moment the political significance of Maclean's extraordinary dinner-invitation, concentrating instead upon the barbaric prodigality of the fare in lines which must owe at least as much to the Canticles as to their Gaelic original:

> We'll bring down the track deer, we'll bring down the black steer,
> The lamb from the breckan, and doe from the glen;
> The salt sea we'll harry, and bring to our Charlie,
> The cream from the bothy, and curd from the pen.

This is far indeed from the beggary and want traditionally associated with the *Gaidhealtachd*. In Hogg's Highland Elysium, even ardent spirits lose their harsher connotations, and illicit poteen is transported into a lyrical and exalted substance:

> Come o'er the stream, Charlie, &c.
> And you shall drink freely the dews of Glen-Sheerly,
>   That stream in the star-light when kings do not ken;
> And deep be your meed of the wine that is red,
>   To drink to your sire, and his friend the Maclean.

> Come o'er the stream, Charlie, &c.
> Our heath-bells shall trace you the maids to embrace you,
>   And deck your blue bonnet with flowers of the brae;
> And the loveliest Mari in all Glen-M'Quarry
>   Shall lie in your bosom till break of the day.

But the banquet is merely a brilliant interlude, a preamble to the business at hand, and waiting outside 'a troop of our bold Highlandmen'

> Shall range on the heather with bonnet and feather,
> Strong arms and broad claymores three hundred and ten.

Thus, with a brisk reminder of the real purpose of Maclean's Welcome, the song draws to a close.

By no means all of Hogg's Jacobite songs found their way into the *Relics*. One of the most famous, 'Bonnie Prince Charlie', was first printed in *The Border Garland*, a pamphlet of nine songs issued in 1819.[42] It reappeared in the edition of the Shepherd's *Songs* in 1831 with the following disparaging note:

> Is it not singular how this song should have been so popular? There can be no dispute that it is one of my worst. The air was...given me by my friend the late Mr Neil Gow, and to it I dashed down the words at random. [43]

The assessment is not wholly unjust, for while it contains some lines in his best manner, 'Bonnie Prince Charlie' is a very uneven song. The female singer urges on the Jacobite forces and dedicates herself and her children to the cause, but her loosely constructed personal testament is largely a framework for a collection of evocative personal and place names:

> Cam ye by Athol, lad wi' the philabeg,
> Down by the Tummel, or banks o' the Garry,
> Saw ye our lads, wi' their bonnets and white cockades,
> Leaving their mountains to follow Prince Charlie...

> I'll to Lochiel and Appin, and kneel to them,
> Down by Lord Murray, and Roy of Kildarlie;
> Brave M'Intosh he shall fly to the field with them;
> These are the lads I can trust wi' my Charlie!

The opening and closing verses and the refrain bear the impress of that dithyrambic abandon which Hogg seems able to realise almost at will, enabling him to achieve a momentarily complete surrender to the mood of whatever he was writing:

> Down through the Lowlands, down wi' the Whigamore!
> Loyal true Highlanders, down wi' them rarely!
> Ronald an' Donald, drive on wi' the broad claymore,
> Over the necks of the foes o' Prince Charlie!

> Follow thee! follow thee! wha wadna follow thee?
> Lang hast thou loved and trusted us fairly!

Charlie, Charlie, wha wadna follow thee,
King o' the Highland hearts, bonny Prince Charlie?

Hogg's most unusual contribution to the Jacobite muse is not his 'gathering songs' or Gaelic paraphrases, but a number of relatively minor pieces all showing to a greater or lesser extent a pervasive sense of *ubi sunt*. For just as songs celebrating the gallantry of the clans gained added point from the recent triumphs of the Highland regiments, so those which deplored the defeat at Culloden began to register something rather larger than military disaster. They seem to be a comment, although indirect, upon the Clearances.

The implications of the Highland Clearances first began to impinge upon the Lowlands during the 1790s with the earliest evictions from the huge Sutherland estates of the Marquess of Stafford. In the next twenty years the successive clearing of Strathglass and Glengarry's country kept the subject before the attention of the public. By 1820, considerable tracts of the Highlands which had once supported a numerous population contained little except a handful of low-country shepherds and a great many Cheviot sheep.[44]

Hogg was a frequent visitor to the Highlands. He had once planned to emigrate as a shepherd to the Isle of Harris and would in any case have been more than ordinarily aware, as a professional sheep-farmer, of conditions in the hills.[45]

It is difficult to accept that lines like the following—the first from 'Why weeps yon Highland Maid?', the second from 'The Highlander's Farewell'—were inspired simply by contemplation of the cruelties which followed the '45:

> Where now her clansman true,
> Where is the bonnet blue,
> Where the claymore that broke
> Fearless through fire and smoke?
> Not one gleam by glen or river,
> It lies dropp'd from the hand for ever.
> Stranger, our fate deplore,
> Our ancient name's no more![46]

> The glen that was my father's own,
>   Maun be by his forsaken;
> The house that was my father's home
>   Is levell'd with the braken...

> Farewell, farewell, dear Caledon,
>   Land of the Gael no longer!
> Strangers have trod thy glory on,
>   In guile and treachery stronger.[47]

The theme of Highland depopulation is clearly suggested in the valedictory 'Stuarts of Appin'. The district's past is celebrated as the homeland of Ossian and the bulwark against the Campbells, but when we come to the deeds of the clan under Montrose and in the Jacobite rebellions, a deeply elegiac note is sounded:

And ne'er for the crown of the Stuarts was fought
  One battle on vale, or on mountain deer-trodden,
But dearly to Appin the glory was bought,
  And dearest of all on the field of Culloden!
Lament, O, Glen-Creran, Glen-Duror, Ardshiel,
  High offspring of heroes, who conquer'd were never,
For the deeds of your fathers no bard shall reveal,
  And the bold clan of Stuart must perish for ever!

While government measures after the rebellion were certainly severe, they were
not so excessive as to extinguish whole clans. Hogg, however, blending the themes
of military defeat with the subsequent expropriations during the rage for Improvement, seizes the occasion of Culloden to mourn the passing of a whole culture:

Clan-Chattan is broken, the Seaforth bends low,
  The sun of Clan-Ranald is sinking in labour;
Glencoe, and Clan-Donnachie, where are they now?
  And where is bold Keppoch, the lord of Lochaber?

Oh-hon, an Righ! and the Stuarts of Appin!
The gallant, devoted, old Stuarts of Appin!
  Their glory is o'er,
  For the clan is no more;
And the Sassenach sings on the hills of green Appin.[48]

Hogg had a much more enthusiastic interest in Gaeldom than Burns and was
less cautious than Scott in accepting its apparent standards. He was moved not so
much by Jacobitism as such—although the subject had laid sporadic claim to his
attention for a number of years—as by the pageant of Highland society, with its
pugnacious mores, evocative eponymy and impending dissolution. It is clear from
his letters that he regarded the notes of the *Relics* as equal in importance to the
songs themselves, and the notes were seen primarily as a means of introducing
various aspects of Highland culture to a Lowland audience. As he wrote in October
1818 to his publisher,

I am now certain that the work will be popular. Many of the songs have a great deal
of spirit and they form such a fine text for Highland anecdote.[49]

Hogg had expended considerable effort on the collection and took a justifiable
pride in its range and comprehensiveness. He intended it to be definitive, complete,
the last word on the subject.[50]
His wrath when the Highland Society withheld one half of the promised fee
was consequently great:

The secretary of the Highland Society refuses to pay me my £50. Colonel Stuart...has
misled me. I conceived I had as good a claim for that money as any I ever won in my
life...I have made a collection which no man on earth could have made but myself,
for Scott could not have collected the music...I am sure there never was a fairer bargain
made between two men on earth...I have a great mind to force him to implement his

bargain, which I find he has made without authority. There is no reason why I should be gulled and cheated by everybody in this manner after the pains I have taken.[51]

The usual view of the ensuing fracas is that in going ahead and actually commissioning the collection the Colonel had rather anticipated his fellow members' wishes. Hogg's anger does not help to make things clearer. At one point he insisted that his work had been approved. He wrote to the song-publisher George Thomson on 14 December 1821 'The Highland Society were not displeased with my work. I have obligations to the contrary'.[52] How he could have managed to believe this after the letter he got from Stewart of Garth, dated 9 September 1821, is difficult to follow (unless he had problems, as the present writer had, with Garth's abominable handwriting). It was huffy enough in all conscience. The Society's views could hardly have been more plainly, indeed brutally, expressed:

> The trouble is, as I told Mr Blackwood the execution of the first volume has not given satisfaction—No communication was made to the Society during its progress—the work having in a manner originated with the Society their object being to show that the people of Scotland and the Jacobites in particular possessed a fund of bravery equal to if not superior to any other Country, they were anxious to preserve those ballads and songs which tended so much to show this talent—
> Fifty pound was advanced to make the experiment—the best and only the best was to be published—the experiment has not been satisfactory—no opportunity was afforded of expressing an opinion—no communication was made to enable them to say what ballads and songs they wished to have for their money—[53]

Hogg, it seems, had interpreted too widely the privileges of editorial independence. Instead of humbly submitting his literary excavations to a committee of grandees in London, he had wantonly gone his own way. Instead of a garland of lyrics breathing the purest spirit of patriotism and self-sacrifice, their £50 had purchased a heterogeneous mishmash of squibs, satires and lampoons. Instead of a budget of 'Bonnie Charlies', they had a superb collection of largely contemporary political songs and they were not amused.

But Garth left the real fly sticking firmly in the ointment. It was left to Jeffrey and the *Edinburgh Review* to voice the Highland Society's ultimate misgiving.

The warblings of the Jacobite muse, he declared,

> have somewhat disappointed us...the proportion of insipid, middling, and positively bad is far greater than we had expected. This may no doubt be owing to the compiler's taste, which is evidently of a coarse and vulgar description...the cardinal defect of Mr Hogg, as the editor of a selection. He praises almost indiscriminately, and he wants delicacy almost entirely.[54]

And Jeffrey went on to deplore the Shepherd's 'gross and coarse taste'.

Hogg's failure, if failure it be, was that he did not confirm the golden illusion of Jacobitism which existed in the minds of his would-be patrons and that he was insufficiently possessed of 'delicacy' or 'taste' to suppress, fabricate and distort the one into conformity with the other. Worst of all, perhaps, he had obviously taken little trouble to 'purify' or 'refine' his material.

Just how careful a contemporary editor had to be, appears in a letter from Allan Cunningham to the ballad specialist Charles Kirkpatrick Sharpe, dated 10 March 1825, when the former was at work on his four-volume *Songs of Scotland*:

> I have still a few curious fragments of old free song, which I shall not use, though I had intended to trim and prime and starch them to correspond with the standard delicacy of the year of grace 1825.[55]

It is clear that what damned the *Relics* was not its occasionally hair-brained notes, or its single avowed forgery, but its approving inclusion of pieces like 'The Sow's Tail to Geordie' (which has great fun with the sexual peculiarities of the Elector of Hanover). Later collectors and editors too often sought to ingratiate themselves by denigrating the Shepherd while, to a man, they used his work as a quarry for their own derivative volumes. The atmosphere of recrimination and mistrust which surrounded Hogg's pioneering and able collection upon its first publication has adhered to it ever since. It is time *The Jacobite Relics of Scotland* took its rightful place in Scottish literature.

Hogg himself is an important songwriter, subtly attuned to the melodic culture of Scotland and capable of using vernacular Scots, at his best, with dazzling virtuosity. This becomes clearer when we consider the range of his personal contribution to the collection. 'Donald Macgillavry' was avowed. But how many songs were not? Obviously one has to be tentative since the evidence is wholly internal and circumstantial, but there a number of pieces with a very strong family likeness to one another which suddenly appear for the first time in the *Relics*. There is not a trace of them in the earlier tradition and it is highly improbable that earlier collectors would have missed them had they been genuinely old. They are artistically of high quality, outstanding in their command of the vernacular, and fitted to their beautiful airs with the utmost guile by somebody who knew in the highest degree what he was about. On the basis of this I think we must include the following songs (at the very least) amongst the works of James Hogg: 'This is no my ain House', 'Cam ye o'er frae France', 'Will ye go to Sheriffmuir' and 'The Piper o' Dundee'.[56] They approach the very summits of the popular art-song as a form. If they are indeed Hogg's, then he has only one rival as a songwriter in Scotland—Robert Burns.

Chapter Ten

'THE RIGHTS AND LIBERTIES OF THE NATION'

'I really expect', the Ettrick Shepherd had written excitedly towards the end of his second volume:

> that the publication of these Jacobite relics will work a revolution in Scottish song, and that, for a time, we shall hear them more generally sung than any other.[1]

And so it proved. Three major new song collections appeared within a few years of the *Relics*—Allan Cunningham's *Songs of Scotland* (London 1825), R. A. Smith's *The Scotish Minstrel* (Edinburgh ?1824-8) and *The Scottish Songs* edited by Robert Chambers (Edinburgh 1829)—each of them featuring Jacobite songs in unprecedented numbers.

Two volumes devoted exclusively to the form quickly followed, *Jacobite Melodies: A Collection of the Most Popular Legends, Ballads, and Songs of the Adherents to the House of Stuart*, (London 1823), and *Jacobite Minstrelsy; with Notes Illustrative of the Text*, (Glasgow 1829). By the end of the 1820s, Jacobite song was confirmed as second only to the great body of love-song in the national canon and it maintained this position throughout the nineteenth century.

But the quality of new writing within the form seldom reached the heights attained by Burns and Hogg. Their most obvious successor, Caroline Oliphant, Lady Nairne, was enormously popular with contemporaries, but is now remembered only for a handful of songs like 'Wha'll be King but Charlie' and 'The Hundred Pipers'.[2]

Burns's career had coincided with the last phase of political Jacobitism in its original form; Hogg's, with its appropriation by the Scottish right as a counter-revolutionary symbol. But for Lady Nairne, reared from infancy in the high Jacobite tradition, the extinction of the direct Stuart line in 1807, really must have marked the passing of an age. After her death, fresh composition continued in quantity—after all, Jacobite song was now one of the major genres within the popular art-tradition of Scotland—but as the years went on it became increasingly apparent that its artistic possibilities as a form were becoming depleted.

But Jacobitism itself did not cease to exist as a mythogenic force.

In 1822, after a period of 170 years during which no *de facto* king had set foot in Scotland, George IV made his famous visit to Edinburgh. This was at the very height of the passion for Highlandry, and when the monarch himself appeared in the philibeg, the enthusiasm for Celticism knew no bounds.

It was at about this time that two young men called Allan first began to attract the attention of Society. Personable, cultivated, and accessible, they were, it seemed, the ultimate authorities on everything concerning clan tartans, and their advice was eagerly sought.[3]

At the same time, rumours began to circulate that there was something rather mysterious and splendid in their background. If pressed on the point the brothers became smiling and evasive. But why, people wondered, did their surname keep changing: Allen, Allan, Hay Allan, Allan Hay? Was it true that they had fought for Napoleon? Were they the lost Earls of Errol? How did they know so much about the private history of the later Stuarts?

The brothers set up house in Edinkillie in Morayshire and spent their time writing, painting, and pursuing historical research. Their means were sufficient, and their acquaintance wide. But there was always something else...something held back. By the mid-1830s, the rumours had taken definite shape, and the names changed again; this time to Stuart: John Sobieski and Charles Edward Stuart. The implication was unmistakable. They were the grandsons of the Young Chevalier; and they were legitimate. 'Will ye no come back again?' had ceased to be a rhetorical question.

Several distinguished Highland families privately acknowledged their claims. In certain circles the company would rise when they entered, and when the toast to 'the King' was proposed, John would remain seated and his brother would incline his glass significantly towards him. Lord Lovat built them an amazing Celtic Xanadu on the island of Eilean Aigas, a simulated mediaeval mansion with stained glass so thick one could hardly see. And in this romantic gloom, surrounded by antique weapons, trophies of the chase, banners, busts, and every conceivable kind of Highland bric-a-brac, the brothers held court, wrote books, and amassed debts.

They had hinted at their descent in print before, but the story did not assume its final form until 1847, and then in the ambiguous form of a novel, *Tales of the Century or Sketches of the Romance of History between the years 1746 and 1846*.[4] Considered simply as a novel, it is rather a good one, using with considerable panache all three of Scotland's literary languages, English, Scots and Gaelic. It possesses, to be sure, superficially conventional elements: there are weepy death-scenes, kidnaps, mysterious assignations, plots, disguises, a sea-rescue, a mad prophetess—and yet it is written in a prose which challenges comparison with some of the best in nineteenth century Scottish fiction.

It takes the form of three detached episodes describing the birth and early career of the fateful Captain O'Haleran, and the narrative is linked by various MacDonnells of Glendulochan whose fortunes are bound up with those of the hero. The opening section is set in London in 1831, and introduces the younger Glendulochan to Dr Beaton, an aged Highland physician, who claims to have been present at the birth of a legitimate son and heir to Charles Edward Stuart and his consort Louise of Stolberg, and to have later witnessed the child conveyed with great secrecy on board a British warship. According to the Doctor, that child survived and grew into manhood.

In the next section the story is taken up by MacDonnell's father. This is done rather adroitly. The young laird, a great gadder-about at galleries and sale-rooms, stumbles into a lost family heirloom in a curio-shop in Wardour Street. This is the famous Black Kist of Glendulochan, brought over by the Fergusian Scots, and said to be the very vessel in which Moses floated down the Nile. And it has a secret: a little-spring-loaded drawer containing the private memoirs of MacDonnell senior. These papers form the narrative of section two.

The writer has been forfeited following his involvement in the '45, and gone soldiering abroad for King George to make ammends. When he comes home, he discovers that he has a mysterious new neighbour, the dashing Captain O'Haleran, whom the locals have christened Iolair Dhearg (or Red Eagle) on account of his piercing gaze and bright red tartans. The writer meets the Iolair on a visit to his chief Glengarve, a gigantic centenarian gifted with the second sight which he uses to penetrate O'Haleran's true identity.

Section three is based on the memoirs of Glengarve's son Eneas, which have come into the possession of the younger Glendulochan. They deal with the Iolair's marriage, a morganatic affair which his advisers try to prevent by having the lady abducted by smugglers. The Iolair rescues her and makes a dramatic escape on a schooner bound for nobody knows where, and there the narrative ends.

Clearly the Iolair Dhearg was the lost Stuart heir, and after 1788, therefore, titular King of England, Scotland, France and Ireland, just as his sons, the brothers Hay Allan, or Sobieski Stuart, or whatever, were titular Prince of Wales and Duke of York.

Could they possibly have been genuine? It hardly seems likely. We know nothing of their early life except what they tell us themselves. Nobody knows where they were born or when. They appear to have been the sons of Thomas Allen, alias Hay Allan, alias Stuart Hay, alias Salmond, a lieutenant in the Navy. But who was he? He was acknowledged as a son in the will of his ostensible father Admiral John Carter Allen. About the year 1798 he left the Service and apparently went to live in France. Somewhere about 1811, it was apparently revealed to his sons John and Charles that they were of high descent, and they seem to have gone through the rest of their lives believing it. If that is so, and they were not mere charlatans, then the most obvious source of this revelation was their father, and the brothers' strange and equivocal lives were the price of his delusion. If it was a delusion. Thomas Allen was a shadowy, footloose, raffish sort of character who drifted in and out of society in several European countries and eventually died in Clerkenwell in 1852. His resemblance to Charles Edward Stuart was said to be striking; and his birth certificate has never been found.

Tales of the Century had a serious purpose over and above any dynastic claims it may have contained. It presented a complex argument about the nature of time, and the importance of mythogenic processes working through it. The brothers carefully discriminated between history and myth as ways of looking at the world. They deplored the rise of modern historiography and the drab and impoverished world-picture it produced, seeking to recover the past as a liberating threshold for the human imagination by identifying figures capable of uniting 'the reality of existence' with the most profound symbolic significance. This higher historical reality, they claimed, had its ultimate embodiment in Charles Edward Stuart:

History, which in the days of chivalry—under the thirst of glory, the division of power, the love of adventure, the grandeur and the gloom, the rudeness and the magnificence of the Gothic arts, edifices, and manners—had borne in its persons and events the true spirit of the 'Romaunt' or Chivalric History—with the world which it accompanied, glided down into a dull and simple narration—the dry obituary of Princes and Prelates—the record of contracted and ruptured treaties—undetailed battles—changes of laws and changes of Ministry; and truth became allied with poverty of action and juste-milieuism of mind, as the events and the characters of men had become subdued and common-place...With the velvet and the gold, the armour and the blazonry, the cross and the sword of chivalry, vanished the heroism and the splendour, the great crimes and the great virtues of the middle ages; and the world and its history declined into that Quakerism of the mind and body, that insensibility to dignity and elevation, splendid arts and abstract glory, which skulks to court in a brougham, worships heaven in a barn, and, awakened to the philosophy of courage, when its flank is turned, feels no morbid sensibility respecting the exhibition of its back. Between all extremes, however, there is a graduating scale, and between the lives of the common herd, and the actions of extraordinary minds, there is the contrast of many ages. Like trees in the forest, nature still creates some to overtop and overshadow; and between the spirit, the projects, and the deeds of each contrast, there lies a disparity as wide, as between the saplings of the crowded thicket and the giants of the forest chase. The superlative actions of these partaking the reality of existence, with the Epic of 'Romaunt,' has properly been called the 'Romance of History'. In this combination of veracity and exaggeration, there has appeared from time to time, even to the present day, a solitary shooting star, which gleams and falls upon the dull blank sky of History, with a transient and mysterious light.

Among these—however little known, and little appreciated—lived CHARLES EDWARD; and to the age of the veracious Romaunt belonged his adventurous and concentrated character, his daring designs, mysterious projects, and years of unknown seclusion. His enterprise in Scotland, now consigned to the shade of other unsuccessful attempts, was prompted by the same spirit which carried his namesake across the Baltic, and Caesar beyond the Rubicon. It is inglorious, because it failed; and it failed, because it was divided. But had the Clans accompanied him to London, he would have been crowned in Westminster Abbey; and had the council of war been unanimous at Culloden...a victory would—not have been disgraced by massacre, nor the glory of a triumph darkened by the blood of murdered peasants, and the smoke of peaceful glens. The attempt which has been reproached for temerity, would have been celebrated for heroic enterprise; and he who is now named an 'Adventurer', would have descended to posterity with the conquerors, who have planned upon no better hopes, and won battles with greater disparity of force.

But if, by his 'Adventures' in Scotland, the chivalry of Charles Edward was most conspicuous to the world, the years of mysterious seclusion which followed his expulsion from Paris were no less deeply tinged with the 'romance of history'. His sudden, secret, and long journeys, his negociations with courts and individuals, his momentary apparition in the most distant parts of Europe, have left traces of occult enterprises and ceaseless activity, filled with a spirit as far from the animation of the ordinary world, as that which threw him alone and unsupported into the bosom of the Clans. Even to the latter days of his existence, mysterious and extraordinary occurrences have left the traces of a deep and secret history, which appear like twinkling sparks through the veil drawn over his seclusion. Recollections of his concealment still exist in various parts of England—in France—Germany—Sweden and Poland, and the working of his mysterious designs may yet be traced in the cabinets of Foreign states, the Senate of Great Britain, and even in the British navy—busy mysterious phantoms of tradition more nearly allied to the 'Romaunt' of the middle ages than the history of modern times, and leaving such evidence of his spirit, and his conception, that there is no event connected with his comprehension, of which it may not be said, 'It is credible, because it is improbable'.[5]

But even as the brothers mourned the departure of the mythic world picture, they were helping to recreate it, combining a full-blown Romantic mediaevalism with the old heroic tradition, in a way that was to occur again and again in the next great upsurge of cultural nationalism in late Victorian Scotland.

This book has examined three themes from the recent Scottish past: firstly, the continuity and vitality of Scottish popular culture in the century after the Union; secondly, the cultural role of Jacobitism and its impact on Scottish national consciousness; and thirdly, the forces within Scottish society resisting English cultural hegemony.

Students of Scottish culture during the eighteenth and nineteenth centuries have too often concentrated their attention upon a handful of Edinburgh intellectuals and accepted the assimilationist Whig ethos they represented at its face value. They have seen Europe swept by successive waves of nationalism and concluded that Scotland was in some mysterious way exempted from this pattern. Scottish nationhood is deemed to have ended with legislative independence in 1707, and anything which happened subsequently must therefore be treated as an empty shadow, or relegated to the limbo of paradox. If we consider Scotland as a European nation rather than as a British region, however, the logic and cohesion of its cultural development becomes more apparent.[6]

The Scots early achieved a sense of nationhood. I have suggested that it was limited in the earlier period by diversity of cultural and linguistic traditions. The essential point is that it was not static. It continued to grow and change, and one of the most important moving forces behind it during the eighteenth century was the Jacobite movement whose main objective, after the restoration of the Stuarts, was the dissolution of the Union and the maintenance of Scottish cultural and political distinctiveness.

At the heart of Jacobitism itself lay the theme of 'Guid Auld Lang Syne' which gave symbolic force to the struggle for 'the rights and liberties of the nation'.[7] During the eighteenth and early nineteenth centuries, it merged with 'the Matter of Prince Charlie', to produce a new national consciousness and transform the Scottish identity.

At the end of the last session of the Scottish parliament, the Chancellor, James Ogilvy, Earl of Seafield, appended his signature to the draft treaty of Union with the wry aside, 'Now there's ane end of ane old song'.[8] He was profoundly wrong.

APPENDIX OF TUNES

The Battle of Killicrankie.

The Highland Laddie.

Maclean's Welcome.

O'er the Water to Charlie.

The Battle of Sheriffmuir.

Dialogue between Will Lickladle and Tom Cleancogue,
twa Shepherds, wha were feeding their Flocks on
the Ochil Hills on the Day the Battle
of Sheriffmuir was fought.

O my King.

Though Geordie reigns in Jamie's Stead.

The Union.

The Curses.

Donald Macgillavry.

NOTES

1 The best modern general studies of Jacobitism are those of Bruce Lenman, namely *The Jacobite Risings in Britain 1689-1746* (London 1980); and *The Jacobite Clans of the Great Glen 1650-1784* (London 1984); for a convenient brief summary of his views, see 'The Scottish Episcopal Clergy and the Ideology of Jacobitism' in Eveline Cruickshanks (ed), *Ideology and Conspiracy: Aspects of Jacobitism, 1689-1759* (Edinburgh 1982), pp 36-48. For an intriguing earlier study of Jacobitism as a cultural force, see George Pratt Insh, The *Scottish Jacobite Movement A Study in Economic and Social Forces* (Edinburgh 1952). Jacobite literature as such has received relatively little attention, but see Douglas Duncan, *Thomas Ruddiman A Study in Scottish Scholarship of the Early Eighteenth Century* (Edinburgh 1965), a pioneering work which contains many revealing insights into the world of Jacobite historians and men of letters at that period; for a brief but useful later study in this field see Ian Ross and Stephen Scobie, 'Patriotic Publishing as a Response to the Union' in T I Rae (ed), *The Union of 1707 Its Impact on Scotland* (London 1974), pp 94-119. On Jacobite song itself, the following may be consulted: Alison S Norton, 'Robert Burns and the 'Forty-Five' in *Burns Chronicle*, 1963, pp 40-57; Thomas Crawford, 'Political and Protest Songs in Eighteenth-Century Scotland 1. Jacobite and Anti-Jacobite' in *Scottish Studies*, Vol XIV, 1970, pp 1-33; and David Daiches, 'Robert Burns and Jacobite Song' in D A Low (ed), *Critical Essays on Robert Burns* (London 1975), pp 137-56.

2 For the late 19th century peak in Jacobite publishing, see Dorothy A Guthrie and Clyde L Grose, 'Forty Years of Jacobite Bibliography' in *Journal of Modern History*, Vol XI, 1939, pp 49-60. For a moderately Whiggish 18th century view of Jacobitism, see David Hume, *The History of England, from The Invasion of Julius Caesar to The Revolution in 1688* (8 vols London 1763), VIII, 310. For Jacobitism as a racial struggle, see Charles Sanford Terry, *The Rising of 1745* (2nd edn London 1903), pp v-vi; for modernism *versus* traditionalism, see George Pratt Insh, *The Scottish Jacobite Movement*, op.cit. p ix; for civilisation against barbarism, see Henry Thomas Buckle, *History of Civilization in England* (2nd edn 2 vols London 1858-1861), II, 299; for a view of Jacobitism as 'anachronistic and historically meaningless' see David Daiches, *The Paradox of Scottish Culture* (London 1964), p 16.

3 James C Dick (ed), *Notes on Scottish Song by Robert Burns Written in an Interleaved Copy of The Scots Musical Museum* (London 1908), pp 4-5.

4 *Scotish Songs. In Two Volumes* (London 1794), I, lxviii.

5 (2nd edn 2 vols Edinburgh 1822), p 100.

6 James Hogg (ed), *The Jacobite Relics of Scotland ; being The Songs, Airs, and Legends, of the Adherents to the House of Stuart* (2 vols Edinburgh 1819-1821), I, vii.

7   See John M Ellis, *One Fairy Story Too Many: The Brothers Grimm and their Tales* (Chicago 1983), pp 1-6; for an intriguing and highly favourable comparison of the scholarly methods of James Macpherson's *Ossian* with those of the brothers Grimm, see pp 94-103.

8   *The Harp of Caledonia: a Collection of Songs, Ancient and Modern*, (chiefly Scottish), (2 vols Glasgow 1819), 1, iii,xiv; see also James Currie (ed), *The Works of Robert Burns...A New Edition. With Additional Pieces* (4 vols Montrose 1816), I, 13, 25-6; and James Kinsley, 'The Music of the Heart', in *Renaissance and Modern Studies*, Vol VIII, 1964, 32-6.

9   *Scottish Song Its Wealth, Wisdom, and Social Significance* (Edinburgh 1889), pp 144, 160, 176. Blackie continues: 'Of all the species of the genus *Volkslied*, so generally appreciated since Cowper and Wordsworth brought poetry back to Nature, the most extensively known and the most largely acknowledged is the Scotch.' p 6. On Jacobite songs further: '...though in point of political significance and lasting good results they can in no wise bear comparison with the war-songs of the German Liberation war in 1813-14, in point of nobility of sentiment, picturesqueness of situation, and dramatic effect, they are vastly superior. In fact these ballads in their natural historical sequence present to the eye a ready-made national opera of the finest elements and the most effective points, possessing as they do an interesting central figure round which every variety of martial enthusiasm, romantic adventure, broad popular humour, delicate pathos, gathers itself with a natural grace and a completeness of effect which no art could improve.' pp 160-61. Evidence of the high esteem in which Scottish songs and Jacobite songs in particular were held is omnipresent in the song collections of the 19th century. For a typical example, see the undated but probably mid-Victorian *The Illustrated Book of Scottish Songs. From the Sixteenth to the Nineteenth Century* (Illustrated London Library, 227 Strand. [n.d.]), p 2. The preface remarks 'this volume contains all, or nearly all, the most celebrated, beautiful, and characteristic of the Scottish songs, whether pastoral, amatory, patriotic, convivial, or Jacobite.' p 14. See also William Gunnyon, *Illustrations of Scottish History Life and Superstition From Song and Ballad* (Glasgow 1879), pp 118-52.

10   For Burns, Hogg and Lady Nairne, see the later chapters of this book; the 'Skye Boat Song' was published in A C Macleod and Harold Boulton (eds), *Songs of the North, Gathered together from The Highlands and Lowlands of Scotland* (London n.d. [but 1885]).

11   For Robert Chambers, see the 'Historical Essay on Scottish Song' in *The Scottish Songs* (2 vols Edinburgh 1829), I, lix. For Gavin Greig, see Ian A Olson, 'Scottish Traditional Song and the Greig-Duncan Collection: Last Leaves or Last Rites?' in Cairns Craig (ed), *The History of Scottish Literature* (4 vols Aberdeen 1987-8), IV, 37-46.

CHAPTER TWO pp 5 to 15

1   See R G Collingwood, *The Idea of History* (London 1961, first published 1946), pp 134-334.

2   The earlier parts of this chapter owe much to William Matthews' excellent article 'The Egyptians in Scotland: the Political History of a Myth' in *Viator: Mediaeval & Renaissance Studies*, i (1970), 289-306. Arthur H Williamson discusses the use made by George Buchanan of Scottish legendary history in *Scottish National Consciousness in the Age of James VI* (Edinburgh 1979); for a recent view of the use of legendary history for political purposes see Roger A Mason, 'Scotching the Brut: Politics, History

and National Myth in Sixteenth-Century Britain' in Roger A Mason (ed), *Scotland and England 1286-1815* (Edinburgh 1987), pp 60-84, which came to my attention as this book was in the press. For a rich and illuminating study of the complex interrelation of myth, 'myth-tale', legend, and folk-tale, see G S Kirk, *Myth its Meaning and Function in Ancient and Other Cultures* (Cambridge 1970). Finally, for some intriguing observations on the survival of the mythogenic tendency in Scottish popular tradition, see Edwin Muir, *Scottish Journey* (London 1935), pp 92-4.

3 George Mackenzie MD, *The Lives and Characters of the most Eminent Writers of the Scots Nation* (3 vols Edinburgh 1708-1722), III, 473; see also Patrick Abercromby, *The Martial Atchievements of the Scots Nation, Being an Account of the Lives, Characters, and memorable Actions, of such Scotsmen as have Signaliz'd themselves by the Sword at Home and Abroad* (2 vols Edinburgh 1711-1715), I, 30-5.

4 Roberta Florence Brinkley, *Arthurian Legend in the Seventeenth Century* (New York 1967, first published 1932), p 61.

5 George Mackenzie MD, *Eminent Writers*, op.cit. I, iii.

6 Thomas Innes, *A Critical Essay on the Ancient Inhabitants of the Northern Parts of Britain or Scotland. Containing an Account of the Romans, of the Britains betwixt the Walls, of the Caledonians or Picts, and particularly of the Scots* (Edinburgh 1879; first published London 1729), pp 126-7, 270; see also Abercromby, *Martial Atchievements*, op.cit. I, 29-30.

7 See, for example, Mathew Kennedy, *Chronological Genealogical and Historical Dissertation of the Royal Family of the Stuarts* (Paris, 1705), pp 1-5.

8 See C A Patrides, *The Phoenix and the Ladder* (Berkeley 1964), *passim.*

9 Kennedy, loc.cit.; see also Thomas Innes, *Critical Essay*, op.cit. pp 268-9; on the ideal of historic legitimacy, see T D Kendrick, *British Antiquity* (London 1950), pp 69-72.

10 See E L G Stones, *Anglo-Scottish Relations 1174-1328* (London 1965), pp 96-117 (I am indebted for some of the argument at this point, and the above reference, to Mr James Galbraith); for the Scottish claim through Mordred, see Innes, op.cit. pp 335-7, and Matthews, 'The Egyptians in Scotland' op.cit. pp 292-5.

11 Matthews, op.cit. p 293; see also James Anderson, *An Historical Essay, Shewing That the Crown and Kingdom of Scotland, is Imperial and Independent* (Edinburgh 1705), preface, pp 4, 12.

12 Abercromby, *Martial Atchievements*, op.cit. I, 2-3, 38.

13 *Seafield Correspondence*, pp 101-2, cited in W C Mackenzie, *Andrew Fletcher of Saltoun His Life and Times* (Edinburgh 1935), p 357 n28.

14 *The Late Lord Belhaven's Memorable Speeches in the Last Parliament of Scotland* (Glasgow 1784), pp 15-21.

15 Ibid. p 22.

16 'Miscellaneous Scottish Poetical Broadsides. 1660-1785', National Library of Scotland, Ry.111.c.34.f.24. For a less sympathetic view of Belhaven's speech, see William Ferguson, *Scotland's Relations with England: a Survey to 1707* (Edinburgh 1977), pp 258-9; and for other contemporary 'Vision' poems, Frank H Ellis (ed), *Poems on Affairs of State Augustan Satirical Verse Vol VII: 1704-1714* (New Haven 1975), pp 208-29.

17 George Mackenzie MD, *Eminent Writers*, op.cit., I, preface, p 1; see also the dedication in William Hamilton of Gilbertfield's *The Life Surprising Adventures and Heroic Actions of Sir William Wallace, General and Governor of Scotland* (New Edition, Aberdeen 1774, first published 1721), p vi.

18 Abercromby, *Martial Atchievements* op.cit. I,22; see also Sir George Mackenzie, *Defence of the Antiquity Of the Royal Line of Scotland* (Edinburgh 1685), pp 19-20.

19 David Symson, *A Genealogical and Historical Account of The Illustrious Name of Stuart* (Edinburgh 1712), p 154, see also p 93. For the heroic legends cited see Abercromby op.cit. I, 80-84, and Mackenzie, *Defence* op.cit. p 107. When James Boswell visited

the exiled Jacobite Earl Marischal in 1764, the latter 'took down Barbour's *Brus* from his bookcase and inscribed it 'Scotus Scoto' before giving it to Boswell with the injunction to read it once every year', see Janet Adam Smith, 'Some Eighteenth-Century Ideas of Scotland' in N T Phillipson and Rosalind Mitchison (eds), *Scotland in the Age of Improvement Essays in Scottish History in the Eighteenth Century* (Edinburgh 1970), p 114.

20   National Library of Scotland, Rosebery Collection, Ry.111.a.10.f.71.

21   'Poems and a few other documents Scottish and English, 1644-1821, n.d.', National Library of Scotland MS.2092.f.38.

22   William Gordon, *History of the Ancient, Noble, and Illustrious Family of Gordon* (2 vols Edinburgh 1726-1727), II, 100-1.

23   'Jacobite Verses', National Library of Scotland MS.2910, pp 33-4.

24   'Come brave boys letts merrie be/and go fetch home our King Jo', Dalhousie Muniments, Scottish Record Office, GD45/26/103.

25   'Old Scotch Ballads Broadsides &c', National Library of Scotland Ry.111.a.10, f.117.

26   Innes *Critical Essay* op.cit. see especially pp 7, 111; for the dedication, see 'Copy of Mr Thomas Innes's Letter to the King', dated Paris 17 October 1729, in *The Miscellany of the Spalding Club* (Vol 2, Aberdeen 1842), pp 353-6.

27   The quotation is from '*Tearlach Mac Sheumais*', in John Lorne Campbell (ed), *Highland Songs of the Forty-Five* (Edinburgh 1984, first published 1933), pp 52-60.

28   See Matthews, 'The Egyptians in Scotland', op.cit. p 303; Brinkley, *Arthurian Legend*, op.cit. p 16; Kennedy, *Chronological...Dissertation*, op.cit. pp 192-3; Mackenzie *Defence*, op.cit. pp 185-9; Symson, *Genealogical...Account*, op.cit. pp 1-5.

29   William Gordon, *History of the...Family of Gordon*, op.cit. II, 101; Brinkley, op.cit. pp 1-10; Kendrick, *British Antiquity*, op.cit. pp 35-6; James A H Murray (ed), *The Romance and Prophecies of Thomas of Erceldoune Printed from Five Manuscripts; with Illustrations from the Prophetic Literature of the 15th and 16th Centuries* (London 1875), pp xxx, xxxvi-xxxvii, xl-xli; Sir George Mackenzie, *The Antiquity of the Royal Line of Scotland Farther Cleared and Defended* (London 1686), p 1.

30   Abercromby, op.cit. I, 6; Innes, op.cit. pp 141-2; Mackenzie, *Defence*, op.cit. 21-2; for Drummond of Hawthornden, see Terence Tobin, 'Popular Entertainment in Seventeenth Century Scotland' in *Theatre Notebook*, 23, Winter 1968-9, 48-9, cited in Terence Tobin (ed), *The Assembly by Archibald Pitcairne* (Lafayette, Indiana 1972), p 100.

31   Mackenzie, *Defence*, op.cit. pp 10-11.

32   Symson, *Genealogical...Account*, op.cit. pp 84-5. See also Abercromby, op.cit. I,16-17; see also George Mackenzie MD, *Eminent Writers*, op.cit. III, 111-86, 235-360, 468-79, 487-513; William Gordon, *History of the ...Family of Gordon*, op.cit. I, xiii-xxix, 182-3, 187-8,202-42, 302-3, 539-40; *Miscellany of the Spalding Club*, op.cit. pp 353-5; and Kennedy, *Chronological...Dissertation*, op.cit. *passim*.

CHAPTER THREE pp 16 to 23

1   For a modern overview of the complex ecclesiastical politics of the time see the relevant volumes of the Edinburgh History of Scotland, namely, Gordon Donaldson, *Scotland James V to James VII* (Edinburgh 1965) and William Ferguson, *Scotland 1689 to the Present* (Edinburgh 1968); for a more recent study of the later Covenanters, see Ian B Cowan, *The Scottish Covenanters 1660-1688* (London 1976). For a detailed account, see the older ecclesiastical histories, for the Presbyterians, John Cunningham, *The Church History of Scotland from the Commencement of the Christian Era to the Present*

Time (2 vols Edinburgh 1882), and for the Episcopalians, W Stephen, *History of the Scottish Church* (2 vols Edinburgh 1894-6). The real flavour of the period, however, can only be got in contemporary or near contemporary texts: see, for example Sir James Stewart and James Stirling, *Naphtali; or, the Wrestlings of the Church of Scotland for the Kingdom of Christ* (Perth 1845, first published 1667); see also, *A Hind let loose, or An Historical Representation of the Testimonies, Of the Church of Scotland, for the Interest of Christ* (n.p. 1687), by 'A Lover of true Liberty' (Alexander Shields); almost anything by Robert Wodrow, but perhaps especially his *History of the Sufferings of the Church of Scotland from the Restoration to the Revolution* (Robert Burns (ed), 4 vols Glasgow 1829-30); best of all, perhaps, the works of Patrick Walker, a treasure-house of Scottish popular prose: the most accessible edition of which is D Hay Fleming (ed), *Six Saints of The Covenant Peden: Semple: Welwood: Cameron: Cargill: Smith* (2 vols London 1901). For a near-contemporary Episcopalian view see the trenchant second volume of John Skinner, (the famous songwriter and author of 'Tullochgorm'), *An Ecclesiastical History of Scotland, From The First Appearance of Christianity in that Kingdom, to The Present Time* (London, 1788).

2 See *The Lockhart Papers: Containing Memoirs and Commentaries upon the Affairs of Scotland from 1702 to 1714, by George Lockhart, Esq. of Carnwath, His Secret Correspondence with the Son of King James the Second from 1718 to 1728, And his other Political Writings* (2 vols London 1817), II, 25-42; see also George Grub, *Ecclesiastical History of Scotland* (4 vols Edinburgh 1861), III, 382-5; see also George T S Farquhar, *Three Bishops of Dunkeld: Alexander, Rose and Watson 1743-1808* (Perth 1915), pp 2-3, 47, 87-90, 98-9, 112-3, 113-4, 121, 136-7, 180-89, *Life of Jonathan Watson Bishop of Dunkeld, 1760-1808* (Selkirk 1915), pp 69-74; Mary E Ingram, *A Jacobite Stronghold of the Church Being the Story of Old St. Paul's, Edinburgh* (Edinburgh 1907), pp 23-66.

3 Shields, *A Hind let loose*, op.cit. pp 5-6.

4 Mackenzie, *Defence*, op.cit. pp 3-10.

5 Shields, op.cit. pp 8-9.

6 See S A Burrell, 'The Apocalyptic Vision of the Early Covenanters' in *Scottish Historical Review*, Vol XLIII, No. 135 April 1964, 1-24. The 'Covenant and...Bishops' quote is taken from *Calendar of State Papers, Domestic Series, of the Reign of Charles II. 1666-1667* (London 1864), p 275. See also Shields, op.cit. pp 93-145, 181ff. For the Sanquhar declarations, see Cowan, *Scottish Covenanters*, op.cit. pp 105, 111, 129, and Fleming, *Six Saints*, op.cit. i, 11, 174-5, n50. The key figure in the persecution in the Westland was John Graham of Claverhouse, Viscount Dundee; his career there has been variously interpreted and was still capable of arousing violent controversy until well into the 19th century. For a pungently written high Tory view, see Mark Napier, *Memorials and Letters Illustrative of The Life and Times of John Graham of Claverhouse, Viscount of Dundee* (3 vols, Edinburgh 1859-62); for a less elegant but equally fierce Whiggish one, see Robert Simpson, DD, of Sanquhar, *Traditions of the Covenanters; or, Gleanings among the Mountains* (new edn Edinburgh n.d.), especially pp 88, 286, 290-1, 426.

7 Shields, op.cit. pp 270, 275, 303.

8 Fleming, *Six Saints*, op.cit. I, 33-4.

9 See Norman Cohn, *The Pursuit of the Millennium Revolutionary millenarians and mystical anarchists of the Middle Ages* (London 1972, first published 1957), *passim*.

10 Fleming, op.cit. I, 91-3; for limited insight into the future as a special mark of sanctity, see James Durham, *A Commentarie Upon the book of the Revelation. Wherein The Text is explained, the Series of the several Prophecies contained in that Book, deduced according to their order and dependance upon each other...Delivered in several Lectures* (London 1658), pp 4, 470.

11   Fleming, op.cit. I, 113-4.
12   Op.cit. I, 230.
13   Cohn, op.cit. p 21.
14   Fleming, op.cit. I, 113-4.
15   George Sinclair, *Satan's Invisible World Discovered, or a Choice Collection of Relations anent Devils, Spirits, Witches, and Apparitions* (T G Stevenson (ed), Edinburgh 1871, first published Edinburgh 1685, preface); Fleming, I, 33-88; see also, Robert Wodrow, *Analecta: or, Materials for a History of Remarkable Providences; mostly relating to Scotch Ministers and Christians* (2 vols Glasgow 1842), *passim*.
16   Fleming, op.cit. I, 229.
17   'Jacob Curate', [?Robert Calder, *et al.*], *Scots Presbyterian Eloquence Displayed; or Their manner of Teaching and Preaching exposed* (London 1767, first published 1692), p 93. For a fuller account of this collection and its influence upon Scott, see Robert Hay Carnie, 'Scottish Presbyterian Eloquence and *Old Mortality*' in *Scottish Literary Journal* Vol III, No.2 December 1976, 51-61. See also the Whig riposte by 'Will Laick' [George Ridpath], *An Answer to the Scotch Presbyterian Eloquence* (London 1693).
18   Op.cit. p 95; for a theoretical justification for this style of preaching, see Durham, *Upon the...Revelation*, op.cit. pp 263-4.
19   Op.cit. p 92.
20   Fleming, op.cit I, 59.

CHAPTER FOUR pp 24 to 35

The standard account of popular song at this period is Thomas Crawford, *Society and the Lyric a study of the Song Culture of eighteenth-century Scotland* (Edinburgh 1979); see also Crawford's accompanying anthology *Love, Labour and Liberty: the eighteenth-century Scottish Lyric* (Cheadle Hulme 1976);for the instrumental tradition see David Johnson, *Music and Society in Lowland Scotland in the Eighteenth Century* (London 1972); see also Francis Collinson, *The Traditional and National Music of Scotland* (London 1966), especially chapters IV and VII; amongst older studies, John Glen, *Early Scottish Melodies: including examples from MSS. and Early Printed Works, along with a number of Comparative Tunes, Notes on Former Annotators, English and other Claims, and Biographical Notices* (Edinburgh 1900), and James C Dick (ed), *The Songs of Robert Burns Now First Printed with the Melodies for which they were Written A Study in Tone-Poetry* (London 1903), may be consulted. On the broadside tradition and popular poetry generally see Claude M Simpson, *The British Broadside Ballad and its Music* (New Jersey 1966); John Holloway and Joan Black (eds), *Later English Broadside Ballads* (London 1975); and V de Sola Pinto and A E Rodway (eds), *The Common Muse an Anthology of Popular British Ballad Poetry XVth-XXth Century* (London 1957).

1   For an account of the air see John Glen, *Early Scottish Melodies*, op.cit. pp 241-3; as to the theme, as well as several broadside versions, there is a text by Ramsay, see B Martin, J W Oliver, A M Kinghorn and A Law (eds), *The Works of Allan Ramsay* (6 vols Edinburgh 1945-75), II, 81-2. For 'Kate Dalrymple' see William Watt, *Poems, on Sacred and other Subjects; and Songs, Humorous and Sentimental* (Glasgow 1860, first published 1835), pp 88-9. For an acute study of the formative influence of melodic tradition upon verbal texts in the case of Burns, see Bertrand Harris Bronson, *The Ballad as Song* (Berkeley 1969), pp 306-12.
2   There are two Killiecrankie songs. The second: 'Whare hae ye been sae braw, lad?/

Whare hae ye been sae brankie, O?' is almost certainly a later composition and does not appear to have been published until 1790 when it was included in the third volume of *The Scots Musical Museum* (6 vols Edinburgh 1787-1803), p 302. The note which follows refers to the original air. See 'An Excellent Song on the present Times, by a Country *Hind*. To the Tune of Killycranky' in 'Broadside Ballads etc. 18th and 19th Centuries', National Library of Scotland, Ry.111.a.1.f.19; 'The Battle of *Preston*. To the Tune of *Killiecranky*', in 'Printed pamphlets, broadsides, Acts of Parliament, ballads, and songs relating mainly to the risings of 1715 and 1745', National Library of Scotland MS.488.f.46; 'The Lasses of Kinghorn *Tune of Clavers and his Highland Men*' in 'Old Scotch Ballads Broadsides &c', National Library of Scotland Ry.111.a.10.f.9; 'Virtue *and Wit, The Preservatives of Love and Beauty*. To the Tune of, *Gillicranky*', in *The Tea-Table Miscellany: Or, a Complete Collection of Scots Sangs* (3 vols Dublin 1729), II, 121-2. See James C Dick (ed), *Notes on Scottish Song*, op.cit. p 91, for the earliest recorded versions of the air.

3   *Jacobite Relics of Scotland*, op.cit. I, 200.

4   See *A Compleat Collection Of All The Poems Wrote by...Alexander Pennecuik. To which is annexed some Curious Poems by other worthy Hands* (Parts 1-11 Edinburgh n.d. but ?1750), pp 125-32. For the general popularity of the piece and its active use against the English see William Cowan (ed), *A Journey To Edenborough in Scotland by Joseph Taylor, Late of the Inner Temple, Esq* (Edinburgh 1903), pp 126-7.

5   'The Old Way of Killicranky' in *Several Scots Poems* (n.p. n.d. but c. 1745), National Library of Scotland, Rosebery Pamphlets, 1.2.85.

6   For a convenient short account of the broadside at its height as a form, see Hyder E Rollins, 'The Black-Letter Broadside Ballad' in *Publications of the Modern Language Association of America*, Vol XXXIV, new ser. Vol XXVII, 1919, 258-339.

7   'The Battle of *Preston*. To the Tune of *Killiecranky*' in 'Printed pamphlets, broadsides, Acts of Parliament, ballads, and songs relating mainly to the risings of 1715 and 1745', National Library of Scotland MS.488.f.46.

8   *The Poetical Works of the Ingenious and Learned William Meston* (Edinburgh 1767), pp 115-8.

9   In 'Jacobite Relics', National Library of Scotland MS.2960.f.48.

10   Dalhousie Muniments, Scottish Record Office GD45/26/103/34.

11   Spottiswoode Papers—'Miscellaneous papers...and poems, chiefly Royalist and Jacobite', National Library of Scotland MS.2935.f.101-2.

12   The most accessible source for the Watson text is Harriet Harvey Wood (ed), *James Watson's Choice Collection of Comic and Serious Scots Poems*, Vol 1 (Edinburgh 1977), pp 8-10. On the question of authorship and an attribution to Sir William Scott of Thirlestane, see Mark Napier, *History of the Partition of the Lennox* (Edinburgh 1835), pp 237-9. The version quoted here is from David Herd's *Ancient and Modern Scottish Songs Heroic Ballads etc* (2 vols Edinburgh 1973, first published Edinburgh 1776), II, 24-6.

13   See P Hume Brown, *History of Scotland* (3 vols Cambridge 1909), III, 113.

14   The text is from [James Maidment](ed), *A Book of Scotish Pasquils 1568-1715* (Edinburgh 1868), pp 366-7.

15   Edinburgh University Library, Laing Collection, La.11.358/6.

16   For the Whig riposte see 'Jacobite Relics', National Library of Scotland MS.2960.f.88; for 'Lord Balmerino's Lament' see 'Collection of Ballads, collected chiefly from tradition, by R Pitcairn...Commenced Edinr., 1817', National Library of Scotland MS.2914.pp 7-9.

17   *Roxburghe Ballads*, op.cit. I, 588-92. See also Claude M Simpson, *British Broadside Ballad*, op.cit. pp 68-71.

18   Allan Ramsay (ed), *The Tea-Table Miscellany* (Edinburgh 1724), pp 25-7. The text is

followed by the letters 'S R' leading some to ascribe the song to Struan Robertson: see Matthew P M'Diarmid (ed), *The Poems of Robert Fergusson* (2 vols Edinburgh 1954-6), II, 292.

19   In 'Old Scotch Ballads Broadsides &c', National Library of Scotland, Ry.111.a.10.f.7.

CHAPTER FIVE pp 38 to 47

1   For the primitive state of land communications see Henry Grey Graham, *The Social Life of Scotland in the Eighteenth Century* (London 1969, first published 1899), pp 39-42, 166-8; for the Grampians as a land barrier, see Stewart, *Sketches of the ...Highlanders of Scotland*, op.cit. I, 4; for southern ignorance of the Highlands see John Home, *The History of the Rebellion in the Year 1745* (London 1802), pp v-vi; for the making of wills, see [Edward Burt], *Letters from A Gentleman in the North of Scotland to His Friend in London* (2 vols London 1754), I, 5; for Lowland fears about the backward state of religion in the Highlands see William Maitland, *The History of Edinburgh, from its Foundation to the Present Time* (Edinburgh 1753), bk.VII, 471-80; for conflict within the Highlands see Audrey Cunningham, *The Loyal Clans* (Cambridge 1932), pp 13-43: and for a contemporary account of the same see the 'Memoir Regarding the State of the Highlands—1716' in [Bindon Blood & James Macknight](eds), *Memoirs of Sir Ewen Cameron of Locheill, Chief of the Clan Cameron* (Edinburgh 1842), pp 377-83.

2   On linguistic barriers see Home, *History of the Rebellion*, op.cit. pp 3,5,n; on lions and elephants, see Daniel Defoe, *A Tour Thro' the whole Island of Great Britain* (2 vols London 1927), II, 821.

3   See Burt, *Letters from a Gentleman*, op.cit. II, 93; and Dr John Macpherson, *Critical Dissertations on the Origin, Antiquities, Language, Government, Manners, and Religion, of the Ancient Caledonians* (London 1768), p 115.

4   There are numerous military histories of the '45; probably the best brief modern account is that of Bruce Lenman, in *The Jacobite Risings*, op.cit. pp 231-59 which deals with the diplomatic and economic aspects and tempers the traditional romantic interpretation with a salutory, perhaps excessive, cynicism; there is an excellent account of what went wrong for the government from a military point of view in Rupert C Jarvis, *Collected Papers on the Jacobite Risings* (2 vols Manchester 1971-2), I, 3-20; for the legal and political tangle which paralysed the Scottish administration, see Rosalind Mitchison, 'The Government and the Highlands, 1707-1745' in N T Phillipson and Rosalind Mitchison (eds), *Scotland in the Age of Improvement* op.cit., pp 39-44, and (what is probably the best of the older accounts), Robert Chambers, *History of the Rebellion of 1745-6* (Edinburgh 1869), pp 74-5.

5   One reason for this was the incredible pace at which Highland infantry attacked which was quite outside the experience of soldiers accustomed to conventional European warfare; another, and more important, was the utter carnage which followed when Highlanders got in amongst orthodox 18th century foot with the broadsword; even hardened career soldiers with long experience of gunshot and bayonet wounds were unnerved by it: see The Chevalier de Johnstone, *Memoirs of The Rebellion in 1745 and 1746* (London 1820), pp 28-9; see also the chapter 'Highland War' in W R Kermack, *The Scottish Highlands A Short History (c. 300-1746)*, (Edinburgh 1957), pp 125-39; and William Wallace (ed), *Robert Burns and Mrs Dunlop* (London 1898), p 78.

6   'The Original and Conduct of the Young Pretender. To the Tune of, *The Broom of Cowden Knowes*', in 'Broadside Ballads etc. 18th and 19th Centuries', National Library of Scotland, Ry.111.a.1.f.21.

7   *'The Rebels bold March into* England, *with their shameful Retreat. Dedicate to the truly loyal the Wights in and about* Ormiston *and* Cousland, *for unmerited Favours'*, in 'Broadside Ballads etc. 18th and 19th Centuries', National Library of Scotland, Ry.111.a.1.f.20.

8   Hugo Arnot, *The History of Edinburgh* (Edinburgh 1779), p 214; Harold William Thompson (ed), *The Anecdotes and Egotisms of Henry Mackenzie 1745-1831 (London 1927), p 23;* David Daiches, *Charles Edward Stuart The Life and Times of Bonnie Prince Charlie* (London 1973), pp 148-9.

9   John, x, 1-10.

10 'An Excellent Song on the present Times, by a country *Hind. To the Tune of* Killycrancy', in 'Broadside Ballads etc. 18th and 19th Centuries', National Library of Scotland, Ry.111.a.1.f.19.

11 *'A Poem on the Rebellion, &c. To the Tune of* William *of* Plymouth' in *A Poem on the Rebellion. Being an Abridgment of our unhappy circumstances, with an Account of the Three Battles, Preston, Falkirk, and Culloden.* Printed in the Year 1746 (n.p.), in 'Printed pamphlets, broadsides, Acts of Parliament, ballads, and songs relating mainly to the risings of 1715 and 1745' National Library of Scotland MS.488.f.68-71.

12 From 'An Excellent Song on the present Times', see note 10 above.

13 John Hill Burton (ed), *The Autobiography of Dr Alexander Carlyle of Inveresk 1722-1805* (London 1910), pp 156-7.

14 See Cohn, *Pursuit of the Millennium,* op.cit.; the biblical text is Ezekiel, xxxviii, 14-16; for an account of the apoclacyptic significance of Gog Magog see J S P Tatlock, *The Legendary History of Britain Geoffrey of Monmouth's Historia Regum Britanniae and its early Vernacular Versions* (Berkeley 1950), pp 53-5; for a revealing account of the mental habits which lay behind the extreme Whiggish world-view, see Alex Fergusson, *Henry Erskine, his Kinsfolk and Times* (Edinburgh 1882), pp 373-4.

15 The lines occur in 'The Prophecie of Bertlington' in *[David Laing] (ed), Collection of Ancient Scottish Prophecies, in Alliterative Verse* (Edinburgh 1833), pp 14-17.

16 See George MacGregor (ed), *The Collected Writings of Dougal Graham 'Skellat' Bellman of Glasgow...Together with a...Sketch of the Chap Literature of Scotland* (2 vols Glasgow 1883), I, 103.

17 The persecuted remnant often denounced Charles II and James VII as agents of Antichrist: 'The Duke of York...a sworn vassal of Antichrist, 'the devil's lieutenant' (as Mr Shields used to call him in publick)', Fleming, *Six Saints of the Covenant,* op.cit. I,225.

18 See P Doddridge, *Some Remarkable Passages in the Life of the Honourable Col. James Gardiner, Who was Slain at the Battle of Preston-Pans, September 21, 1745* (London 1748), pp 16-46; see also Alex Charles Ewald, *The Life and Times of Prince Charles Stuart Count of Albany* (London 1883), p 125.

19 The text is taken from 'An Elegy and a Ballad' in the *Scottish Historical Review,* Vol VI, No.24, July 1909, 357-61, from a broadside then in the possession of C H Firth.

CHAPTER SIX pp 49 to 66

The present chapter is based on my article 'Bonny Highland Laddie: the Making of a Myth' in the *Scottish Literary Journal*, Vol III, No.2, December 1976, 30-50.

1   W Mackay Mackenzie (ed), *The Poems of William Dunbar* (London 1932), p 123.

2   Tom Scott (ed), *The Penguin Book of Scottish Verse* (Harmondsworth 1970), p 80.

3   *A Collection of Several Poems and Verses Composed upon Various Occasions By Mr.*

William Cleland Lieutenant Collonel to my Lord Angus's Regiment. Printed in the year 1697 (n.p.), pp 7-47.

4   [James Maidment] (ed), *Scotish Elegiac Verses. M.DC.XXIX.—M.DCC.XXIX.* (Edinburgh 1842), pp xxxix-xl; for a fuller account of this episode see Burt, *Letters from a Gentleman,* op.cit. II, 170-3. A letter from Clunie to the Jacobite court at Rome stating the MacPherson side of the affair is quoted in Henrietta Tayler (ed), *Jacobite Epilogue A Further Selection of Letters from Jacobites among the Stuart Papers at Windsor* (London 1941), pp 162-4.

5   The text is in 'Old Scotch Ballads Broadsides &c', National Library of Scotland, Ry.111.a.10.f.36.

6   'Jacobite Papers, 1623-1869, n.d.' National Library of Scotland MS.1696.f.90. This was part of a collection formed by Sir Henry Steuart of Allanton which was bought by Robert Chambers and used by him for his *History of the Rebellion.* On the usefulness of Highland arms in Lowland disputes see [Thomas Morer], *A Short Account of Scotland. Being a Description of the Nature of that Kingdom, and what the Constitution of it is in Church and State* (London 1702), pp 11-12.

7   The text is taken from *A Full Collection of all Poems upon Charles, Prince of Wales, Regent of the Kingdoms of Scotland, England, France and Ireland, and Dominions thereunto belonging. Printed in the Year MDCCXLV.* (n.p.), pp 3-11.

8   *The Earl of Mar marr'd. With the Humours of Jockey, the Highlander: a Tragi-Comical Farce* (London 1716). A similar note is struck in the introductory verses of another London publication, William Thomson's *Orpheus Caledonius: or, a Collection of Scots Songs* (2 vols London 1733): 'Love's brightest Flames warm Scottish Lads,/Tho' coolly clad in High-land Plads;/They scorn Brocade, who like the Lass,/Nor need a Carpet, if there's Grass/...Thus merrily they court the Fair,/And love and sing in Northern Air:'

9   *Tea-Table Miscellany* (1724), op.cit. pp 169-70.

10 'Old Scotch Ballads Broadsides &c', National Library of Scotland, Ry.111.a.10.f.89.

11 Ibid. f.45. For songs similar in theme see 'Bonny Baby Livingston' (Child 222), 'Lizzie Lindsay' (Child 226), 'Rob Roy' (Child 225), 'The Duke of Gordon's Daughter' (Child 237); 'Ettrick *Banks*', in *Orpheus Caledonius,* op.cit. II, 102-3; 'Had awa' frae me, Donald' in *The Lark: being a Select Collection of the most celebrated and newest songs, Scots & English* (Edinburgh 1765), pp 125-8; for bawdy Highland Laddie songs, see James Barke, Sydney Goodsir Smith and J De Lancey Ferguson (eds), *The Merry Muses of Caledonia* (Edinburgh 1959), pp 76, 110-11, 113; in manuscript sources, see 'Donald M'Queen's Flight wi Lizie Menzie', National Library of Scotland MS.210.f.92; 'Miscellaneous Verses' in Scottish Record Office, RH13/40, contains an early 18th century text cognate with 'As I cam o'er the Cairney mount.'

12 *A Collection of Loyal Songs. For the Use of the Revolution Club. Some of which never before printed* (Edinburgh 1748), pp 13-14.

13 Ibid. pp 14-15.

14 Ibid. pp 56-8.

15 Evan Charteris, *William Augustus Duke of Cumberland His Early Life and Times (1721-1748),* (London 1913), p 248.

16 *Loyal Songs, Poems,* op.cit. pp 33-4.

17 Andrew Bisset (ed), *Memoirs and Papers of Sir Andrew Mitchell, KB, Envoy Extraordinary and Minister Plenipotentiary from the Court of Great Britain to the Court of Prussia, from 1756 to 1771* (2 vols London 1850), i,19. James Ray dryly observed, 'It is remarkable, many of the prettiest Ladies in *Scotland* are *Jacobites*', see his *Compleat History of the Rebellion, From its first Rise, in MDCCXLV. To its total Suppression at the glorious Battle of Culloden, in April, 1746* (Bristol 1750), pp 294-6; see also Robert Chambers, *The Threiplands of Fingask a Family Memoir* (London 1880), p 43; James

Dennistoun, *Memoirs of Sir Robert Strange...and of his Brother-in-Law Andrew Lumisden, Private Secretary to the Stuart Princes* (2 vols London 1855), II, 213; and Alex Fergusson, *Henry Erskine,* op.cit. p 187, n2.

18 From *Three Excellent New Songs* (n.p. n.d.), in 'Printed pamphlets, broadsides, Acts of Parliament, ballads, and songs relating mainly to the risings of 1715 and 1745', National Library of Scotland MS.488.f.64-7.

19 'A Song. Tune,—*Bonny laddie, Highland laddie*', in *True Loyalist,* op.cit. p 50.

20 Ibid. pp 40-3. Under the title 'Charlie Stuart and his Tartan Plaidy' it appears on song-slips until well into the 19th century: see the copies preserved in the National Library of Scotland, LC.70 where it is printed along with 'The Tinker's Wedding' and 'The Banks of sweet Primroses'; and LC1270 where it appears alongside 'The Inniskillen Dragoon'. At least one version has been found in oral circulation during the present century: see Collinson, *Traditional and National Music,* op.cit. pp 154-5.

21 *Loyal Songs, Poems,* op.cit. pp 41-3.

22 'A Song *for Joy of our ancient Race of* Stewarts', in *Four new Songs, and a Prophecy* (n.p. n.d.), National Library of Scotland, Rosebery Pamphlets, 1-2-85.

23 *True Loyalist,* op.cit. pp 96-7.

24 *The Scots Nightingale: or, Edinburgh Vocal Miscellany. A New and Select Collection of the Best Scots and English Songs* (Edinburgh 1778), pp 233-4.

CHAPTER SEVEN pp 67 to 71

1 Certain Jacobite tunes begin to appear in the general collections in the generation after the '45: such as 'Over the Water to Charlie' and 'Miss Flora M'Donald's Reel' in Robert Bremner's *Collection of Scots Reels or Country Dances* (Parts I-IV, Edinburgh n.d. [but 1757-9]); 'The Eight Men of Moidart', 'Auld Stuarts back again', 'The Whigs of Fife' and 'the Highland Dress', in Neil Stewart's *Collection of the Newest and best Reels or Country Dances* (Edinburgh n.d. [but 1761]); and 'There are few good Fellows when Jamie's awa'', 'Up and ware them a Willie', 'Gilly Cranky', 'Over the Water to Charlie', 'There's three good fellows down in yon Glen', 'Will you go to Sheriff Muir', 'Carl an the King Come', 'Away Whigs Away', and 'The Old Stewarts back Again' in James Oswald's *Caledonian Pocket Companion* (London, n.d. [but 1743-59]); three of the older songs, 'Killiecranky', 'A Race at Sheriffmuir' and 'Tranent Muir', which in any case were not distinguished by hot partisanship, began to figure in general song collections like *The Scots Nightingale: or Edinburgh Vocal Miscellany* (Edinburgh 1778), pp 211-2, 212-5, 215-8, (although all three were dropped from the second edition, Edinburgh 1779), and *The Gold-Finch, A Choice Collection of the Most Celebrated Songs, Scots & English* (Edinburgh 1777), pp 179-81, 181-4, 184-7. For the relatively pallid and decorative quality of fresh composition within the form at this time see *The True Loyalist,* op.cit. pp 10-11, 46-7.

2 For the numerical decline of the Episcopalians see Skinner, *Ecclesiastical History of Scotland* , op.cit. II, 666-71; the fullest account of Charles Edward's career and Jacobite affairs after the '45 is contained in Andrew Lang, *Pickle the Spy or The Incognito of Prince Charles* (London 1897); Winifred Duke, *In the Steps of Bonnie Prince Charlie* (London 1953), may also be consulted.

3 A number of Jacobite fragments are preserved amongst Herd's MSS; see Hans Hecht (ed), *Songs from David Herd's Manuscripts* (Edinburgh 1904, songs nos. LXI and CXIX. Little is known about Herd, but see *Letters from Thomas Percy, DD afterwards Bishop of Dromore, John Callander of Craigforth, Esq. David Herd, and others, to George Paton* (Edinburgh 1830).

4   *Jacobite Relics*, op.cit. II, 118-20. For a study of Hamilton, a fascinating figure in his
     own right, see Nelson S Bushnell, *William Hamilton of Bangour Poet and Jacobite*
     (Aberdeen 1957). For an intriguing mid-century republican use of the legendary past
     in an anti-Union context, see James Fergusson (ed), *Letters of George Dempster to Sir
     Adam Fergusson 1756-1813 With Some Account of his Life* (London 1934), p 32.
5   The earliest printing of this celebrated piece appears to have been in *The Land of
     Cakes Book the First containing Six Songs set to Musick in the true Scots Taste. To
     which is added, The Tears of Scotland* (London [1746]): see Lewis Mansfield Knapp,
     Tobias Smollett Doctor of Men and Manners (Princeton 1949), pp 60-1. The poem
     was set to music by James Oswald: see O E Deutsch, 'Poetry Preserved in Music
     Bibliographical Notes on Smollett and Oswald, Handel, and Haydn' in *Modern Language
     Notes*, Vol LXIII, No.2 February 1948, 73-88.
6   For Burns and Foxite Whiggism, see William Donaldson, 'The Glencairn Connection:
     Robert Burns and Scottish Politics, 1786-1796', in *Studies in Scottish Literature*, Vol
     XVI, 1981, 61-79; for Burns as a Jacobite, see chapter 8 of this book.
7   For the tartan war in Edinburgh, see Alexander Allardyce (ed), *Scotland and Scotsmen
     in the Eighteenth Century* (2 vols Edinburgh 1888), II, 85n: on the use of tartan by
     English Tories, see Keith Grahame Feiling, *The Second Tory Party 1714-1832* (Lon-
     don 1938), p 49; the text of 'Plaid Hunting' is taken from *Loyal Songs For the Use of
     the Revolution Club*, op.cit. pp 16-17.
8   For the Highlands as a source of fighting men see Home, *History of the Rebellion*,
     op.cit. pp 20-23; see also N T Phillipson and Rosalind Mitchison (eds), *Scotland in
     the Age of Improvement*, op.cit. pp 28-9; on the raising of the Black Watch, see
     Kermack, *The Scottish Highlands*, op.cit. p.147, and Cunningham, *Loyal Clans*, op.cit.
     pp 474-5; the quotation is taken from *A Short History of the Highland Regiment;
     Interspersed with Some Occasional Observations As to the Present State of the Country,
     Inhabitants, and Government of Scotland* (London 1743), p 1.
9   Quoted in John Scott Keltie, *A History of the Scottish Highlands Highland Clans and
     Highland Regiments* (2 vols Edinburgh 1877), II, 334.
10   See Ferguson, *Scotland 1689 to the Present*, op.cit. pp 263-5.
11   On the composition of 'The Garb of Old Gaul', see Keltie, op.cit. II, 347n; see also
     Robert T Fitzhugh (ed), *Robert Burns His Associates and Contemporaries* (Chapel Hill,
     1943), p 92n, 102;for Reid as a composer of military march tunes see Johnson, *Music
     and Society in Lowland Scotland*, op.cit. pp 60-1; for a fuller account of his musical
     career see Henry George Farmer, *A History of Music in Scotland* (London 1947), pp
     337-8, 389-90. The song text is quoted from *The Lark*, op.cit. pp 11-12.

CHAPTER EIGHT pp 72 to 89

During the past two centuries there has been an enormous body of critical and biographical
writing on Robert Burns. The authoritative general study is Thomas Crawford, *Burns A
Study of the Poems and Songs* (2nd edn Edinburgh 1965). John Strawhorn's pioneering
studies of society and culture in contemporary Ayrshire are also a *sine qua non*: see
particularly his *Ayrshire at the time of Burns* (Kilmarnock 1959). Burns's politics have been
variously interpreted; the following may be considered as representative: W L Renwick,
English Literature 1789-1815 (Oxford 1963), p 196; James Kinsley (ed), *The Poems and
Songs of Robert Burns* (3 vols Oxford 1968), III, 1313; David Daiches, 'Robert Burns and
Jacobite Song' in Donald A Low (ed), *Critical Essays on Robert Burns* (London 1975),
p.141; Sir Henry Craik, *A Century of Scottish History* (2 vols Edinburgh 1901), II, 85n,
123.

1   *The Scots Musical Museum*, op.cit. I, iii.

2   J De Lancey Ferguson and G Ross Roy (eds), *The Letters of Robert Burns* (2 vols Oxford 1985), I, 168.

3   See Donaldson, 'The Glencairn Connection', op.cit.

4   Ibid. For a more detailed account of the British Whig ethos in Scotland, see Michael W M'Cahill, 'The Scottish peerage and the House of Lords in the late eighteenth century', in the *Scottish Historical Review*, Vol LI, No. 152 1972, 172-96.

5   See, for example, Hans Hecht, *Robert Burns The Man and His Work*, (London 1936), p 63; Christina Keith, *The Russet Coat A Critical Study of Burns' Poetry and of its Background* (London 1956), pp 40-1, 48. See, for example, *Letters*, op.cit. I, 165; I, 195; I, 231; I, 348. Of the common people in late 18th century Ayrshire, Aiton remarks in his *General View of the Agriculture of the County of Ayr* (1811), that 'The people had been taken from the plough and other peaceful labours to assist the reformers in demolishing churches...and it was not till near the end of the last century that they returned to their proper occupations; they were busy with reformation in the church, but in a great measure overlooked the improvements of the soil...The ambition of the people, at that time, was not to improve the soil, but to reform the church—not to destroy weeds and brambles, but to root out heresy—not to break up the stubborn soil, but to tread down the Scarlet Woman and the Man of Sin.' quoted in D M'Naught, *Kilmaurs Parish & Burgh* (Paisley 1912), pp 10-11. See also, Andrew Edgar, *Old Church Life in Scotland: Lectures on Kirk-Session and Presbytery Records* (Paisley 1885): Edgar was minister of Mauchline, and draws his examples predominantly from his own parish.

6   For the martyr-stone, see the entry for the parish of 'Machlin', Presbytery of Ayr, in Sir John Sinclair (ed) *The Statistical Account of Scotland* (21 vols Edinburgh 1791-99), II, 115. For Peden as schoolmaster of Tarbolton, see Fleming, *Six Saints*, op.cit. I, 45.

7   For the influence of Burns's mother, see De Lancey Ferguson, *Pride and Passion Robert Burns 1759-1796* (New York 1939), pp 42-5; see also Wodrow, *Analecta*, op.cit. *passim*.

8   See, for example verse VIII of the 'Elegy on Captain Matthew Henderson', Kinsley, op.cit. p 1286.

9   See John Muir, 'The Jacobite Ancestry of Burns', in John D Ross (ed), *Burnsiana: a Collection of Literary Odds and Ends Relating to Robert Burns* (6 vols London 1892-7), vi, 42-4. For further particulars of the North-East Burnses see George Henderson Kinnear, *The History of Glenbervie, the Fatherland of Burns a Parish in the County of Kincardine* (Edinburgh 1910), *passim*. The poet's brother Gilbert was very anxious to play down the family's Jacobitical connections, see James Currie, *Works of Robert Burns*, op.cit. I, 65-6; One contemporary, Dr Robert Anderson, noted of Burns 'He was a tory, an idolater of monarchy, and a Jacobite as much as he could be.' quoted in Robert T Fitzhugh, *Robert Burns The Man and the Poet A Round, Unvarnished Account* (London, 1971), p 132.

10 Allardyce, *Scotland and Scotsmen*, op.cit. II, 554.

11 For the Moore letter, see *Letters*, op.cit, I, 134; for Lady Winifred Maxwell Constable, ibid. I, 461.

12 Kinnear, op.cit. pp 39, 68, 87, 93-6 ; most of the cluster of Burnes farms were in the estate of Inchbreck, but one of them, Elfhill, seems to have lain in the adjoining Marischal estate of Fetteresso, see Muir, 'Jacobite Ancestry' op.cit.

13 The main source for the Edinburgh Episcopalians is Mary E Ingram, *A Jacobite Stronghold of the Church*, op.cit. *passim*, but see especially pp 27-42, 57, 67, 81, 92. See John M'Vie, 'Burns's Letter to James Steuart' in *Burns Chronicle*, 3rd series Vol XI, 1953, 42-3; recently discovered evidence shows that Burns actually attended the

celebrations at Cleland's Garden, a point long in doubt: see Donald A Low, 'A Last Supper with Scotland's Bard' in *Weekend Scotsman*, 22 January, 1983. (I am indebted to Dr Hamish Henderson for bringing this reference to my attention). For the Company of Archers, see Farquhar Mackenzie, '*Sir* Robert Burns' in *Burns Chronicle*, 4th series Vol I, 1976, 62-6.

14 Kinsley, op.cit. I, 348.
15 *Letters*, op.cit. I, 91.
16 Ibid. I, 151.
17 See, James Currie, *Works of Robert Burns*, op.cit. I, 138.
18 *Letters*, op.cit. I, 332-5.
19 Ibid. I, 341-2.
20 All song texts are from Kinsley, op.cit.
21 *Scots Musical Museum*, op.cit. II, 138, 195, 195-6; J C Dick (ed), *Notes on Scottish Song*, op.cit. p 27.
22 Kinsley, op.cit. 349-50.
23 *True Loyalist*, op.cit. 53-4.
24 Kinsley, op.cit. 411-2.
25 Hans Hecht (ed), *Songs from David Herd's Manuscripts*, op.cit., Song No.61.
26 Kinsley, op.cit. pp 529-30.
27 See chapter VII, n 1.
28 *True Loyalist*, op.cit. pp 58-9.
29 Ibid. pp 82-4.
30 Kinsley, op.cit. 400.
31 Reprinted in Joseph Ritson's *Scotish Songs*, op.cit. II, 67-73. Burns obviously had access to a broadside or chap version.
32 The 'vain carnal spring' quote comes from *The Heart of Midlothian*, ch.XVIII—the words are Davie Deans's, borrowed by Scott from Patrick Walker, see Fleming, *Six Saints*, I, 237-41; for the song text, see Kinsley, op.cit. 534-6.
33 *Letters*, II, 82.
34 For a discussion of one possible source for this song, see T F Henderson, '"Charlie he's My Darling" and other Burns' Originals' in the *Scottish Historical Review*, Vol III, No.10 January 1906, 171-8; for the text, see Kinsley, op.cit. 846-7.
35 Ibid, 637-8.
36 See Donaldson, 'Glencairn Connection' op.cit.; for further insight into the hierarchical and corrupt nature of contemporary Scottish civic life, see Robert Kerr (ed), *Memoirs of the Life, Writings, & Correspondence of William Smellie* (2 vols Edinburgh 1811), especially I, 321-2, II, 90-7.
37 Just as his song of international brotherhood 'Is there, for honest poverty' was set to a Jacobite tune, 'Tho' Geordie Reigns in Jamie's stead': *True Loyalist*, op.cit. pp 41-3.
38 *Letters*, op.cit. II, 236.
39 Ibid. II, 276.
40 My account of Herder owes much to F M Barnard, *Herder's Social and Political Thought From Englightenment to Nationalism* (Oxford 1965). Burns could possibly have been aware of Herder's work through his friend Alexander Fraser Tytler who was one of the earliest enthusiasts for German literature and translated Schiller's 'The Robbers': see J G Lockhart, *Memoirs of the Life of Sir Walter Scott, Bart*, (7 vols Edinburgh 1837-8), I, 204-5. Likewise Herder and his circle were early aware of Burns, thanks to the advocacy of the Highland scholar James Macdonald, see Alexander Gillies, *A Hebridean in Goethe's Weimar The Reverend James Macdonald and the Cultural Relations between Scotland and Germany* (Oxford 1969). I am indebted for the latter reference to Dr Hamish Henderson.

41   Barnard, *Herder's Social and Political Thought*, op.cit. p 18.

CHAPTER NINE pp 90 to 108

1   *Harp of Caledonia*, op.cit. 1, iii, xiv.
2   See, for example, Andrew Hook, 'Scotland and Romanticism: The International Scene' in *History of Scottish Literature*, op.cit. II, 307-22.
3   One may note here, Burns's unusual openness to Highlanders and the Highlands, and his readiness to present Scotland as a basically Celtic country: see, for example 'The Author's Earnest Cry and Prayer', verses 18, 29; 'Esopus to Maria', 'Address of Beelzebub', 'On Glenriddell's Fox Breaking his Chain', 'The Young Highland Rover', and his numerous other versions of Highland Laddie songs, such as 'As I came o'er the Cairney Mount'; 'The Highland Balou',and 'The Highland Widow's Lament'; indeed the later volumes of the *Museum* contain song after song upon Highland and Jacobite subjects; on the tartan as a symbol of old Scottish virtue and independence see Kinsley, op.cit 1076. The poet may possibly have had first hand experience of Highlanders from boyhood, thanks to the great annual 'Comb's day' fair at Largs to which large numbers of Gaels came and would 'spend the whole night in rustic sports, carousing and dancing on the green to the sound of the bagpipe', *Statistical Account*, op.cit. II, 360-66. For Highland Laddie songs from the later 18th century see, for example, '*Donnel and Flora*. On the late misfortune of General Burgoyne and his gallant army. By a Lady', in *The British Songster, Being A Select Collection of Favourite Scots and English Songs, Catches, &c*, (Glasgow 1786), pp 160-2; and 'The Tartan Plaidie', in *The Edinburgh Musical Miscellany: A Collection of the Most Approved Scotch, English, and Irish Songs, set to music* (2 vols Edinburgh 1792-3), II, 74-6.
4   *The Lyre: A Collection of the Most Approved English, Irish, and Scottish Songs, Ancient and Modern* (Edinburgh 1824), pp 62-3. For an attribution of the original 'Campbells are coming' to Burns, see Kinsley, *Poems and Songs of Robert Burns*, op.cit. 542-3, 1340.
5   James Hogg, *Songs, by The Ettrick Shepherd. Now first collected* (Edinburgh 1831), pp 1-5.
6   For an example of how these latter-day Highland Laddie songs were patched together to fit contemporary circumstances see J Cuthbert Hadden, *George Thomson The Friend of Burns His Life & Correspondence* (London 1898), p 176.
7   James Anton, *Retrospect of a Military Life, During The Most Eventful Periods of the Last War* (Edinburgh 1841), pp 247-52. See also, Philip Howard, *The Black Watch* (London 1968), pp 55-6.
8   See Lady Strachey (ed), *Memoirs of a Highland Lady The Autobiography of Elizabeth Grant of Rothiemurchus* (London 1911), pp 88-9; see also D B Horn, 'George IV and Highland Dress', in the *Scottish Historical Review*, Vol XLVII,2: No.144 Oct. 1968, 209-10. See also Nina, Countess of Minto, Life and Letters of Sir Gilbert Elliot (3 vols London 1874), I, 326. For the European currency of Highland dress as a symbol, see *The Correspondence of Sir John Sinclair* (2 vols London 1831), I, 43, and for much learned and curious matter concerning the antiquity of the garb of old Gaul, ibid. I, 471-3.
9   See [James Browne], *A Critical Examination of Dr Macculloch's Work on the Highlands and Western Isles of Scotland* (Edinburgh 1825), pp 4-5; see also Sir Arthur Mitchell, 'A List of Travels, Tours, Journeys, Voyages, Cruises, Excursions, Wanderings, Rambles, Visits, etc., Relating to Scotland', in *Proceedings of the Society of Antiquaries of Scotland*, 3rd series Vol XXXV, 1900-1, 431-638; also Vol XXXIV, 1905, 500-27;

and Vol XLIV, 1910, 390-405. Alexander Ramsay, *History of the Highland and Agricultural Society of Scotland* (Edinburgh 1879). *Albyn's Anthology Or A Select Collection of the Melodies & Vocal Poetry Peculiar to Scotland and the Isles* (2 vols Edinburgh 1816-1818).

10 *Albyn's Anthology*, op.cit. I, 25.

11 Ibid. I, 90-7, 82-9; II, 54-7.

12 Charles Rogers (ed), *Life and Songs of the Baroness Nairne* (Edinburgh 1905), pp 17-26. The first thirty years of the 'Life' were written by T L Kington Oliphant, the poetess's grand-nephew: see his *Jacobite Lairds of Gask* (London 1870), p 433 *n*. Something of the living atmosphere of Jacobitism at Gask may be seen in Lady Nairne's MS Journals: see, for example, the entry for Sunday 7 June 1789, concerning Cumberland's sack of the old house during the '45, National Library of Scotland MS.981A.f.1. For a similar ambience, see Robert Chambers, *Threiplands of Fingask*, op.cit. p 43, referring to Sir Stuart Threipland who kept up his political attachment to the house of Stuart and toasted the Pretender until his death in 1805. For generally increasing tolerance of Jacobitism and interest in it as a subject before the issue of *Waverley*, see Barbara L H Horn (ed), *Letters of John Ramsay of Ochtertyre 1799-1812* (Edinburgh 1966), pp 39, 74, 96, 103, 153, 185, 189, 240; see also 'Letters written by Mrs Grant of Laggan concerning Highland Affairs and Persons connected with the Stuart Cause in the Eighteenth Century' in J R N Macphail (ed), *Wariston's Diary and Other Papers* (Edinburgh 1896), *passim*.

13 Rogers, op.cit. p 34.

14 *Albyn's Anthology*, op.cit. I, 62 *n*. See also, David Stewart, *Sketches of the...Highlanders of Scotland*, I, 101*n*; See also, *A Series of Original Portraits and Caricature Etchings, by the late John Kay, Miniature Painter, Edinburgh; with Biographical Sketches and Anecdotes* (2 vols, Edinburgh 1842), I, 419-22; and Sarah Tytler and J L Watson, *The Songstresses of Scotland* (2 vols London 1871), II, 113-4.

15 Willmott Dixon and J Logie Robertson, *The Jacobite Episode in Scottish History and its Relative Literature* (Edinburgh n.d.), p 143.

16 See, for example, [H R Duff] (ed), *Culloden Papers: comprising an Extensive and Interesting Correspondence from the year 1625 to 1748* (London 1815); J S Clarke (ed), *The Life of James the Second King of England, &c* (2 vols London 1816); *The Lockhart Papers: containing Memoirs and Commentaries upon the Affairs of Scotland from 1702 to 1715* (2 vols London 1817); Dr William King, *Political and Literary Anecdotes of His Own Times* (London 1818); K Macleay, *Historical Memoirs of Rob Roy and the Clan Macgregor* (Glasgow 1818); [James Maidment] (ed), *Miscellanea Scotica. A Collection of Tracts Relating to the History, Antiquities, Topography and Literature of Scotland* (4 vols Glasgow 1818-20): vol III contained 'Memoirs of the Lord Viscount Dundee, the Highland Clans, The Massacre of Glencoe: with An Account of Dundee's Officers after they went to France'; P Buchan, *An Historical and Authentic Account of the Ancient and Noble Family of Keith, Earls Marichal of Scotland* (Peterhead 1820); *The Chevalier de Johnstone, Memoirs of The Rebellion in 1745 and 1746* (London 1820). Many items of Jacobite interest appear in contemporary periodicals; for an account of one of these, see Alan Lang Strout, *A Bibliography of Articles in Blackwood's Magazine...1817-1825* (Lubbock 1959).

17 George Borrow, *The Romany Rye* (2 vols London 1857), II, 308.

18 William Hazlitt, *The Spirit of the Age: or Contemporary Portraits* (London 1825), pp 137-41. See also Francis Jeffrey in *The Edinburgh Review*, Vol XXXIV, No.67 August 1820, 148-50.

19 'James Hogg—correspondence, poems, and papers of and concerning (1813-1905, n.d.)', National Library of Scotland MS.2245.f.28.

20 For a general account of Hogg's career, see Alan Lang Strout, *The Life and Letters of*

James Hogg, The Ettrick Shepherd (1770-1825) (Lubbock 1946), Edith C Batho, *The Ettrick Shepherd* (Cambridge 1927), and Louis Simpson, *James Hogg A Critical Study* (Edinburgh 1962); see also Douglas S Mack (ed), *James Hogg Memoir of the Author's Life and Familian Anecdotes of Sir Walter Scott* (Edinburgh 1972), pp vii-xviii, 3-91; ibid. *James Hogg Selected Poems* (Oxford 1970), pp xi-xxix; Douglas Gifford (ed), *The Three Perils of Man War, Women and Witchcraft by James Hogg* (Edinburgh 1972), pp vii-xvi; and David Groves (ed), *James Hogg Selected Poems and Songs* (Edinburgh 1986), pp ix-xxxiii.

21   'Blackwood Papers', National Library of Scotland MS.4003.f.99.
22   *Jacobite Relics*, op.cit. I, v-vi, vii-xvi.
23   Ibid. I, vi.
24   Ibid, I, v-vi.
25   Ibid. I, viii.
26   Ibid. I, vii.
27   Ibid. I, 292.
28   See David Hogg, *Life of Allan Cunningham* (Dumfries 1875), pp 103-6.
29   *Jacobite Relics*, op.cit. II, 370-1.
30   Ibid. I, 218.
31   Ibid, I, 282.
32   Ibid. I, 129-30; II, 282.
33   Ibid. I, 137-8, 138-41.
34   Ibid. I, 282.
35   Ibid. I, xvi; for Hogg's debt to Ritson, compare the passage in the *Relics* Introduction, beginning 'Though the government and revolutionary principles...' I, xiv, with the passage from Ritson's 'Historical Essay', 'The gallant attempt made by a delicate young prince...' I, lxviii-lxix*n*; also *Relics* II, 244-8 with Ritson, II, 57-66 *n*; and *Relics* II, 336-7 with Ritson, II, 77-8 *n*.
36   *Relics*, op.cit. I, 279-80.
37   Edgar Johnson, *Sir Walter Scott The Great Unknown* (2 vols London 1970), I, 398, 401, 409-10.
38   For Jeffrey's review, see *Edinburgh Review*, Vol XXXIV, No.67 August 1820, 148-60. For a note of the avowal, see Hogg, *Songs*, op.cit. p 90.
39   *Relics*, op.cit. I, 90-3.
40   Ibid. II, 300-1. Hogg wrote to the publisher William Blackwood, 1 June 1820, 'I am still keeping all the songs subsequent to *Preston pans* in my hand in case of intervening ones but they are every one ready and will be sent as soon as required by the printers. They are very numerous and varied and those from the Gaelic I flatter myself of the first water.' 'Blackwood Papers, National Library of Scotland MS.4005.f.154.
41   Ibid. II, 90-2.
42   See Edith C Batho, 'Notes on the bibliography of James Hogg, the Ettrick Shepherd' in *The Library*, Vol XVI, 1935-6, 309-26.
43   Hogg, *Songs*, op.cit. pp 13-14.
44   See Eric Richards, *A History of the Highland Clearances Agrarian Transformation and the Evictions 1746-1886* (London 1982), pp 209-245.
45   Douglas Mack (ed), *James Hogg Memoir of the Author's Life*, op.cit. pp 16*n*, 31.
46   Hogg, *Songs*, op.cit. pp 83-4.
47   Ibid. pp 133-5.
48   Ibid. pp 59-62.
49   'Blackwood Papers', National Library of Scotland MS.4003.f.99. See also his letter to J Wallace of Peterhead, 25 November 1818: 'I am anxious to have all the curious anecdotes about the families that rose in behalf of the Stuarts that I possibly can...I have a great horde of songs far more than I can publish what I want chiefly at present

is *heroic anecdotes of highlanders.*' Quoted in Alan Lang Strout, *Life and Letters of James Hogg*, op.cit. pp 160-2.

50 See, for example, Hogg's letter to Blackwood of 1 June 1820: 'I send you a large parcel of jacobites today with a kind of regret lest something valuable should cast up that should have been preserved and it is a serious thing to think that the last chance of preserving a Jacobite Relic is going out of one's power and lost for ever for a farther collection of these will never be attempted nor does any one need.' 'Blackwood Papers', National Library of Scotland MS.4005.f.154. In August he added that volume two 'will be a little thicker than the first as I wished to exhaust the subject.' MS.4005.f.160.

51 Hogg to George Thomson, 14 December 1821, 14 February 1822; quoted in Hadden, *George Thomson*, op.cit. pp 180, 182-3.

52 Hadden,loc.cit.

53 'James Hogg—correspondence, poems, and papers of and concerning (1813-1905, n.d.)', National Library of Scotland MS.2245.f.62-3. For the composition of the Highland Society's committee at this period, see *The Correspondence of Sir John Sinclair*, op.cit. I, 330,n.

54 Vol XXXIV, No.67 August 1820, 154,6,7.

55 Alexander Allardyce (ed), *Letters from and to Charles Kirkpatrick Sharpe, Esq* (2 vols Edinburgh 1888), II, 332.

56 *Jacobite Relics*, op.cit. I, 57-8, 87-8, 149-50; II, 43-4.

CHAPTER TEN pp 109 to 113

1 *Jacobite Relics of Scotland*, op.cit. I, 224.

2 Rogers, *Life and Songs of the Baroness Nairne*, op.cit. is the standard source for Lady Nairne; see also [Margaret Stewart Simpson], *The Scottish Songstress Caroline Baroness Nairne by her Great Grand-Neice* (Edinburgh 1894), and George Henderson, *Lady Nairne and her Songs* (Paisley 1901). There are brief accounts of her life and works in Tytler and Watson, *Songstresses of Scotland*, op.cit. II, 108-79, and Oliphant, *Jacobite Lairds of Gask*, op.cit. pp 433-40.

3 This account of the Sobieski Stuarts is based on my article 'Inside the Kist of Glendulochan' in *Cencrastus*, No.4 Winter 1980-81, 20-22; for further information see Hugh Beveridge, *The Sobieski Stuarts* (Inverness 1909), Archibald Craig, *The Sobieski Stuarts* (Edinburgh 1922), Lady Strachey (ed), *Memoirs of a Highland Lady*, op.cit. pp 368-9, and Adam Philip, *Songs and Sayings of the Gowrie* (Edinburgh 1901), pp 142-53.

4 The Edinburgh edition, 1851, is the text cited here.

5 Ibid. pp vii-xii.

6 This view is firmly entrenched in Scottish literary studies. For two influential recent examples see David Daiches, *The Paradox of Scottish Culture: The Eighteenth-Century Experience* (London 1964), *passim*, and David Craig, *Scottish Literature and the Scottish People 1680-1830* (London 1961), *passim*, but especially pp 11-16. For the way that workers in related fields have been misled, see Tom Nairn, *The Break-Up of Britain Crisis and Neo-Nationalism* (London 1977), pp 126-69; a brief earlier summary of Nairn's views may be found in 'The Three Dreams of Scottish Nationalism', in Karl Miller (ed), *Memoirs of a Modern Scotland* (London 1970), pp 34-54. For a recent interpretation challenging some of these assumptions see Cairns Craig, 'Twentieth Century Scottish Literature: An Introduction', in Cairns Craig (ed), *The History of Scottish Literature* , op.cit. IV, 1-9. Finally, for a statement of the limited goals of the Union and its failure to achieve a unified British nation, see Brian P Levack, *The*

Formation of the British State England, Scotland and the Union 1603-1707 (Oxford 1987), particularly pp 169-79, 204-9.

7   The phrase is Belhaven's: see Chapter 2 *n* 14.
8   *Lockhart Papers*, op.cit. I, 223.

BIBLIOGRAPHY

Abercromby, Patrick, *The Martial Atchievements of the Scots Nation, Being an Account of the Lives, Characters, and memorable Actions, of such Scotsmen as have Signaliz'd themselves by the Sword at Home and Abroad* (2 vols Edinburgh 1711-1715)

Allardyce, Alexander (ed), *Letters from and to Charles Kirkpatrick Sharpe, Esq* (2 vols Edinburgh 1888)

——*Scotland and Scotsmen in the Eighteenth Century* (2 vols Edinburgh 1888)

Anderson, James, *An Historical Essay, Shewing That the Crown and Kingdom of Scotland, is Imperial and Independent* (Edinburgh 1705)

Anton, James, *Retrospect of a Military Life, During The Most Eventful Periods of the Last War* (Edinburgh 1841)

Arnot, Hugo, *The History of Edinburgh* (Edinburgh 1779)

Barke, James, Smith, Sydney Goodsir and Ferguson, J De Lancey (eds), *The Merry Muses of Caledonia* (Edinburgh 1959)

Barnard, F M, *Herder's Social and Political Thought From Englightenment to Nationalism* (Oxford 1965)

Batho, Edith C, *The Ettrick Shepherd* (Cambridge 1927),

——'Notes on the bibliography of James Hogg, the Ettrick Shepherd' in *The Library*, Vol XVI, 1935-6, 309-26

Belhaven, John Hamilton, Lord, *The Late Lord Belhaven's Memorable Speeches in the Last Parliament of Scotland* (Glasgow 1784)

Beveridge, Hugh, *The Sobieski Stuarts* (Inverness 1909)

Bisset, Andrew (ed), *Memoirs and Papers of Sir Andrew Mitchell, KB, Envoy Extraordinary and Minister Plenipotentiary from the Court of Great Britain to the Court of Prussia, from 1756 to 1771* (2 vols London 1850)

Blackie, John Stuart, *Scottish Song Its Wealth, Wisdom, and Social Significance* (Edinburgh 1889)

[Blood, Bindon and Macknight, James] (eds), *Memoirs of Sir Ewen Cameron of Locheill, Chief of the Clan Cameron* (Edinburgh 1842)

Borrow, George, *The Romany Rye* (2 vols London 1857)

Bremner, Robert (ed), *Collection of Scots Reels or Country Dances* (Parts I-IV, Edinburgh n.d. [but 1757-9])

Brinkley, Roberta Florence, *Arthurian Legend in the Seventeenth Century* (New York 1967, first published 1932)

The British Songster, Being A Select Collection of Favourite Scots and English Songs, Catches, &c, (Glasgow 1786)

Bronson, Bertrand Harris, *The Ballad as Song* (Berkeley 1969)

[Brown, James], *A Critical Examination of Dr Macculloch's Work on the Highlands and Western Isles of Scotland* (Edinburgh 1825)

Brown, P Hume, *History of Scotland* (3 vols Cambridge 1909)

Buchan, P, *An Historical and Authentic Account of the Ancient and Noble Family of Keith, Earls Marichal of Scotland* (Peterhead 1820)

Buckle, Henry Thomas, *History of Civilization in England* (2nd edn 2 vols London 1858-1861)

Burrell, S A, 'The Apocalyptic Vision of the Early Covenanters' in *Scottish Historical Review*, Vol XLIII, No. 135 April 1964, 1- 24.

[Burt, Edward], *Letters from A Gentleman in the North of Scotland to His Friend in London* (2 vols London 1754)

Burton, John Hill (ed), *The Autobiography of Dr Alexander Carlyle of Inveresk 1722-1805* (London 1910)

Bushnell, Nelson S, *William Hamilton of Bangour Poet and Jacobite* (Aberdeen 1957)

[Calder, Robert ('Jacob Curate')], *Scots Presbyterian Eloquence Displayed; or Their manner of Teaching and Preaching exposed* (London 1767, first published 1692)

Calendar of State Papers, Domestic Series, of the Reign of Charles II. 1666-1667 (London 1864)

Campbell, Alexander (ed), *Albyn's Anthology Or A Select Collection of the Melodies & Vocal Poetry Peculiar to Scotland and the Isles* (2 vols Edinburgh 1816-1818)

Campbell, John Lorne (ed), *Highland Songs of the Forty-Five* (Edinburgh 1984, first published 1933)

Carnie, Robert Hay, 'Scottish Presbyterian Eloquence and *Old Mortality*' in *Scottish Literary Journal* Vol III, No.2 December 1976, 51-61.

Chambers, Robert, *History of the Rebellion of 1745-6* (Edinburgh 1869)

———*The Scottish Songs* (2 vols Edinburgh 1829)

———*The Threiplands of Fingask a Family Memoir* (London 1880)

Chappell, W and Ebsworth, J W (eds), *The Roxburghe Ballads* (9 vols Hertford 1871-97)

Charteris, Evan, *William Augustus Duke of Cumberland His Early Life and Times (1721-1748)*, (London 1913)

Child, Francis James (ed), *The English and Scottish Popular Ballads* (5 vols Boston 1882-98)

Clarke, J S (ed), *The Life of James the Second King of England, &c* (2 vols London 1816)

Cleland, William, *A Collection of Several Poems and Verses Composed upon Various Occasions By Mr. William Cleland Lieutenant Collonel to my Lord Angus's Regiment*. Printed in the year 1697 (n.p.)

Cohn, Norman, *The Pursuit of the Millennium Revolutionary millenarians and mystical anarchists of the Middle Ages* (London 1972, first published 1957)

Collingwood, R G, *The Idea of History* (London 1961, first published 1946)

Collinson, Francis, *The Traditional and National Music of Scotland* (London 1966)

Cowan, Ian B, *The Scottish Covenanters 1660-1688* (London 1976)

Cowan, William (ed), *A Journey To Edenborough in Scotland by Joseph Taylor, Late of the Inner Temple, Esq* (Edinburgh 1903)

Craig, Archibald, *The Sobieski Stuarts* (Edinburgh 1922)

Craig, Cairns (ed), *The History of Scottish Literature* (4 vols Aberdeen 1987-8)

———'Twentieth Century Scottish Literature: An Introduction', in Cairns Craig (ed), *The History of Scottish Literature*, op.cit. IV, 1-9.

Craig, David, *Scottish Literature and the Scottish People 1680-1830* (London 1961)

Craik, Sir Henry, *A Century of Scottish History* (2 vols Edinburgh 1901)

Crawford, Thomas, *Burns A Study of the Poems and Songs* (2nd edn Edinburgh 1965)

———*Love, Labour and Liberty: the eighteenth-century Scottish Lyric* (Cheadle Hulme 1976)

———'Lowland Song and Popular Tradition in the Eighteenth Century' in Craig (ed), *History of Scottish Literature*, op. cit. II, 123-39

———'Political and Protest Songs in Eighteenth-Century Scotland 1. Jacobite and Anti-Jacobite' in *Scottish Studies*, Vol XIV, 1970, pp 1-33.

———*Society and the Lyric a study of the Song Culture of eighteenth-century Scotland* (Edinburgh 1979)

Cunningham, Audrey, *The Loyal Clans* (Cambridge 1932)

Cunningham, John, *The Church History of Scotland from the Commencement of the Christian Era to the Present Time* (2 vols Edinburgh 1882)

Currie, James (ed), *The Works of Robert Burns...A New Edition. With Additional Pieces* (4 vols Montrose 1816)

Daiches, David, *Charles Edward Stuart The Life and Times of Bonnie Prince Charlie* (London 1973)

———*The Paradox of Scottish Culture: The Eighteenth-Century Experience* (London 1964)

Defoe, Daniel, *A Tour Thro' the whole Island of Great Britain* (2 vols London 1927)

Dennistoun, James, *Memoirs of Sir Robert Strange...and of his Brother-in-Law Andrew Lumisden, Private Secretary to the Stuart Princes* (2 vols London 1855)

Deutsch, O E, 'Poetry Preserved in Music *Bibliographical Notes on Smollett and Oswald, Handel, and Haydn*' in *Modern Language Notes*, Vol LXIII, No.2, February 1948, 73-88

Dick, James C (ed), *Notes on Scottish Song by Robert Burns Written in an Interleaved Copy of The Scots Musical Museum* (London 1908)

———*The Songs of Robert Burns Now First Printed with the Melodies for which they were Written A Study in Tone-Poetry* (London 1903)

Dixon, Willmott and Robertson, J Logie, *The Jacobite Episode in Scottish History and its Relative Literature* (Edinburgh n.d.)

Doddridge, P, *Some Remarkable Passages in the Life of the Honourable Col. James Gardiner, Who was Slain at the Battle of Preston-Pans, September 21, 1745* (London 1748)

Donaldson, Gordon, *Scotland James V to James VII* (Edinburgh 1965)

Donaldson, William 'Bonny Highland Laddie: the Making of a Myth' in *Scottish Literary Journal*, Vol III, No.2, December 1976, 30-50

———'The Glencairn Connection: Robert Burns and Scottish Politics, 1786-1796', in *Studies in Scottish Literature*, Vol XVI, 1981, 61-79

———'Inside the Kist of Glendulochan' in *Cencrastus*, No 4 Winter 1980-81, 20-22

[Duff, H R] (ed), *Culloden Papers: comprising an Extensive and Interesting Correspondence from the year 1625 to 1748* (London 1815)

Duke, Winifred, *In the Steps of Bonnie Prince Charlie* (London 1953)

Duncan, Douglas, *Thomas Ruddiman A Study in Scottish Scholarship of the Early Eighteenth Century* (Edinburgh 1965)

Durham, James, *A Commentarie Upon the book of the Revelation. Wherein The Text is explained, the Series of the several Prophecies contained in that Book, deduced according to their order and dependance upon each other...Delivered in several Lectures* (London 1658)

The Earl of Mar marr'd. With the Humours of Jockey, the Highlander: a Tragi-Comical Farce (London 1716)

Edgar, Andrew, *Old Church Life in Scotland: Lectures on Kirk-Session and Presbytery Records* (Paisley 1885)

The Edinburgh Musical Miscellany: A Collection of the Most Approved Scotch, English, and Irish Songs, set to music (2 vols Edinburgh 1792-3)

Ellis, Frank H (ed), *Poems on Affairs of State Augustan Satirical Verse Vol VII: 1704-1714* (New Haven 1975)

Ellis, John M, *One Fairy Story Too Many: The Brothers Grimm and their Tales* (Chicago 1983)

Ewald, Alex Charles, *The Life and Times of Prince Charles Stuart Count of Albany* (London 1883)

Farmer, Henry George, *A History of Music in Scotland* (London 1947)

Farquhar, George T S, *Three Bishops of Dunkeld: Alexander, Rose and Watson 1743-1808* (Perth 1915)

Feiling, Keith Grahame, *The Second Tory Party 1714-1832* (London 1938)

Ferguson, J De Lancey and Ross Roy, G (eds), *The Letters of Robert Burns* (2 vols Oxford 1985)

Ferguson, De Lancey, *Pride and Passion Robert Burns 1759-1796* (New York 1939)

Ferguson, William, *Scotland 1689 to the Present* (Edinburgh 1968)

——— *Scotland's Relations with England: a Survey to 1707* (Edinburgh 1977)

Fergusson, Alex, *Henry Erskine, his Kinsfolk and Times* (Edinburgh 1882)

Fergusson, James (ed), *Letters of George Dempster to Sir Adam Fergusson 1756-1813 With Some Account of his Life* (London 1934)

Firth, C H, 'An Elegy and a Ballad' in *Scottish Historical Review*, Vol VI, No.24, July 1909, 357-61

Fitzhugh, Robert T (ed), *Robert Burns His Associates and Contemporaries* (Chapel Hill, 1943)

———*Robert Burns The Man and the Poet A Round, Unvarnished Account* (London, 1971)

Fleming, D Hay (ed), *Six Saints of The Covenant Peden: Semple: Welwood: Cameron: Cargill: Smith* (2 vols London 1901)

'Full Collection', *A Full Collection of all Poems upon Charles, Prince of Wales, Regent of the Kingdoms of Scotland, England, France and Ireland, and Dominions thereunto belonging.* Printed in the Year MDCCXLV. (n.p.)

Gifford, Douglas (ed), *The Three Perils of Man War, Women and Witchcraft by James Hogg* (Edinburgh 1972)

Gillies, Alexander, *A Hebridean in Goethe's Weimar The Reverend James Macdonald and the Cultural Relations between Scotland and Germany* (Oxford 1969)

Glen, John, *Early Scottish Melodies: including examples from MSS. and Early Printed Works, along with a number of Comparative Tunes, Notes on Former Annotators, English and other Claims, and Biographical Notices* (Edinburgh 1900)

The Gold-Finch, A Choice Collection of the Most Celebrated Songs, Scots & English (Edinburgh 1777)

Gordon, William, *History of the Ancient, Noble, and Illustrious Family of Gordon* (2 vols Edinburgh 1726-1727)

Graham, Henry Grey, *The Social Life of Scotland in the Eighteenth Century* (London 1969, first published 1899)

Groves, David (ed), *James Hogg Selected Poems and Songs* (Edinburgh 1986)

Grub, George, *Ecclesiastical History of Scotland* (4 vols Edinburgh 1861)

Gunnyon, William, *Illustrations of Scottish History Life and Superstition From Song and Ballad* (Glasgow 1879)

Guthrie, Dorothy A and Grose, Clyde L, 'Forty Years of Jacobite Bibliography' in *Journal of Modern History*, Vol XI, 1939, pp 49-60

Hadden, J Cuthbert, *George Thomson The Friend of Burns His Life & Correspondence* (London 1898)

Hamilton, William, *The Life Surprising Adventures and Heroic Actions of Sir William Wallace, General and Governor of Scotland* (New edn Aberdeen 1774, first published 1721)

Hazlitt, William, *The Spirit of the Age: or Contemporary Portraits* (London 1825)

Hecht, Hans, *Robert Burns The Man and His Work* (London 1936)

Hecht, Hans (ed), *Songs from David Herd's Manuscripts* (Edinburgh 1904)

Henderson, George, *Lady Nairne and her Songs* (Paisley 1901)

Henderson, T F, ' "Charlie he's My Darling" and other Burns' Originals' in *Scottish Historical Review*, Vol III, No.10 January 1906, 171-8

Herd, David (ed), *Ancient and Modern Scottish Songs Heroic Ballads etc* (2 vols Edinburgh 1973, first published Edinburgh 1776)

———*Letters from Thomas Percy, DD afterwards Bishop of Dromore, John Callander of Craigforth, Esq. David Herd, and others, to George Paton* (Edinburgh 1830)

[Highland Regiment], *A Short History of the Highland Regiment; Interspersed with Some Occasional Observations As to the Present State of the Country, Inhabitants, and Government of Scotland* (London 1743)

Hogg, David, *Life of Allan Cunningham* (Dumfries 1875)

Hogg, James (ed), *The Jacobite Relics of Scotland ; being The Songs, Airs, and Legends, of the Adherents to the House of Stuart* (2 vols Edinburgh 1819-1821)

———*Songs, by The Ettrick Shepherd. Now first collected* (Edinburgh 1831)

Holloway, John and Black, Joan (eds), *Later English Broadside Ballads* (London 1975)

Home, John, *The History of the Rebellion in the Year 1745* (London 1802)

Hook, Andrew, 'Scotland and Romanticism: The International Scene' in Cairns Craig (ed) *The History of Scottish Literature* (4 vols Aberdeen 1987-8), II, 307-22

Horn, Barbara L H (ed), *Letters of John Ramsay of Ochtertyre 1799-1812* (Edinburgh 1966)

Horn, D B, 'George IV and Highland Dress', in *Scottish Historical Review*, Vol XLVII, 2: No.144 Oct. 1968, 209-10

Howard, Philip, *The Black Watch* (London 1968)

Hume, David, *The History of England, from The Invasion of Julius Caesar to The Revolution in 1688* (8 vols London 1763)

The Illustrated Book of Scottish Songs. From the Sixteenth to the Nineteenth Century (Illustrated London Library, 227 Strand. [n.d.])

Ingram, Mary E, *A Jacobite Stronghold of the Church Being the Story of Old St. Paul's, Edinburgh* (Edinburgh 1907)

Innes, Thomas, *A Critical Essay on the Ancient Inhabitants of the Northern Parts of Britain or Scotland. Containing an Account of the Romans, of the Britains betwixt the Walls, of the Caledonians or Picts, and particularly of the Scots* (Edinburgh 1879, first published London 1729)

Insh, George Pratt, *The Scottish Jacobite Movement A Study in Economic and Social Forces* (Edinburgh 1952)

Jarvis, Rupert C, *Collected Papers on the Jacobite Risings* (2 vols Manchester 1971-2)

Johnson, David, *Music and Society in Lowland Scotland in the Eighteenth Century* (London 1972)

Johnson, Edgar, *Sir Walter Scott The Great Unknown* (2 vols London 1970)

Johnstone, The Chevalier de, *Memoirs of The Rebellion in 1745 and 1746* (London 1820)

Keith, Christina, *The Russet Coat A Critical Study of Burns' Poetry and of its Background* (London 1956)

Keltie, John Scott, *A History of the Scottish Highlands Highland Clans and Highland Regiments* (2 vols Edinburgh 1877)

Kendrick, T D, *British Antiquity* (London 1950)

Kennedy, Mathew, *Chronological Genealogical and Historical Dissertation of the Royal Family of the Stuarts* (Paris, 1705)

Kermack, W R, *The Scottish Highlands A Short History (c. 300-1746)* (Edinburgh 1957)

Kerr, Robert (ed), *Memoirs of the Life, Writings, & Correspondence of William Smellie* (2 vols Edinburgh 1811)

King, Dr William, *Political and Literary Anecdotes of His Own Times* (London 1818)

Kinnear, George Henderson, *The History of Glenbervie, the Fatherland of Burns a Parish in the County of Kincardine* (Edinburgh 1910)

Kinsley, James, 'The Music of the Heart', in *Renaissance and Modern Studies*, Vol VIII, 1964, 5-52

Kinsley, James (ed), *The Poems and Songs of Robert Burns* (3 vols Oxford 1968)

Kirk, G S, *Myth its Meaning and Function in Ancient and Other Cultures* (Cambridge 1970)

Knapp, Lewis Mansfield, *Tobias Smollett Doctor of Men and Manners* (Princeton 1949)

[Laing, David] (ed), *Collection of Ancient Scottish Prophecies, in Alliterative Verse* (Edinburgh 1833)

Lang, Andrew, *Pickle the Spy or The Incognito of Prince Charles* (London 1897)

The Lark: being a Select Collection of the most celebrated and newest songs, Scots & English (Edinburgh 1765)

Lenman, Bruce, *The Jacobite Risings in Britain 1689-1746* (London 1980)

———*The Jacobite Clans of the Great Glen 1650-1784* (London 1984)

———'The Scottish Episcopal Clergy and the Ideology of Jacobitism' in Eveline Cruickshanks (ed), *Ideology and Conspiracy: Aspects of Jacobitism, 1689-1759* (Edinburgh 1982), pp 36-48

Levack, Brian P, *The Formation of the British State England, Scotland and the Union 1603-1707* (Oxford 1987)

Lockhart, George, *The Lockhart Papers: Containing Memoirs and Commentaries upon the Affairs of Scotland from 1702 to 1714, by George Lockhart, Esq. of Carnwath, His Secret Correspondence with the Son of King James the Second from 1718 to 1728, And his other Political Writings* (2 vols London 1817)

Lockhart, J G, *Memoirs of the Life of Sir Walter Scott, Bart.* (7 vols Edinburgh 1837-8)

Low, Donald A (ed), *Critical Essays on Robert Burns* (London 1975)

———'A Last Supper with Scotland's Bard' in *Weekend Scotsman*, 22 January, 1983

'Loyal Songs', *A Collection of Loyal Songs. For the Use of the Revolution Club. Some of which never before printed* (Edinburgh 1748)

The Lyre: A Collection of the Most Approved English, Irish, and Scottish Songs, Ancient and Modern (Edinburgh 1824)

M'Cahill, Michael W, 'The Scottish peerage and the House of Lords in the late eighteenth century', in *Scottish Historical Review*, Vol LI, No. 152, 1972, 172-96.

M'Diarmid, Matthew P (ed), *The Poems of Robert Fergusson* (2 vols Edinburgh 1954-6)

MacGregor, George (ed), *The Collected Writings of Dougal Graham 'Skellat' Bellman of Glasgow...Together with a...Sketch of the Chap Literature of Scotland* (2 vols Glasgow 1883)

Mackenzie, Farquhar, '*Sir* Robert Burns' in *Burns Chronicle*, 4th series Vol I, 1976, 62-6

Mackenzie, George M D, *The Lives and Characters of the most Eminent Writers of the Scots Nation* (3 vols Edinburgh 1708-1722)

Mackenzie, Sir George, *The Antiquity of the Royal Line of Scotland Farther Cleared and Defended* (London 1686)

————*Defence of the Antiquity Of the Royal Line of Scotland* (Edinburgh 1685)

Mackenzie, W C, *Andrew Fletcher of Saltoun His Life and Times* (Edinburgh 1935)

Mackenzie, W Mackay (ed), *The Poems of William Dunbar* (London 1932)

Macleay, K, *Historical Memoirs of Rob Roy and the Clan Macgregor* (Glasgow 1818)

Macleod, A C and Boulton, Harold (eds), *Songs of the North, Gathered together from The Highlands and Lowlands of Scotland* (London n.d. [but 1885])

M'Naught, D, *Kilmaurs Parish & Burgh* (Paisley 1912)

Macphail, J R N (ed), *Wariston's Diary and Other Papers* (Edinburgh 1896)

Macpherson, Dr John, *Critical Dissertations on the Origin, Antiquities, Language, Government, Manners, and Religion, of the Ancient Caledonians* (London 1768)

M'Vie, John, 'Burns's Letter to James Steuart' in *Burns Chronicle*, 3rd series Vol II, 1953, 42-3

Mack, Douglas S (ed), *James Hogg Memoir of the Author's Life and Familiar Anecdotes of Sir Walter Scott* (Edinburgh 1972)

————*James Hogg Selected Poems* (Oxford 1970)[Maidment, James](ed), *A Book of Scotish Pasquils 1568-1715* (Edinburgh 1868)

————*Miscellanea Scotica. A Collection of Tracts Relating to the History, Antiquities, Topography and Literature of Scotland* (4 vols Glasgow 1818-20)

————*Scotish Elegiac Verses. M.DC.XXIX.—M.DCC.XXIX.* (Edinburgh 1842)

Maitland, William, *The History of Edinburgh, from its Foundation to the Present Time* (Edinburgh 1753)

Martin, B, Oliver, J W, Kinghorn, A M and Law, A (eds), *The Works of Allan Ramsay* (6 vols Edinburgh 1945-75)

Mason, Roger A, 'Scotching the Brut: Politics, History and National Myth in Sixteenth-Century Britain' in Roger A Mason (ed), *Scotland and England 1286-1815* (Edinburgh 1987)

Matthews, William, 'The Egyptians in Scotland: the Political History of a Myth' in *Viator: Mediaeval & Renaissance Studies*, I (1970), 289-306

Meston, William, *The Poetical Works of the Ingenious and Learned William Meston* (Edinburgh 1767)

Minto, Nina Countess of, *Life and Letters of Sir Gilbert Elliot* (3 vols London 1874)

Mitchell, Sir Arthur, 'A List of Travels, Tours, Journeys, Voyages, Cruises, Excursions, Wanderings, Rambles, Visits, etc., Relating to Scotland', in *Proceedings of the Society of*

Antiquaries of Scotland, 3rd series Vol XXXV, 1900-1, 431-638; also Vol XXXIV, 1905, 500-27; and Vol XLIV, 1910, 390-405.

[Morer, Thomas], *A Short Account of Scotland. Being a Description of the Nature of that Kingdom, and what the Constitution of it is in Church and State* (London 1702)

Muir, Edwin, *Scottish Journey* (London 1935)

Murray, James A H (ed), *The Romance and Prophecies of Thomas of Erceldoune Printed from Five Manuscripts; with Illustrations from the Prophetic Literature of the 15th and 16th Centuries* (London 1875)

Nairn, Tom, *The Break-Up of Britain Crisis and Neo-Nationalism* (London 1977)

Nairn, Tom, 'Three Dreams of Scottish Nationalism', in Karl Miller (ed), *Memoirs of a Modern Scotland* (London 1970), pp 34-54

Napier, Mark, *History of the Partition of the Lennox* (Edinburgh 1835)

————*Memorials and Letters Illustrative of The Life and Times of John Graham of Claverhouse, Viscount of Dundee* (3 vols Edinburgh 1859-62)

Norton, Alison S, 'Robert Burns and the 'Forty-Five' in *Burns Chronicle*, 1963, pp 40-57

Oliphant, T L Kington, *Jacobite Lairds of Gask* (London 1870)

Olson, Ian A, 'Scottish Traditional Song and the Greig-Duncan Collection: Last Leaves or Last Rites?' in Cairns Craig (ed), *The History of Scottish Literature* (4 vols Aberdeen 1987-8), IV, 37-46

Oswald, James (ed), *Caledonian Pocket Companion* (London, n.d. [but 1743-59])

Paton, Hugh, *A Series of Original Portraits and Caricature Etchings, by the late John Kay, Miniature Painter, Edinburgh; with Biographical Sketches* (Edinburgh 1843)

Patrides, C A, *The Phoenix and the Ladder* (Berkeley 1964)

Pennecuik, Alexander, *A Compleat Collection Of All The Poems Wrote by...Alexander Pennecuik. To which is annexed some Curious Poems by other worthy Hands* (Parts 1-11 Edinburgh n.d. but [?1750])

Philip, Adam, *Songs and Sayings of the Gowrie* (Edinburgh 1901)

Phillipson, N T and Mitchison, Rosalind (eds), *Scotland in the Age of Improvement Essays in Scottish History in the Eighteenth Century* (Edinburgh 1970)

Pinto, V de Sola and Rodway, A E (eds), *The Common Muse an Anthology of Popular British Ballad Poetry XVth-XXth Century* (London 1957)

Ramsay, Alexander, *History of the Highland and Agricultural Society of Scotland* (Edinburgh 1879)

Ramsay, Allan (ed), *The Tea-Table Miscellany* (Edinburgh 1724)

————*The Tea-Table Miscellany: Or, a Complete Collection of Scots Sangs* (3 vols Dublin 1729)

Ray, James, *Compleat History of the Rebellion, From its first Rise, in MDCCXLV. To its total Suppression at the glorious Battle of Culloden, in April, 1746* (Bristol 1750)

Renwick, W L, *English Literature 1789-1815* (Oxford 1963)

Richards, Eric, *A History of the Highland Clearances Agrarian Transformation and the Evictions 1746-1886* (London 1982)

[Ridpath, George ('Will Laick')], *An Answer to the Scotch Presbyterian Eloquence* (London 1693)

Ritson, Joseph (ed), *Scotish Songs. In Two Volumes* (London 1794)

Rogers, Charles (ed), *Life and Songs of the Baroness Nairne* (Edinburgh 1905)

Rollins, Hyder E, 'The Black-Letter Broadside Ballad' in *Publications of the Modern Language Association of America*, Vol XXXIV, new ser. Vol XXVII, 1919, 258-339

Ross, Ian and Scobie, Stephen, 'Patriotic Publishing as a Response to the Union' in T I Rae (ed), *The Union of 1707 Its Impact on Scotland* (London 1974), pp 94-119

Ross, John D (ed), *Burnsiana: a Collection of Literary Odds and Ends Relating to Robert Burns* (6 vols London 1892-7)

The Scots Musical Museum (6 vols Edinburgh 1787-1803)

The Scots Nightingale: or, Edinburgh Vocal Miscellany. A New and Select Collection of the Best Scots and English Songs (Edinburgh 1778)

Scott, Tom (ed), *The Penguin Book of Scottish Verse* (Harmondsworth 1970)

[Shields, Alexander], *A Hind let loose, or An Historical Representation of the Testimonies, Of the Church of Scotland, for the Interest of Christ* (n.p. 1687), by 'A Lover of true Liberty'

Simpson, Claude M, *The British Broadside Ballad and its Music* (New Jersey 1966)

Simpson, Louis, *James Hogg A Critical Study* (Edinburgh 1962)

[Simpson, Margaret Stewart], *The Scottish Songstress Caroline Baroness Nairne by her Great Grand-Niece* (Edinburgh 1894)

Simpson, Robert, *Traditions of the Covenanters; or, Gleanings among the Mountains* (new edn Edinburgh n.d.)

Sinclair, George, *Satan's Invisible World Discovered, or a Choice Collection of Relations anent Devils, Spirits, Witches, and Apparitions* (T G Stevenson (ed), Edinburgh 1871, first published Edinburgh 1685)

Sinclair, Sir John, *The Correspondence of Sir John Sinclair* (2 vols London 1831)

Sinclair, Sir John (ed), *The Statistical Account of Scotland* (21 vols Edinburgh 1791-99)

Skinner, John, *An Ecclesiastical History of Scotland, From The First Appearance of Christianity in that Kingdom, to The Present Time* (2 vols London 1788)

Smith, Janet Adam, 'Some Eighteenth-Century Ideas of Scotland' in N T Phillipson and Rosalind Mitchison (eds), *Scotland in the Age of Improvement* (Edinburgh 1970), pp 107-24

Spalding Club Miscellany (Vol 2, Aberdeen 1842)

Stephen, W, *History of the Scottish Church* (2 vols Edinburgh 1894-6)

Stewart, David, *Sketches of the Character, Manners, and Present State of the Highlanders of Scotland* (2nd edn 2 vols Edinburgh 1822)

Stewart, Sir James and Stirling, James, *Naphtali; or, the Wrestlings of the Church of Scotland for the Kingdom of Christ* (Perth 1845, first published 1667)

Stewart, Neil (ed), *Collection of the Newest and best Reels or Country Dances* (Edinburgh n.d. [but 1761])

Stones, E L G, *Anglo-Scottish Relations 1174-1328* (London 1965)

Strachey, Lady (ed), *Memoirs of a Highland Lady The Autobiography of Elizabeth Grant of Rothiemurchus* (London 1911)

Strawhorn, John (ed), *Ayrshire at the time of Burns* (Kilmarnock 1959)

Strout, Alan Lang, *A Bibliography of Articles in Blackwood's Magazine...1817-1825* (Lubbock 1959)

———*The Life and Letters of James Hogg, The Ettrick Shepherd (1770-1825)* (Lubbock 1946)

Struthers, John (ed), *The Harp of Caledonia: a Collection of Songs, Ancient and Modern, (chiefly Scottish.)*, (2 vols Glasgow 1819)

Stuart, John Sobieski and Charles Edward, *Tales of the Century or Sketches of the Romance of History between the Years 1746 and 1846* (Edinburgh 1851, first published 1847)

Symson, David, *A Genealogical and Historical Account of The Illustrious Name of Stuart* (Edinburgh 1712)

Tatlock, J S P, *The Legendary History of Britain Geoffrey of Monmouth's Historia Regum Britanniae and its early Vernacular Versions* (Berkeley 1950)

Tayler, Henrietta (ed), *Jacobite Epilogue A Further Selection of Letters from Jacobites among the Stuart Papers at Windsor (London 1941)*

Terry, Charles Sanford, *The Rising of 1745* (2nd edn London 1903)

Thompson, Harold William (ed), *The Anecdotes and Egotisms of Henry Mackenzie 1745-1831* (London 1927)

Thomson, William (ed), *Orpheus Caledonius: or, a Collection of Scots Songs* (2 vols London 1733)

Tobin, Terence (ed), *The Assembly by Archibald Pitcairne* (Lafayette, Indiana 1972)

Tytler, Sarah and Watson, J L, *The Songstresses of Scotland* (2 vols London 1871)

Wallace, William (ed), *Robert Burns and Mrs Dunlop* (London 1898)

Watt, William, *Poems, on Sacred and other Subjects; and Songs, Humorous and Sentimental* (Glasgow 1860, first published 1835)

Williamson, Arthur H, *Scottish National Consciousness in the Age of James VI* (Edinburgh 1979)

Wodrow, Robert, *History of the Sufferings of the Church of Scotland from the Restoration to the Revolution* (Robert Burns (ed), 4 vols Glasgow 1829-30)

————*Analecta: or, Materials for a History of Remarkable Providences; mostly relating to Scotch Ministers and Christians* (2 vols Glasgow 1842)

Wood, Harriet Harvey (ed), *James Watson's Choice Collection of Comic and Serious Scots Poems*, Vol 1 (Edinburgh 1977)

GLOSSARY

a' all
aboon above
aft often
amang among
ane one
anither another
arles hiring fees
auld old
awa' away

Banachadee Gaelic phrase of greeting
banes bones
bannocks scones
baukit denied
bawbee coin of small value
bees-skeps bee-hives
begowth began
beuk, book
billy term of endearment
blads fables, false promises
blas Gaelic word meaning 'flavour'
blin' blind
blutter blether
boord table
bouk man
brake broke
braw fine, handsome
breeks trousers
brig bridge
brochen oatmeal gruel
brose similar to drammoch, crowdie, etc., but hot
bruik to wear as of a favourite or prized garment
buckies whelks
Butter-box a Dutchman
bygone past, former

cairny piled-up bed
cald coals to blaw to attempt an
impossible, thankless or frustrating task
callan a young lad
caller fresh
cam' came
canty blithe, cheerful
cappet ill-humoured, peevish
cauld-steer see 'crowdie' and 'drammock'
cess taxation
chafts jaws
cla' claw, scratch
climkum/clankum sounds of ringing blows
club-law brute force
cog/cogue bowl
correnoch/cronoch dirge
craw, crow, boast
creach raid
crowdie as 'drammock', also known as 'cauld steer'
cultors plough blades

daur dare
Deel Devil
deads deaths
devit deafened
dike wall
dinna do not
door targe
dows doves
drammock cold oatmeal mixed with water
drie endure, suffer
drucken drunken
dulse edible seaweed
durk dirk, highland dagger

elwand measuring rod
enew enough
Ersche Gaelic

Erschemen Highlandmen
ether adder

fa' fall
fadges loaves
fa'n fallen
failzie fail
fautes faults
feelabeg kilt
ferlie wonder, marvel
fery foray
flang flung
fleshcruik meat-hook
flyting scolding
fouth plenty
fu' full
furich Gaelic word meaning 'stay'
fyl'd befouled

gabbock portion
gades goads
gade-men persons who goad plough-
  oxen
gae go
Gaidhealtachd the Highlands
gait way, direction
gane gone
gang go
gar make
gentie well-bred
gie give
glaum'd grasped
goodman husband
gouk cuckoo, fool
gowden golden
grane groan
guid good

ha' door house door
hae have
hame home
hech hey expression of greeting
hing hang
hodding gray hodden grey
houghs hamstrings
hough'd cut down
hur Lowland version of Gaelic personal
  pronoun
hur nane-sell comic sobriquet for
  Highlandman
huskiebae whisky

ilkane every one
ill bad

jimped tripped

kebbecks cheeses
ken know
kennis knows
kits containers

laigh low
lang long
lav'rock lark
lawland lowland
lingel bind
louns boys, villains

Mahoun the Devil
mains moans
mair more
maukin hare
maun must
maut malt
meggs hands, paws
meikle large
mirds chicanery
moals earth of a grave
mony many
mou' mouth
muckle large
mumpit deceived

nane none
nowt beef cattle
nowtfeet calves foot

o' of
o'ercome refrain, burden

pa' feeble movement, pall, trick
padyane pageant
paikes blows
parten large edible crab
pig, earthenware dish or crock
phow 'how' in pseudo-Highland
  pronunciation
pleding tartan
pockmohon indelicate Gaelic phrase
  expressive of extreme contempt
pouches pockets
powsowdie sheep's head broth

pra braw, bonnie
press imposition
prie/pree savour

ra' row
rane roch blustering blether
rax stretch, reach for
reave to steal violently
red-shank highland
reif theft
rerd confusion
riggings heads
roup cry harshly
rug piece

sair sore, painful
saul soul
sawt salt
scaud punish
scroggy covered with undergrowth or scrub
servitor retainer
sey sea
sheugh ditch
sic such
simmer summer
sine/syne since, ago, then
singit sheepheads sheepheads rendered palatable by singeing and boiling
skelp smack, run energetically
skitter-raw slitherly, squelchy, resembling diarrhoea
skyrin glaringly brightly coloured
sla/slaw slow
sma small
smorit smothered
snishing snuff
sough whistle, pant
spaldings dried white fish
spence larder, store-room
stane stone
stank small stream
stent stop

stirks beef cattle
stoure dust, conflict
straikes strokes
straught straight
strid led with legs apart
swarf faint, 'tak a dwam'
swingle-trees part of plough to which *theats* (q.v.) are attached
swoor swore

tailzie entail
tangles kind of seaweed
teuch tough
theats ropes attaching plough to horse or oxen
thrissles thistles
tinkler tinker
tirled at the pin rang for entrance
tocher dowry
trow believe
trows trews
trumps jews harp
twa two

unco much, great
uncos strangers

wa' wall
wad would
wae woe
wan won
wauken waken
weal good fortune
weel/weell well
weigh-bauk balance for weighing
weir war
whytens whitings
winna will not
wist guessed
wud mad, berserk

yestreen yesterday evening

INDEX